Glasses in the Grass

Devotions for My Friends

by

R.E. Clark

GnG Publishers

122 Skinner St.

Centerton, AR 72719

Second Edition

Published 10/01/15

ISBN-13: 978-0692544389

ISBN-10: 0692544380

Printed in the United States of America

DEDICATION

To all those who have been a part of my life
and
in doing so have become bits and pieces
of
the mosaic that is me.
Without you these devotional thoughts
would not have been written.

ACKNOWLEDGEMENTS

I am grateful to so many who encouraged me to write this book. Though I will not attempt to name you individually, you know who you are. I thank you for your friendship and the many comments that have come my way as I wrote these devotionals and posted them on Facebook over the past several years.

I would be amiss in not thanking my daughter and administrative assistant, Kayre. During the writing of this book, she has helped divert some of the interruptions that would have kept me from completing it on time. Her grasp of English grammar has been a tremendous blessing. Since she was home-schooled, we have joked about her wonderful teacher. But truthfully, the student has well surpassed the teacher!

I am especially thankful for my wife, Trudy, who was among the first to suggest compiling my daily thoughts and publishing this book. She has been a daily encourager as I worked to get the finished manuscript to the publisher. She has served as my proofreader and editor. But more than that she has been my friend as I have written to my friends. I love you, Trudy! I am so blessed that God has brought you into my life and filled such a huge void.

PREFACE

These daily devotionals were written for my Facebook friends over
several years. They are written for the most part in a pastoral format
with a little exegesis thrown in here and there. They are concise and
can be quickly read. Some of the devotionals contain personal stories
that have become the parables of my life in which God has shown me
insight into His word.

I have included in each day's devotional a QR-code like the one printed above,
which can be scanned with your smart phone or other device that has a built-in
camera. An excellent free app can be found here: www.i-nigma.com. Of course,
there are others that you can download from any app store for free.

These codes will take you to *The Bible Study Tools* website which has been
developed by Broadman and Holman Publishers. From here you can deepen
your study using online commentaries or simply read the daily verses in context.

My desire in writing this devotional and including the QR-codes for you is that
your daily devotional time will not stop with my words, but that my words might
be a gateway for you to delve into the depths of God's word. You can join King
David in his love for the unchanging word of God.

January 1

Leaving a Year Behind

Thomas Mann, in his novel, *The Magic Mountain,* said when writing about the beginning of a new year, "Time has no divisions to mark its passage; there is never a thunderstorm to announce the beginning of a new year. It is only we mortals who ring bells and fire off pistols."

In Exodus 12 God gave to the Hebrews in Egyptian slavery the instructions for the observance of the Passover. He told them that their deliverance from Egypt would be marked by the Passover and that month would be from that day forward the beginning of months. "Now the LORD spoke to Moses and Aaron in the land of Egypt, saying, 'This month shall be your beginning of months; it shall be the first month of the year to you.'"~Exodus 12:1–2

We do not need to observe the Passover because Jesus, the Lamb that takes away the sins of the world, has already been offered once and for all as our sacrifice! Praise God! We can learn from this New Year observance, however.

From the Exodus account we learn these things about our relationship to The Lamb. A lamb was to be brought into the Hebrew home, so He must be taken into our home. This lamb had to be slain even as He had to be slain to provide the answer to our sin condition. The blood of that sinless lamb was applied to the doorposts and mantle of that home in Egypt as His blood must be applied to our lives to be effective. The family then ate that lamb in celebration of their departure. He, too, must become our very sustenance as we consume Him in joy.

Then LEAVE EGYPT BEHIND!

Make this first day of this New Year your first day of a new journey with Jesus! Have a blessed New Year!

Lord, help me to leave Egypt behind and never look back.

January 2

Caught You Looking

 We are the best advertisement for Jesus that exists. I am speaking of the Christian of course. As a matter of fact I come across people all the time who have very negative feelings about Christ and His Church. Where did they get that idea?

FROM ME AND YOU UNFORTUNATELY! This is how Micah said it in the book named for him. "For all people walk each in the name of his god, but we will walk in the name of the Lord our God forever and ever."~Micah 4:5 Do you see the truth here? The word *walk* has in its deepest meaning the idea of behavior. Our behavior belies who our god really is. If our habits constantly disclose behavior that is not in sync with the character of Christ then those around us will easily conclude who our god really is. CHECK YOUR WALK!

It may be time to set a new course or make a course correction. Let's be people who disclose who our God really is as they see His character displayed openly in our everyday living. We are God's advertisement of Himself. Like a company who pays big money to have billboards along highways, we are God's billboard along our pathway. As others cross our path, let them see the evidence of God in us.

Sometimes billboards are left un-rented and the company that owns the board will post catchy phrases to prove the value of advertising there. I saw one the other day that read, "CAUGHT YOU LOOKING!" Let your life be like that billboard along the highway of your everyday living. May you be saying all the time, "Caught you looking!" Now you have their attention; what exactly do they see in your life?

Lord, help me be the best advertising for You that the world might see.

God is in Control

In the midst of Job's suffering his friends came to "instruct" him. Even though they were misinformed as to the cause of Job's suffering their words are recorded for us and therefore are inspired and valuable for our learning.

Here is one statement that Elihu made: "Behold, God is exalted by His power; who teaches like Him?"~Job 36:22 Two truths come from this statement. First, God does not need any help in being exalted. He is promoted by His own limitless capacity! We really need to understand this. God is not waiting on us to contrive the next event so He can be shown on stage. God is exalted in and of Himself! His power is sufficient!

Second, it is somewhat strange that His teaching is connected to His power. At least it was to me, until I realized that He has the power to teach me truth in every situation because His power is always sufficient in every case. So when I am taught by Him in seemingly out of control situations, I learn that He is exalted by His own ability to always be in control!

Are you in a Job-like situation today? Instead of asking *why*, ask a better question: *what?* Ask God what He is teaching you. See that you are in this trouble or trial so that God can show His power. In that display you will learn what others only dream about knowing. You will learn that God is always in control no matter the circumstances or the friends who are trying to give you their little piece of wisdom. What a mighty God we serve! May He be exalted in power as He teaches you today!

Lord, help me live like You are in control.

3

January 4

The Captivity of Pride

 If there is one thing of which there is no shortage in the world today it is pride. Not only does it come very naturally to us human beings, it is only reflected in our character as humans. You simply will not find an element of pride anywhere else in all of creation. No lion today roars out of pride because of its strength. The sun does not shine in its glory while boasting in pride that it has thus made itself shine. No wind blowing upon a tree will boast of its power to bend the branch. No, pride belongs to man alone.

In our time pride has become second nature and is even promoted. Yet even in its promotion as being something good it leaves the person affected by it unaware of its existence. "Pride," says Oswald Sanders, "is a sin of whose presence its victim is least conscious." God hates pride and had much to say about it throughout the Bible. He said this about pride in Jeremiah 13:15-17. "Hear and give ear: do not be proud, for the Lord has spoken. But if you will not hear it, My soul will weep in secret for your pride; My eyes will weep bitterly and run down with tears, because the Lord's flock has been taken captive."

Did you get that? When God sees His people filled with pride it brings Him to tears! Not the pride itself, but the resulting captivity that pride brings to us. Captivity holds the concept of being carried away and held against one's will. Someone said that pride is the one thing that makes everyone sick except the one who has it.

Amazing isn't it? The proud moment that places us into pride's grip is that which takes us away into pride's prison. There is no safe level of pride. It always leads to captivity and to tears on the face of God.

Lord, help me to keep my pride in check.

January 5

A Willing Student

A high-school student was part of a band which performed on a Caribbean cruise. His friends tried to entice him into the ship's bar, but the young man, whose mother was an alcoholic, had memorized verses from Proverbs about alcohol abuse. He explained to his friends that addiction ran in his family and that he would not yield to their suggestion. Then he had the courage to quote Scripture to them: "Wine is a mocker, strong drink is a brawler, and whoever is led astray by it is not wise." (Proverbs 20:1) They replied, "Come on, man. Just one beer won't hurt." He replied, "At the last it bites like a serpent and stings like a viper" (Proverbs 23:32). They accused him of not being a good friend and a spoil sport, to which he said, "If sinners entice you, do not consent." (Proverbs 1:10) "Leave him be," he heard one of the young men say to the others. "He's so full of Scripture we can't do a thing with him!"

Nothing is more enjoyable than sitting under an excellent teacher and there is no better teacher than God's word. But no teacher will be capable of sharing truth without willing students. God speaks to us with these words, "Give ear and hear my voice, listen and hear my speech. For He instructs him in right judgment, his God teaches him."~Isaiah 28:23,26

As you journey through this year make sure that you are a willing student. God is always teaching. In some of the most insignificant moments God is speaking. Are you listening?

His charge against Israel in this same chapter was that they never came to the knowledge of the truth. They were like a farmer who plowed forever, but never planted. Nice looking fields. Straight rows. No fruit. God's intent is for us to be fruitful. That means plowing, seeding, watering, weeding, and harvesting. Be fruitful! No shortcuts though! Learning is a lifelong process!

Lord, help me to always be willing to learn.

5

January 6

Focus on the Task

 We live in a time where multi-tasking is honored. I do it. You do it. They do it. The better we are at it the more we brag about how much we can get done simultaneously. But truthfully, true multi-tasking is impossible for us. Our minds can only focus on one thing at a time. It may seem that things are happening simultaneously, but in reality they are sequential.

We are like the little boy who went with his family on vacation to the Grand Canyon. The guide said that the canyon at that point was one-mile deep. The little fellow couldn't help himself, so he leaned over the rail to spit as hard as he could. That night he wrote in his diary, "Today, I went to the Grand Canyon. I spit a whole mile." We tend to make a lot more of abilities than what is true. It may seem like you are spitting a mile, but we both know better!

As the army of Israel was being formed the captains were instructed to allow all distracted soldiers to go take care of their distractions be it home or vineyard or family and then return to the battle. We read of this in Deuteronomy 20. Here's how it concludes: "And so it shall be, when the officers have finished speaking to the people, that they shall make captains of the armies to lead the people."~Deuteronomy 20:9

To lead you must put aside the distractions. Capable leaders are focused on the task. Quit spitting in the wind or down the canyon wall. Ask God to help you lay down your multi-tasking lifestyle. Simplify and serve!

Lord, help me stay focused today.

January 7

Shine On

I read somewhere that it is possible to push a needle through a concrete block if you just take your time and exert a steady pressure. Too much you break the needle; too little you have no influence on the block.

As Christians we live in a concrete block world. It's hard and difficult to make changes, but NOT IMPOSSIBLE! Jesus said our influence should be like a bright light shining in a dark world. "'You are the light of the world. A city that is set on a hill cannot be hidden. Nor do they light a lamp and put it under a basket, but on a lampstand, and it gives light to all who are in the house. Let your light so shine before men, that they may see your good works and glorify your Father in heaven.'"~Matthew 5:14-16

Three verbs are used to describe us as light. First, we *are* light. It is not artificial light. Second, we *give* light. Light is not meant to be hidden. It simply shines to all without prejudice. Third, we are to *let* our light shine not to bring glory to the light, but to the one who brought us into the light in the first place. Remember, light makes NO NOISE! It just silently shines as it pierces the darkness.

Our responsibility is not to destroy the block or remove the darkness. We are to insert ourselves into our surroundings and have an influence. We are like that city on a hill. Even though small it cannot be hidden. Press on! Shine bright! Make a difference where you live, in the time you live, and by the way you live!

Lord, help me to shine forth into the darkness.

January 8

Faithful in the Small Stuff

 We live in a world that promotes everything that is BIG. If it's big it gets all of the attention and that makes big seem like the best. We can be so affected by this that we begin to overlook the small in favor of the big. In Perth, Australia the world's largest hamburger was constructed. It weighed in at 1000 pounds. Though the largest on record, the health department deemed it inedible. So, a tiny one dollar burger in this case would provide more use than a 1000 pound monstrosity. There is nothing inherently bad about big. Big just has a way of tricking us into thinking that unless it is big it's just not important.

Jesus told his disciples that our faithfulness is measured by our response to the small things not the big stuff. "He who is faithful in what is least is faithful also in much; and he who is unjust in what is least is unjust also in much."~Luke 16:10 Do you feel like you are in a small place doing small things? Has no one recognized the work you are doing? The words of Jesus give us great hope in a world of bigness. We are simply required to be faithful right where we live and in what we do. Be faithful in the small things and there will be no doubt as to your faithfulness in larger things.

BE FAITHFUL!

Your day of big things may come, but if not, the day will come in which you will hear, "Well done, good and FAITHFUL servant!" Our big God takes note of the small stuff. Never forget: It's stuff that is small; not people. There are no big you's and little me's. BE FAITHFUL!

Lord, help me to be faithful in the small stuff.

January 9

Song of Praise

Ever heard the phrase, "Well, it's nothing to sing about!" The idea is that we just aren't impressed or the outcome was not to our liking. When Robert Ingersoll, the noted agnostic died, his funeral notice informed those who would attend that there would be no singing at his funeral. I guess it would have been useless anyway, since he was probably not impressed with the outcome of his life. How this contrasts to the lives of Christian martyrs who were noted by Roman officials as a people who sang while they were carted off to be slaughtered in the great coliseums.

When Israel returned to build the second temple a spontaneous reaction occurred at the completion of the foundation. "And they sang responsively, praising and giving thanks to the Lord: 'For He is good, for His mercy endures forever toward Israel.' Then all the people shouted with a great shout, when they praised the Lord, because the foundation of the house of the Lord was laid."~Ezra 3:11

This verse says that they sang responsively. The word responsively means to eye and take heed. The singing was the result of them regaining something lost, i.e., the temple. You and I, as believers, should sing because we have something that can never be taken away from us. We are born again and now we are the temple of God. God is in us and with us at all times. Now that's something to sing about!

How about it? Is there something for you to sing about today? No? I sure hope it doesn't take a loss and a regaining for you to see that for which God can be praised. Stop now! Take heed! Look for a reason to praise Him and respond with a song of thanks!

Lord, help me to always have a song in my heart.

January 10

Vanilla World

 There is a new ice cream shop in town. It's called Baskin and Robbins Vanilla. I'm not sure if it's going to make it though. It seems that some people have other preferences than vanilla.

Can you believe that? Of course you can, because if you are like me vanilla is an insult to my ice cream taste buds. I'll eat it in a pinch, but I'd prefer lots of stuff thrown in the mix.

Have you ever noticed that your church is not First Church of Vanilla? Furthermore, if you are a vanilla person this just makes for a miserable time for you. The early church was quite cosmopolitan. Is that a new flavor? Excuse me, I digress to the ice cream once again!

The church of Paul's day was filled with new believers who had lots of baggage. So he instructed the church in Romans 12:10, "Be kindly affectionate to one another with brotherly love, in honor giving preference to one another..."

Do you see it? We are to give way in our vanilla world and realize that we must love and even honor those who are different. The idea is that of leading out in this process so that others will follow. Let's make an effort to love our differences. We must keep the truth in place; that is a given. That's what makes us all ice cream first. We start there. Then we can accept a little fruit and nuts along the way!

James Dobson spoke of differences in marriage and said that if both spouses were the same, then one would be unnecessary. I think it is the same in the church. God knew what he was doing when he put you into the mix. Remember, you just may be one of the nuts!

Lord, help me to respect every "flavor" you have placed in the church.

January 11

A Cloak and a Cigar Box

When I was a little boy and big fancy malls didn't exist, we used to go to a place called Delmont Village in Baton Rouge to shop. There were about ten stores, the anchor store being J.C. Penny. I still remember a man who sat on a board that had casters mounted on the bottom. This was his method of movement for he had no legs. Sitting next to him was a cigar box where people could give some money to help him. In return he would offer a pencil.

I always looked for him because I knew my daddy would give me some change to put in his box. He would always give me a pencil, which as a little boy, I would readily take. I took the pencil knowing what would happen next. As soon as my daddy saw the pencil, he would make me take it back to the man. I knew this, but I always went through the double transaction anyway.

Just outside of Jericho sat a blind man named Bartimaeus. He was always there I suppose, like the legless man at the shopping center. But this day was different. Jesus was passing by. When Bartimaeus heard the noise of the crowd and the name of Jesus, he began to cry out for mercy from his perpetual darkness. Then the sweetest words I have ever read are recorded for us. "So Jesus stood still and commanded him to be called. Then they called the blind man, saying to him, 'Be of good cheer. Rise, He is calling you.'"~Mark 10:49

JESUS STOOD STILL! Oh, the day that Jesus stood still to my cry is as fresh as ever in my heart. I was like Bartimaeus–blind in my sins and trespasses. I was like the man at Delmont Village–no longer able to run from the one who loved me so. I was like both of these men–only able to beg my way through this life. But, JESUS STOOD STILL!

Calling unto Bartimaeus, Jesus watched a blind man by faith leave his cloak behind. Blind folks don't lay things down with little hope of finding them again. Bartimaeus knew by faith that he would *look* for his cloak with his own eyes after going to Jesus. And so it was. "Then Jesus said to him, 'Go your way; your faith has made you well.' And immediately he received his sight and followed Jesus on the road.'"~Mark 10:52

Is it time to cry out to Jesus? He's passing by your way today. Call out to him and watch Him stand still. You can leave your cloak and your cigar box behind!

Lord, help me call out to You today and watch you stand still.

January 12

Shipwrecked

When you think about accidents most of them fall in the arena of cars or the occasional aircraft, but there were at least 27 major ships that went down to the bottom of the sea last year. Shipwrecks don't seem to make the news as much anymore unless they cause great loss of life. In nearly every case the ship is lost by careless operation in uncharted waters or the warning signs of foul weather are ignored.

Paul warned Timothy about shipwrecks of faith. "...having faith and a good conscience, which some having rejected, concerning the faith have suffered shipwreck,..."~1 Timothy 1:19 This word *shipwreck* in biblical times was never used generically. It would always be spoken of in context of the cause of the ship's loss. Even so, Paul describes the cause of this shipwreck of faith. The ship was lost when a good conscience was rejected.

Conscience is that moral bearing that helps us make the right decisions. It might be likened in this context to the ship's mate who takes regular soundings to determine the water's depth. When a ship sails in deep open water, this may not be as necessary, but as a ship comes into proximity of obstacles it is very necessary to the survival of the ship and all on board. The person who rejects the moral sounding of a God-given conscience is a shipwreck waiting to happen.

When a ship slips beneath the waves it is a total loss. Take care as you sail life's seas lest in a careless moment you suffer total loss and like the news of shipwrecks today you are just second page news. Take regular soundings in your life. The obstacles will not move, you must. Avoid the dangers that lie just beneath the surface and enjoy blessed sailing!

Lord, help me to guard against the unseen dangers.

January 13

Companion of Fools

 Scientists tell us that our sense of smell is more connected to our memories than any other sense. How many times has a memory come rushing back to your mind when you were confronted with a scent? Of course, that scent has the potential of bringing back good or bad memories. For example, if you smell spoiled milk, you don't need to taste it to verify that it is bad. Your sense of smell quickly reminds you of the taste that you once experienced. On the other hand, the scent of chocolate chip cookies baking summons fond memories of a handful of those cookies and a cold glass of milk.

Here's another question. Who do you smell like? Maybe that's a little personal, but you and I know that we quickly pick up the smell of those with whom we've been in company. I've never smoked, but I grew up in a home where both parents did. Now when I come into contact with a smoker I can smell their habit even though they are not smoking at the moment. I wonder how many people thought I was a smoker. I was affected by the company I was keeping.

Proverbs puts it this way, "He who walks with wise men will be wise, But the companion of fools will be destroyed."~Proverbs 13:20

Our lives are affected deeply by the company we keep. The phrase "companion of fools" literally means to station oneself in the sheepfold of stupid sheep. It's hard to live in the sheepfold and not smell like sheep. On the positive side of this if you associate with wise folks wisdom will rub off on you!

So, do you smell smart or stupid? If you're not sure, ask a friend. They can tell you what you smell like because of their close association with you in your daily walk. THEY KNOW! THEY'RE USED TO YOUR SMELL!

Lord, help me to smell like I've been close to You.

January 14

Making Room

Most of us are notorious for holding on to stuff. Somewhere in your house is a junk drawer or a junk closet. No, I haven't been looking in your window! It's just our nature to keep stuff for some reason and we can usually find justification for doing so. And besides, I have my own junk drawer!

When Nehemiah rode into Jerusalem with a desire to rebuild the walls he could have gotten discouraged. There were places that he and his horse could not pass through because of the rubble. Not only did the junk pose a problem for the new construction, but it provided a place for the enemy to hide and sling insults.

"Then Judah said, 'The strength of the laborers is failing, and there is so much rubbish that we are not able to build the wall.' And our adversaries said, 'They will neither know nor see anything, till we come into their midst and kill them and cause the work to cease.'"~Nehemiah 4:10-11

What is God calling you to do? Have you been discouraged and slow in getting started? Perhaps a trip to the dump is in order. Look closely at the stuff you've been hoarding. LET GO AND LET GOD! You'll be surprised how much room there is for God's plan when our junk is removed.

Happy sorting!

Lord, help me to get rid of my junk today.

January 15

Enlarge Your Heart

 The human heart is an amazing organ. It is about the size of an adult fist and with its four chambers pumps about five quarts of blood through our bodies every sixty seconds. Though it is very small we cannot survive if it is severely damaged. In some cases, because of health issues the heart will become enlarged and dilated. But in the case of an athlete, the heart will increase in size with no apparent concerns for health.

Hear the Psalmist as he speaks these words. "I will run the course of Your commandments for You shall enlarge my heart."~Psalms 119:32 Jesus said, "If you love me, keep my commandments."~John 14:15 How are we to follow Him and keep His commands while having such little hearts? Remember: Big God. Little me. When I look in the mirror I see me–little me. But I serve a big God!

We can keep His commands because the answer does not lie within, but without. It is God who commands and then prepares within us the ability to obey. God lays a course for us and then gives us the stamina to run well. Like a well-trained athlete our heart grows in its capacity to support the demands of the race.

What a great God we serve! He knows we are feeble and frail as dust. So in mercy He equips us to keep that which He commands! Now run! It's all up to Him!

Lord, help me keep in spiritual shape so I can run the race.

January 16

Turn Around

I like to ask people where they are from as a way of understanding better who they are. Sometimes after they tell me of their hometown, I will jokingly tell them that their hometown sounds like a good place to be from. That statement can be taken two ways. Your hometown may hold great memories and be a good place to talk about, but sometimes our hometowns are just a good place to be away from at this point in our lives.

Egypt has always held a bad connotation for the children of God. Abram fled there in the famine, lied to Pharaoh, allowed Hagar into his home and the rest as they say is history. It is a good place to be from spiritually.

Again and again scripture tells us about the bad things that happened when Israel trusted in Egypt instead of God. Turning to Egypt is synonymous with trusting the world or the flesh, i.e., our own strength. Where does this turn to "Egypt" begin for us?

Acts 7:39 tells us the source of failure to trust God as we make the turn towards our spiritual Egypt. "...And in their hearts they turned back to Egypt..." It always begins in the heart. Our affections are misplaced and our dependence is displaced and suddenly we wake up in the shadow of the pyramids.

Satan will convince you that it's just a little side trip, but remember this. Sin will always take you further than you wanted to go and keep you longer than you wanted to stay! Put up a spiritual roadside in your heart. WELCOME TO THE CITY LIMITS OF EGYPT! When you see this sign: TURN AROUND IMMEDIATELY!

Lord, help me to know when I need to turn around.

January 17

Doing God's Will

 Many folks have a deep desire to know God's will. Not so many have as deep a desire to *do* God's will. This is much like a person who desires to learn a second language. They will add lots of new words to their vocabulary, but unless that person takes those new words and puts them to use in everyday life they will never really learn the language. Knowing is not particularly doing.

Take for example the command to forgive others. We know the will of God concerning this. We are to forgive unconditionally, but we don't! We are hesitant as we wait for a move on the other person's part. We won't until they will. But until we will they most likely won't.

Stop now and make the decision that you will even if they won't! God put it this way, "And the world is passing away and the lust of it; but he who does the will of God abides forever."~1 John 2:17 We cannot wait for the doing of God's will to become fashionable or even acceptable. We must get out there and just do His will. When we do this it will become like a second language to us. It will become more and more comfortable to us and will help us to communicate God's perfect will.

Do the will of God regardless! Even if others will not! After all, the promise of doing God's will is that we will live forever! Wouldn't you like to live forever? Get busy doing God's will...

Lord, help me to do Your will today.

January 18

Sold Out

God declares His power and sovereignty in many ways, but none so amaze me as His ability to use the ungodly and/or unbeliever for His own magnificent purpose. God sends the rain on the just and the unjust alike. He will prosper the wicked and allow his possessions to increase all the while preparing them for His own use. Everything that is, belongs to the God of this universe, and He can and will call it into His use.

So with Cyrus the king of Lebanon. Scripture tells us that God raised him up and then used him to provide all of the timber from the great cedar forest of Lebanon for the rebuilding of the temple. "Thus says the Lord to His anointed, to Cyrus, whose right hand I have held—'I am the Lord, and there is no other; there is no God besides Me. I will gird you, though you have not known Me that they may know from the rising of the sun to its setting that there is none besides Me. I am the Lord, and there is no other.'"~Isaiah 45:1;5-6

God called Cyrus "anointed." Literally set aside for service. And in doing so, He declared Himself to be the one and only true God. If God can use a pagan king to demonstrate His own power and glory I wonder what the world would think of our God if they saw just one Christian totally sold out to His service?

You can be that person today! Not in your strength or self-righteousness, but clothed in His mercy and grace. You may not own the cedars of Lebanon, but you can lay down the seed of faith through your life and perhaps even after you are long passed from the scene God will say, "You were my anointed and because you freely gave your life to Me, I have raised up a giant forest of the faithful that declare, 'Our God is the Lord; there is no other!'"

Lord, help me to live my life knowing that it belongs to You.

January 19

Under God's Hand

 There is a familiar thought that seems prevalent among some congregations relative to their pastor. It goes something like this: LORD YOU KEEP HIM HUMBLE AND WE WILL KEEP HIM POOR! Now that will bless your socks off, don't you think?

In reality, humility is not the responsibility of God in the Christian life. Peter said it this way in his first epistle, "Therefore humble yourselves under the mighty hand of God, that He may exalt you in due time, casting all your care upon Him, for He cares for you."~1 Peter 5:6-7

Did you catch that? YOU humble YOURSELF! Could God humble you? Of course, and I believe that sometimes God does put us in circumstances that promote humility, but the actual act comes as we place ourselves under His hand.

Now here's where it gets interesting. We humble ourselves under His hand when we place our cares and concerns in His hand! You see humility is not self-abasement. Humility is the release of the pride-filled attitude that says I can take care of this myself.

What are you facing today? Whatever it is may be in your life through God's hand so you will place it in God's hand and thereby be under God's hand! And that's where you will be exalted in due time! Being humbled may seem a bad place to be, but it certainly reduces your chance of making a wrong decision when the only way out is up!

Lord, help me to be humbled at all times today.

January 20

The Lord's Doing

I am a little slow on the uptake at times. God moves mightily, I miss
it while it's happening, and then I respond with an astounding,
"WOW!" I wish there was an instant replay on life. It would be worth
watching it all in slow motion, just so I could grasp it all.

The Psalmist stated it this way, "This was the Lord's doing; it is marvelous in our
eyes."~Psalms 118:23 This verse was written in response to the fact that even
though Christ was rejected He will become the Chief Cornerstone. None of us
do well at reconciling something like rejection as the Lord's doing. We quickly
attribute anything that causes us hurt or pain as coming from Satan, but the
Psalmist says in this verse that it was not only God's doing that Jesus was rejected;
it was marvelous! Again, that just leaves me saying, "Wow!"

The things that happen in my life certainly do not compare to the rejection of
Jesus by His own people, but I am still amazed at what God can do to turn around
a situation. Remember this when it's dark and hopeless: God is at work! It is the
Lord's doing! We cannot trust our opinion on the matter. God's thoughts are
greater than ours. His ways are past understanding.

Be prepared to be amazed. No matter how dark this day may be for you, the sun
will shine again, and you will stand in jaw-dropping amazement at what God has
done. In that day, you can join me with a simple word of amazement...Wow!

Lord, help me to never lose my amazement at Your great works.

January 21

Perfect

 Oh well, nobody's perfect! I am sure you have heard that one a thousand times. Sometimes we hear it...sometimes we say it! It is a true statement, but it is not a complete statement. It does not take into account what happens in a person who meets the living God and has their life changed by the encounter.

Yes, nobody is perfect in this flesh that we live yet God told Abraham, "I am Almighty God; walk before Me and be blameless."~Genesis 17:1 The word blameless could be translated perfect. Now that leaves us in a quandary. We know that no one is perfect yet God tells Abraham to be so.

Was God just not aware of the propensity of man to be anything but perfect? Of course not!

Here's the answer. God never commands that which He cannot perform in the one to whom the command is given. With every command comes the ability to perform! Time and again Jesus performed miracles in lives and concluded by saying, "You've been made whole. Go and sin no more." The word *whole* holds the same thought as being blameless or perfect. Again, the command is followed by the ability to perform. When Jesus said you've been made whole He was revealing to those people who had been touched by Him that their wholeness, i.e., perfection, was based on Him living in them. It was not on the condition that brought them to Him!

We are commanded to be holy as He is holy; perfect as He is perfect; as whole as He is whole. HE MAKES THIS HAPPEN! He fills us with His Spirit who guides us into His righteousness and perfection. If you have trusted Him then God sees Him not you. When God sees Him, He sees the Lamb without spot or blemish. And that is just perfect!

Lord, help me to live in Your perfection.

January 22

This Generation

Have you noticed that righteousness does not easily pass from generation to generation? Josiah was the godly boy king who came to the throne and brought revival to Israel. He turned the nation's heart back to God. Each generation is responsible, however, to pass along the promises of God and to seek Him for themselves.

Now listen to these words which God spoke to Josiah's son: "I spoke to you in your prosperity, but you said, 'I will not hear.' This has been your manner from your youth that you did not obey My voice."~Jeremiah 22:21

You've heard it before. It only takes one generation to forsake God and turn a nation away from following Him. Is God that judgmental and unforgiving? No! This verse tells us that God spoke in the day of prosperity and spoke even from the days of youth, but they would not hear! When tragedy befalls a nation it is caused not so much by a misuse of hands, but by a deafened ear. There will always be those who are engaged in ungodliness. But God is still speaking and waiting on us to hear His voice even in a moral wilderness.

Listen! God is speaking. You and I need only listen. If we hear, then obedience will be quite naturally the next step. If we obey, I believe God will bring the day of prosperity back to this land. No president, no congress, no government can create prosperity unless God is heard.

Shhh! Listen! God still speaks in that still small voice. Hear Him. Obey Him. Be prosperous.

Lord, help me to hear Your voice today.

January 23

Our Team Wins

 Fame is a fleeting characteristic that exalts one day and evaporates the next. Our heroes come and go in this day that we live. Records seem to be broken before the ink is dry. Again and again human frailty rises to engulf the victor and we experience the truth of our own mortality.

Not so with our God! Habakkuk puts it this way: "Lord, I have heard of your fame; I stand in awe of your deeds, O Lord. Renew them in our day, in our time make them known..."~Habakkuk 3:2 The prophet was writing in a day when it seemed that the glory of God's fame had faded.

Like one mulling over old record books he begins to remember the days when God's power had been revealed among His people. These memories caused him to be awestruck at God's ability. Then as if he remembered that time nor circumstance can weaken the God of heaven he calls for God to come back on the field, take up His former position, and let today's "fans" see what God can do!

WHAT A MIGHTY GOD WE SERVE!

Show yourself Lord and may the crowds bow before you in awe of your deeds. Let us raise the banner! Let the cheers resound as we lift up our voices! Spend no time looking at the scoreboard! We win in spite of the score or the time left on the clock! Our God has taken the field as the captain of our team! Hallelujah and amen!

Lord, help me to never forget that we win in the end.

January 24

Mirror, Mirror

There are times when heaven seems silent. The doors of the gate appear shut and made of brass. We have sought the Lord in prayer, but there is no answer. What should you do at these times? There is no one else to turn to in our time of need. We know that He holds the answer. Should we not with open mouth continue to plead with heaven? I suggest that you take a look in the mirror!

Stay with me now... Go ahead... Take a long look... Study especially your face. See those two things sticking out from the side if your head. EARS! See those two big round objects just above and on either side of your nose. EYES!

Now ask this question. Who made these eyes and ears? Stay with me... You know that God made both and He did so to make us aware of our world, but more importantly aware of Him.

The Psalmist declares, "Can the One who shaped the ear not hear, the One who formed the eye not see?"~Psalms 94:9 Now answer those questions with a resounding, YES! God does see and God does hear even when we think heaven doesn't care anymore.

Keep praying and keep knocking, but never stop using your God-given senses to see and hear what God is doing. You will be surprised what God is up to in your life. Now, get up and go look in the mirror and while you're there be amazed at the great things that God has done!

Lord, help me to see myself just as You do.

January 25

Thinking About You

 Have you ever developed the idea that you are a middle child? Not physically, though that may be, but spiritually. You feel like God paid a lot of attention to the first borns like Adam and Abraham and even David. And it seems that He pays a lot of attention to the newborns too. Everyone coos over the new Christian and keeps talking about how happy they are to have them in the family. We are really happy, but what about us middle kids?

Do you just wish God would send you a "Just Thinking About You" card? Come on now! You know you do... Well, guess what? He has and it's found in Psalm 40:5. "Many, O Lord my God, are Your wonderful works which You have done; and Your THOUGHTS toward us cannot be recounted to You in order; if I would declare and speak of them, they are more than can be numbered."

See there it is! Just a little thinking about you note to bump you out of your middle-child doldrums! As a matter of fact the Psalmist declares that God thinks so much about us that it is impossible to put it all in logical order or begin to speak of them.

Go ahead...try writing them all down and you will quickly run out of numbers to ascribe to your list. When you are done why not take a moment and drop a "Just Thinking About You" note to someone you know. Remind them of how much God really loves them and that He has continual thoughts of their welfare. It could be that this person is feeling like a middle child today and they just need to know that you are thinking of them. Both of you will have a blessed day just for the thought!

Lord, help me give a word of encouragement to someone today.

January 26

Today

"So he said, 'Tomorrow.'"~Exodus 8:10 This was the word of Pharaoh spoken to Moses.

Here's the context. God brought frogs upon the land as part of the plagues that affected all of Egypt. The frogs were EVERYWHERE! In the people's beds, in their water, and in their food. Pharaoh summoned Moses and implored him to seek God's hand to remove the frogs.

I HATE FROGS! And I'm going to assume at the least that by this time Pharaoh hated them also. This is where the story gets funny, but sad. Moses said to Pharaoh, "Accept the honor of saying when I shall intercede for you, for your servants, and for your people, to destroy the frogs from you and your houses, that they may remain in the river only."~Exodus 8:9 And Pharaoh gave Moses the answer that is seen in the opening words of this devotional. TOMORROW! Tomorrow? You've got to be kidding me! Tomorrow? Why not NOW?

Tomorrow is the day of dieters and drunkards. Today is the appointed time, even the day of salvation. What have you been seeking from the Lord? It is time to act. Say, "Today, Lord! Not tomorrow! For I am weary of frogs in my soup. I cannot put this off another day. TODAY...LORD! Or I die!"

Sometimes the answer to our prayer comes in accordance to the urgency of our asking. And Moses said, "Let it be according to your word, that you may know that there is no one like the LORD our God. Don't wait for another tomorrow. The time will come when tomorrow won't. Ask boldly today; ask that it be done today that it may be according to your word.

Lord, help me to not put off to tomorrow what I should do today.

January 27

The Game of Life

 I have a card game that we play once in a while. It is called Flux. The unusual thing about this game is that the rules are constantly changing, therefore, the name Flux. Cards are drawn which change direction of play, cause you to exchange cards with other players, rewrites how you win, etc. It's a fun game, but it can be frustrating.

There is just something about not being sure what the rules are. As much as most of us despise rules we like them at the same time. We take comfort in them. This is why people spend so much time seeing just how far they can go. We really are trying the limits. It's the old "I'm going to count to three" game that parents play with their children.

Solomon showed us the limit in Proverbs 4. "My son, give attention to my words. Incline your ear to my sayings. Do not let them depart from your eyes. Keep them in the midst of your heart. For they are life to those who find them and health to all their flesh. Keep your heart with all diligence for out of it spring the issues of life."~Proverbs 4:20-23 The word *issues* would be well translated as limits. It is our heart that sets the limits in our life. But wait! Isn't the heart of man desperately wicked?

Yes, so Solomon preceded the idea of trusting our hearts to limit our actions by telling us to fill it with God's word. Like an antiseptic it cleanses and like an immunization it works as a preventative. With God's word firmly planted in our hearts our lives will never be in flux. Now let's go play the game of life within the limits of God's word!

Lord, help me to always know Your word before I play the game of life.

January 28

Posthaste!

The word "posthaste" came into usage during the reign of Henry VIII of England. Relays of horses were stationed in principal towns in England. When a letter was stamped "posthaste," it meant "ride for your life!" If a carrier was caught delaying on route, he was hanged! Letters of the sixteenth century often bore a drawing of a letter carrier suspended from the gallows. Beneath the drawing occurred the words: "Haste! Post haste! Haste for thy life!"

This illustration might help us understand the words of Paul to Archippus, "Take heed to the ministry which you have received in the Lord, that you may fulfill it."~Colossians 4:17

Archippus evidently was a deacon and the same word translated ministry here is where we derive our word deacon. But Paul's instruction carries weight for all believers today. Each of us have a ministry and knowing that time is short we too should make haste!

Thank God we are not in danger of being hanged for dilly-dallying, but we serve a King greater than Henry VIII. Our ministry is not complete until it has been fulfilled. The idea is that of cramming until nothing can be added. Like the postman of old England our lives are stamped "posthaste."

Now ride! Don't stop until the message from heaven is delivered. We must be faithful to deliver the good news that others may be waiting to hear! HASTE! POSTHASTE!

Lord, help me share the good news with someone today.

January 29

Face to Face

 I have been on a lot of retreats during my years in the ministry. Usually the retreat is a long way from home. This is necessary to get to a neutral environment, away from the office, etc. Then the schedule is handed out to the attendees. Breakfast is thirty minutes before sunrise and bedtime is somewhere around midnight. The program is jam packed with activity. The retreat becomes a workshop. They're called retreats, but they make me tired. At least it's nice to get back to the routine of the office and plan the next retreat!

All of us need to retreat now and again. So spoke the Psalmist, "Restore us, O God, cause Your face to shine and we shall be saved!"~Psalms 80:3

The restoration he spoke of did not mean to return to the start, but to allow a "do-over". Our error may have been minor or major, but the only way to get it right is to go back to the point of departure from truth. This brings a couple of questions to mind. How far back are we supposed to go? And how will we know that we've gone back far enough? There is one answer to both questions. Ask God to restore you to the point where His face shines again!

In Hebrew the word for face is plural, but it is always used singularly. God is One and has one face, yet shows each of us the face we need to see as He restores and saves us.

Here's my rendition of this verse. "Take me back Lord to the place where your face shines again so I will know the joy of my salvation." You'll never do this by yourself. Ask Him to restore you in the race. Seek His shining face. Be refreshed in His saving grace. Feel the warmth of His embrace. Have a blessed retreat and never let it become just another workshop!

Lord, help me to spend some face-to-face time with You today.

January 30

Pursuing God

The pursuits of life can take us in many directions. Very few people have life-time jobs or spend their entire existence in one town anymore. We are highly mobile and ultra-connected. We want to get where we are going quicker and never lose touch while we are getting there. Nothing blesses us more than a fast Internet connection! Our pursuit of these things keeps us so occupied that we can forget the greatest pursuit: the knowledge of God.

Clearly this is a lifelong endeavor. Truly knowing him is beyond our capacity, but we are still given the word to do just that. "Let us know; let us pursue the knowledge of the Lord. His going forth is established as the morning; He will come to us like the rain, like the latter and former rain to the earth."~Hosea 6:3

Do you see the command? To know Him is to pursue Him. Not some casual past time, but a carefully designed attempt to overtake Him and thereby gain all that He is. Here's where it gets exciting!

We discover God like the dawn of the day springing out of the darkness of night. It comes to us sometimes like the cold drizzle of fall and sometimes like the downpour of a spring rain. As water upon a dry thirsty piece of ground, receive the knowledge of Him who made you and loves you. He wants to be known by you! Make this your passionate pursuit and be surprised! Not only will you have the joy of being known by the God of heaven, but you will know Him in all of His glory. This revelation of God will be like the bounty of the harvest that is produced by the former rain upon the planted seed and the latter rain upon the mature plant. You may need a bigger barn!

Lord, help me to get ready for Your blessing.

January 31

He's Holding Us

 In a New Orleans cemetery is a monument which has created much interest. It represents a ship in the midst of a storm- tossed sea. On the bow of the ship is a mother clinging to her child. On the base of the monument is an inscription saying that they were lost at sea on July 4, 1900.

The mother and child were sole survivors of a large estate, and the question needed to be resolved as to whose name the estate be administered—the name of the mother or the daughter. The court decided it should be in the name of the child, reckoning that the little girl went down last, because the mother would hold her in a place of safety to the end. A wonderful tribute to a mother's love!

How much more does God love us?

No matter the storm or tide He holds us close. Yes, there are times we cry out like the Psalmist did in the Psalms. "Lord, do not abandon me; my God, do not be far from me."~Psalms 38:21 But be not dismayed at the wind nor the waves!

HE is the sovereign of the storm and the tamer of the tide! When the winds howl and the waters rise be sure that you know in that moment, it is He that tightens His grip upon us. Remember His promise to always be with us; even to the end of the age. Against your own intuition relax. He is holding you; not vice versa! The mother who held her child up to safety could only do so for so long. Not so with our God! His strong arms of salvation shall hold us to the end. Yea, beyond the end to all of eternity, we are safe in the arms of Jesus.

Lord, help me to never forget that You are always holding me.

February 1

Following the Example

I have some great memories of all the churches I have pastored over three decades. In each one we were involved in either a building program or remodeling of existing buildings. Even though these churches were a blessing to serve, each one was both unique and a challenge. I am blessed to have learned so much from these congregations over these years.

While building the two story educational building at FBC, Livingston it came time to install the pre-fabricated joists that would be the ceiling for the first floor and the floor of the second level. I learned something that day as Mike Lott, our builder and fellow church member, helped us install these very large and cumbersome pieces of the puzzle that would become our building.

The man on each end of these long joists was given a piece of board cut to represent the exact distance these joists had to be apart from each other. Mike called these templates a "preacher". They are called this because they are cut precisely and keep a project true to the plan. That has stuck with me to this day. The Apostle Paul spoke to the Philippians using a similar example. "Brethren, join in following my example, and note those who so walk, as you have us for a pattern."~Philippians 3:17

Is your life a pattern that can be laid out for all to see and even use to gauge their own lives? Ask God to make you the pattern that others can model. Thanks Mike for a great lesson so many years ago.

Lord, help me to be a faithful pattern that others can follow.

February 2

The Fear of the Lord

 Fear is a strong emotion. It can cause people to freeze, flee, or fight. Fear, therefore, can protect us from great harm. It has taken on a bad connotation in our day and we can find ourselves avoiding fear altogether. There may be times that we should apply Franklin D. Roosevelt's thoughts on fear: "The only thing we have to fear is fear itself." But this rejection of fear should not enter into our relationship with God.

We are fully in the "God is my buddy" mind set in the religious arena. Now hear me. God is a friend. But He is a friend that deserves an aura of fear. "In the fear of the Lord there is strong confidence and His children will have a place of refuge. The fear of the Lord is a fountain of life to turn one away from the snares of death."~Proverbs 14:26-27

Note the value of a healthy godly fear. In this state of reverence and awe we are filled with strong confidence. This is bold assurance based in the holiness of God and His ability not ours.

Now the greatest thing most people fear is death, but in these verses we learn that fear properly rendered toward the Lord does not lead to death, but to life. And not just life, but a fountain of life. The idea is of a water source flowing of its own accord. This source issues forth and gives not only life, but the ability to turn away from death.

Unless Christ comes first, we ALL will die. But for the believer here is the good news! We may die, but we never have to experience death! Now engage this day in the fear of the Lord and enjoy the abundant, overflowing life promised to all who believe!

Lord, help me to live today with a sense of holy fear.

February 3

Rattled!

It never ceases to amaze me having walked with the Lord now for many years, watching Him intercede multiple times, and perform miracles beyond comprehension that I still get rattled. Excuse me:

I STILL GET RATTLED!!!

We (that makes me feel better using the plural) can take comfort that we are not experiencing this as a first nor do we walk this corridor alone.

Listen carefully to the words of the Psalmist and you can hear the rattle across 3000 years of humanity: "Why are you cast down, O my soul? And why are you disquieted within me? Hope in God, for I shall yet praise Him for the help of His countenance."~Psalms 42:5 That one word *disquieted* says it all. It means to make noise, clamor, be unsettled, RATTLE!

It's loud! It doesn't stop when you do. It can even wake you up at night as if you have heard the sound of an intruder, but it's not someone or something trying to get in; it's something trying to get out of us.

How can you quiet the rattle? Two steps: (1) redirect your focus from the rattle and place your hope in the only One who can do soul surgery; (2) get into the face of God. This last one is important. The psalmist said he received help from the face of God. Like a lost child that suddenly sees the face of a parent our rattle will calm down when we make sure that we see the face of God. Now this can either be a noisy day for you or a calm one and the decision is all yours...

Lord, help me not get rattled today.

February 4

Hide and Seek

 It's fun to remember childhood games. Silly little games like Red Rover, Colored Chicks, and Hide-and-Go-Seek. We even played a version of that last one in the dark! It was called Ghost in the Graveyard. I still have a scar on my shin from running over the water hydrant in the pitch dark as I was being chased. Oh sweet memories of childhood and the risk we take as kids!

Sometimes it may seem that God is playing hide and seek with us. But He really wants to be found! These words from 2 Chronicles occurred during the reign of Asa. Clearly, God desires to be found. "And Azariah went out to meet Asa, and said to him: 'Hear me, Asa, and all Judah and Benjamin. The Lord is with you while you are with Him. If you seek Him, He will be found by you; but if you forsake Him, He will forsake you. For a long time Israel has been without the true God, without a teaching priest, and without law; but when in their trouble they turned to the Lord God of Israel, and sought Him, He was found by them.' Then they took an oath before the Lord with a loud voice, with shouting and trumpets and rams' horns."~2 Chronicles 15:2-4;14

Just like it was when you were discovered playing hide and seek, you would let out a scream and everyone knew you had been found. Israel sounded forth with shouts and trumpets that God had been found and was with them again. Take the risk even though it is dark. Seek Him today. He wants to be found. Seek Him early and He WILL allow Himself to be discovered. Then sound forth the good news. Let out a shout and tell the whole land that you walk in fellowship with the God of the universe!

Lord, help me find You early in the morning.

February 5

Known By God

Let's be honest. Worship isn't what it used to be. Nearly everything we do seems focused on us not Him who made us. Let this verse realign your worship: "Lord, what is man, that You take knowledge of him? Or the son of man, that You are mindful of him?"~Psalms 144:3

Two words jump out for our consideration. The words *knowledge* and *mindful* from this verse give us insight into what God thinks of us and how this should frame our worship.

The idea of God having knowledge of us is not one of expectation or right on our part. It holds the concept of recognition and care in a familiar relationship as of close kin. We approach God in worship as a child would a parent out of deepest respect and understanding that our very existence and maintenance depends on Him. We did not bring ourselves into this relationship! We cannot keep ourselves in it!

The second word is the word mindful. The Hebrew word translated *mindful* means to plait or weave like one would do with hair. God has intertwined us into Himself! We are woven into His very being by His Holy Spirit!

So, as you approach Him in worship think not how impressed He is that you showed up, but be filled with awe that He has accepted you into Himself and welcomes you as a child upon His lap of dependency!

Lord, help me approach You as a child today.

February 6

God Alone

 We continue to peer deeper and deeper into space with the aid of such incredible telescopes like the Hubble space telescope that orbits the earth. When I hear of some new discovery it seems always couched in the thought of somehow getting a look back to our origin. What a futile experiment?

Scripture clearly gives us the origin of the universe. "He alone spreads out the heavens and treads on the waves of the sea."~Job 9:8 Notice He did it alone. This one verse finishes the discussion for me. I accept it by faith and need no further explanation. The evolutionists on the other hand need to arise every day, take a long look into the past and extrapolate a theory about what they see in the dark.

You may well say to me that words alone prove nothing. I would agree except for the conclusion of this verse. I know He has stretched out the heavens because He has come walking on the roaring waves of my life in the dark and stormy times!

Men will continue to look far away into the darkness of space with the hope of finding hope. I need only look to my last rescue from the dark of my own soul and there he is walking with authority and power upon the heights of the waves. As Peter said, "If it be you Lord, bid me come!" Listen my friend. It's the voice of God on the stormy sea. "COME!"

Lord, help me to hear Your voice both near and far.

February 7

Glasses in the Grass

Parables are always interesting. They are earthly stories with heavenly meaning. God is always ready to speak to us in our everyday lives. Parables are unfolding before our very eyes if we will just take time to see.

Here's a parable that unfolded for me one frosty morning. I took my usual walk along my usual route at my usual time. Nearing the end of my journey the sun was just coming up and those first rays were glancing across the frost covered ground.

That light which has shown forth daily since creation today fell on a glint in the grass and there almost nestled down and out of sight was a pair of glasses. From the size I assumed them to belong to a child, but what child? In my hand was the recovery of sight and somewhere in my neighborhood was a child whose vision was impaired.

Just before I arrived back to my house I saw a lady scraping the same frost from her windshield that had revealed the lost glasses. I knew that she had several children in her home so I asked if any of them had lost a pair of glasses. To my surprise and I believe to her relief she said, "Yes!"

In a moment lost glasses were restored to the tiny face upon which resting could give clear vision. Only a sovereign God could have worked all of those details out to the point that He did. This "parable" showed me the lengths God is willing to go to bring spiritual sight (salvation) to the blind.

The following words come from Psalm 119 and Luke 19. I have melded these two verses into one. "I have gone astray like a lost sheep; the Son of Man has come to seek and to save that which was lost."~Psalms 119:176 and Luke 19:10

I was that lost pair of glasses. Jesus sought me out and found me, but He has done more than just find me. For as in my "parable" the glasses found were of no use until reunited with the face upon which they belonged. God in His mercy has put me into use in His blessed Kingdom.

You see, I wear glasses, but I do not wear them to see my glasses. I wear glasses to see the world clearer through their aid. God wants to use our lives like a pair of glasses. He can use your life to help others see Jesus. Not you...Jesus!

This is my parable. What's yours? Take the time today to SEE what God is saying!

Lord, help me Lord, help me help someone else see You clearly today.

February 8

God Wins!

There are days that can only be categorized as "one of those days!" We all have them. We take a wary look at the scoreboard to see our team behind and time running off the clock rapidly. I sure hope I'm not the only one that has experienced this. I doubt it very much!

What do we do when it seems that evil is winning and the wicked are openly renouncing our God. It is like the days of David and Goliath with the giant coming out day after day to ridicule us and our God. Take heart!

"[The wicked] has said in his heart, 'God has forgotten. He hides His face. He will never see.' Arise, O Lord! O God, lift up Your hand! Do not forget the humble. Why do the wicked renounce God? He has said in his heart, 'You will not require an account.'"~Psalms 10:11-13

Yes, take heart, my friend! Your God has not forgotten you nor has He forsaken forever. The wicked have made a serious mistake. They assume since they do not serve God that He will not hold them to an answer for their actions. Oh, how wrong they are!

See! God is in the valley gathering smooth stones. Already the sling is in motion and soon the rock will fly. Victory is coming! The wicked will indeed answer! Oh, victory in Jesus! My Savior forever! He sought me and He bought me! And He calls me His own! Don't mind the clock...GOD WINS!

Lord, help me to remember that You have not forgotten me.

February 9

Look to the Fruit

 This is the day of talking heads. Hour after hour of commentary by people who may or may not know one iota about what they are saying. Especially during times of elections, sales pitches on infomercials, or seemingly endless newscasts. So what are we to do? How do you sort all of this so that it makes sense?

The first place to look is to the tree from which the information is coming. More precisely check what's hanging on the end of the branch. Jesus put it this way, "Either make the tree good and its fruit good, or make the tree bad and its fruit bad; for a tree is known by its fruit."~Matthew 12:33

He was speaking to the Pharisees of His day. They were literally talking heads entering into hours of discourse as they argued the finest detail of the law, yet never experiencing the righteousness of a changed heart. Jesus said that it was the overflow of the heart that passed over the lips. "...For out of the abundance of the heart the mouth speaks. A good man out of the good treasure of his heart brings forth good things, and an evil man out of the evil treasure brings forth evil things."~(Matthew 12:34)

What are we to do? Don't be fooled by the shade of the tree, the beauty of the foliage, nor the design of the bark. The truth lies in the fruit. It is either good or bad. It either has intrinsic goodness produced by its connection to the root of the tree or it is filled with rottenness by the same connection.

In this day of information overload look to the fruit. Is it good or bad? Never be fooled by the flower. Wait for the fruit! Have a happy picking day and quickly discard any rotten fruit in your basket. It tends to only draw flies anyway!

Lord, help me to be good fruit in a rotten world.

February 10

Rats!

What did you want to be when you were growing up? I was sure that I would be a scientist. My folks bought me a chemistry set for Christmas one year. The way I figured it I needed to do some experiments. To do experiments I needed some rats. At least that's what a ten year old kid thinks when he has a chemistry set and a desire to be a famous scientist! So I built a trap and placed it in my neighbor's shed. My friend told me there were several rats in there and they all could be mine.

I still remember the excitement of setting the trap I had built with a three pound coffee can and a piece of heavy gauge wire. The next morning I was amazed to see the door of my trap closed. But to my dismay the rat had eaten through the wire door! I changed my dream right on the spot. I wasn't messing around with anything that could eat wire!

Scripture tells us that we should avoid the devil's trap. "Furthermore, he must have a good reputation among outsiders, so that he does not fall into disgrace and the devil's trap."~1 Timothy 3:7 This verse speaks expressly to those called to serve as a pastor, but holds true for all believers. The trap is always set for us and the devil is patiently waiting for us to stumble into it. We move towards capture when we lose our testimony with those who are not believers. GUARD YOUR REPUTATION!

The word *reputation* used here in this verse comes from the same word translated as martyr. So live your life in the presence of the world that when they hear your name they think of you as a martyr for the faith.

My rat ate his way out of captivity. You and I cannot get out of the devil's trap so easily. The best thing is to never enter the snare. Be a witness today and the victory and freedom will be yours!

Lord, help me to watch out for the devil's trap.

43

February 11

The Grace Filter

 I remember when my son discovered one day that he could think without speaking. It was quite a revelation to him. Until that day his mouth and brain were intricately connected and thus he talked a lot about everything. You probably know someone like that. I think we all suffer the malady from time to time. Who hasn't regretted a word too quickly spilled?

God's word speaks over and again concerning our speech. One of those verses is from the Apostle Paul as he gave us insight into this matter of using our speech as an instrument of grace. He wrote to the Ephesians: "Let no corrupt word proceed out of your mouth, but what is good for necessary edification, that it may impart grace to the hearers."~Ephesians 4:29

This is a very strong directive as to the use of our words. Paul uses intense language as he gives instruction to the church. The word *corrupt* could have been translated rotten. Now think about this. You wouldn't dare put anything rotten in your mouth so why would you allow rottenness to come out of your mouth?

Here's the test for our speech. Will it build up (edify) the person to whom I am speaking? Will my words deliver grace to the ears of the hearer? Wow! God in His grace has given us the ability to impart grace to others by our very words. How often we only think of receiving grace, but few times think of giving grace. Gracious speech has divine influence on the human heart and is reflected in the everyday life of the one who benefits thereby. The next time you get ready to open your mouth make sure that the grace filter is in place. You'll know if it is so by the reflection on the face of the one listening. If you must talk today, be gracious.

Lord, help me to say everything through a filter of grace.

February 12

A Little Help from My Friends

In some ways I still act like a two year old. I know that surprises you, but it is true! I have learned to control my words, but often my actions are saying, "I can do it myself!" Now a little independence is okay I guess, but a little goes a long way.

Moses was acting a like a two year old as he tried to be judge and jury in every matter that came before him. He was trying to do this for a couple of million people no less!

His father-in-law, Jethro, was used by God to deliver instructions concerning this matter. In essence God said, "You need a little help from your friends." Now you know where that song title came from a few years back. Moses was instructed to take some of the people and appoint them to assist him so that he would not be over burdened by the massive load. The results of doing this would be two-fold. "If you do this thing, and God so commands you, then you will be able to endure, and all this people will also go to their place in peace." ~Exodus 18:23

Asking for help would give Moses endurance. The idea is that of standing, abiding, continuing, repairing, and being established. Here's the amazing part of this, however. The effect of Moses asking for a little help from his friends is that the people whom he had been helping would begin to stand on their own. The verse above says they would return to their own place in peace. This holds the meaning of standing on your own, being established, rising up against the foe, or to be strengthened.

The next time you think about saying you can do it all by yourself remember that you will be weakening those around you. Jethro said, "If you do this thing and oh, by the way, GOD HAS COMMANDED IT!" We are in this thing called life together. Now go get a little help from your friends.

Lord, help me seek a little help from a friend today.

February 13

Alone with God

 God never intended for us to be alone. This is evident from the beginning of His creative acts. He arranged for Adam to discover his aloneness as he named all of the animals. God purposefully brought the animals before Adam male and female. Through this Adam discovered his aloneness and God provided for him a helpmate, Eve.

Spring ahead to Jacob's story in Genesis 32 and we find a man alone. "Then Jacob was left alone; and a Man wrestled with him until the breaking of day."~Genesis 32:24

As much as God never intended for us to be alone, He arranges times in our lives for us to be so. It is in those moments that God Himself enters in to speak and change us. It is a time of wrestling. Can you imagine that? Who in their right mind would attempt wrestling with God? I see that hand! And mine is raised with yours.

Know this for sure. God wants us to be changed and such change comes only as He touches our lives. In this same chapter we see the Angel of the Lord (Jesus) as He touches Jacob's hip and he was immediately immobilized. He could do nothing, but cling to the Angel.

That's exactly where God wants to get you and me. He wants us at the point of holding on for dear life. It is at this moment that we are blessed. Alone: not good; but necessary from time to time. Take time to spend time alone with God. You'll be changed forever.

Lord, help me to take the time needed to be alone with You.

February 14

Who Will You Love?

Who will you love today? Will your love only be reciprocal…loving only after you are loved? When asked what the greatest commandment was Jesus compressed ten commandments into one: LOVE! That love was to be directed towards the Lord and our neighbors. "Jesus said to him, 'You shall love the Lord your God with all your heart, with all your soul, and with all your mind. This is the first and great commandment. And the second is like it: You shall love your neighbor as yourself.'"~Matthew 22:37–39

Love God totally and your neighbor as yourself. That degree of love is defined in the sacrifice of Christ. A love that falls short of sacrifice, i.e. death, is not real love. Most of what we see and hear of love today does not have a heart of sacrifice, but a root of selfishness.

Moments after Jesus had washed the feet of the disciples he told his disciples, "A new commandment I give to you, that you love one another; as I have loved you, that you also love one another."~John 13:34

The depth of our love is measured by the love of Jesus for us. Let me rephrase the first question. WHO WILL YOU DIE FOR TODAY?

Lord, help me to love others as deeply as You have loved me.

February 15

Order

 ZBFGAJMEILD Do you have any idea what this word means? Don't worry, neither do I. It's just a few letters of the alphabet all jumbled up and out of order.

It's amazing what we can do with a mere 26 letters placed in the correct order. Hundreds of thousands of possible words can be formed. I like order! Its possibilities are endless.

God is a God of order. From the first moments of creation He was about the process of bringing order. The Apostle Paul enjoyed order as well and said so to the Colossians. "For though I am absent in the flesh, yet I am with you in spirit, rejoicing to see your good order and the steadfastness of your faith in Christ."~Colossians 2:5

There is a direct connection between order and steadfastness found here. Order brings stability to our Christian walk. This does not mean that our lives are boring or lack adventure. Paul's life was full of twists and turns as he traveled on his missionary journeys. Yet he found joy when he saw the orderliness of Christian living among the Colossians.

Your life may be topsy-turvy today, but that does not mean that you cannot maintain a sense of order. Remember what happens in a cartoon sketch when the person loses control? A thought bubble appears above their head and is filled with something that looks something like this: #h&*()?jy@!

Now such thoughts or actions make no sense, but you and I have been in similar situations where our order turns into chaos. Ask God to bring order to your chaos today. You will be happier and others will receive joy from seeing God at work in your life.

Lord, help me to seek Your order in a world of turmoil.

February 16

Houdini

There will always be another Houdini. I don't mean by this that anyone might be as adept at illusions as Houdini, but there will always be those who follow in his footsteps. At least some will follow up to the point of his greatest error. He tried to cheat death, but died trying.

As a matter of fact we all have been a little Houdini at times, especially when it comes to the attempt to escape death. Everyone knows that it's coming, yet all are attempting to escape it. And like Houdini we spend part of our days seeing how close we can come to it without it taking us.

As a believer, I know how to escape death. Not on my own through some feat of illusion, but through the One who holds the keys of death and declares victory over it. David phrased it this way in Psalm 68. "Our God is the God of salvation; and to God the Lord belong escapes from death."~Psalms 68:20

He uses some interesting words in this verse. He declares that God is the God of salvation. Clearly there is only one salvation and one way to that salvation. But he uses a plural collective form in speaking of escaping death. How can there be one salvation yet many ways to escape?

God in His infinite wisdom has made provision for us to be saved from every attempt upon our lives. He delivers first from the very cause of death, the sin of our nature. He delivers time and again in many ways that we never recognize as deliverance, i.e., what we call near misses. However, the greatest joy is to know that He has also provided an escape from that final moment when we exit this life. Oh, death where is your sting? Oh, grave where is your victory?

Stop being a Houdini! God has given to us the "escapes" from death. He is the God of our salvation! All of the applause belongs to Him!

Lord, help me to rest knowing my final escape is in Your hands.

February 17

The Overlook

 When I am driving along highways that run through mountain areas I sometimes notice a sign that says something like this: OVERLOOK–NEXT RIGHT. You have probably joined me at some time or another when you had a few extra minutes in turning aside to take a look—at least an overlook. The best we can do in this exercise is to take a very broad view of that afforded to us from our perch on a hillside. For the most part we do not really see what's below us.

I think that this is our perception of God's attention to our valley. We get the idea that God's up there somewhere giving us a casual glance–an overlook of our situation. It seems that He is just not fully aware of our need at the moment.

The children of Israel were in just such a predicament in Egypt. The Pharoah that had showed kindness toward Joseph was now dead and a new ruler was on the throne who had no affinity to the people of God. The people began to cry out to God. "So God heard their groaning, and God remembered His covenant with Abraham, with Isaac, and with Jacob. And God looked upon the children of Israel, and God acknowledged them."~Exodus 2:24-25 This was no casual overlook on God's part.

The words *looked* and *acknowledged* hold a treasure trove of truth for us. Together they mean that God showed concern by knowing their situation and giving recognition by demonstrating His care for them. This was no mere overlook on God's part. His full deliberative gaze fell upon them in their time of need.

Are you crying out to God about today? Be assured of this: He hears you! He has turned off the thoroughfare, stopped at your valley and is overlooking your particular situation. He hears your cry! He sees you!

Lord, help me to take a new look at my situation today.

February 18

Strange

I have had the joy of meeting many strangers in my life. My life as a pastor and then as an associational missionary has given me many opportunities to cross paths with folks that I did not know previously. Some of these strangers were in foreign lands as we traveled there to share the good news of the gospel.

I also have had the interesting experience of eating some strange foods. Of course, they were only strange to me because I had never tried them before. Some turned out to be quite good. Others were a one-time experience! In times like that you pray the missionary's prayer, "Lord, I'll put it down. You please keep it down!"

Peter reminds us that as believers, trials will come our way, but we will not be alone in this experience. "Beloved, do not think it strange concerning the fiery trial which is to try you, as though some strange thing happened to you."~1 Peter 4:12 Others have walked and some are walking the same path as you walk today. The phrase *think it strange* means that we should not let the thought of our trial being strange take up residence or lodge in our minds. Remember the missionary's prayer from above? "Lord, I'll accept this thing that's happening and I'll put it down. Would you please keep it down?"

Do not fear the fiery struggles of life if you are a child of God. They are the blessed hand of the Father working the stuff out of our lives so you might be filled with more and more of Him! This life is all preparatory for an eternity in His presence! Lord, help me to submit to your plan of preparation! AMEN!!!

Lord, help me to be ready for the fiery trial today.

February 19

Remembering

It is always an enjoyable time to meet with old friends and talk about yesterday. Somehow days gone by seem sweeter and simpler even though we know better.

In First Chronicles 16 we join the celebration of the return of the ark of the covenant. The ark of the covenant was for Israel a symbol of the very presence of God. The ark had been lost in battle with the Philistines some time before. A failed attempt to return it to Jerusalem had resulted in death and tragedy. Now with fear and trepidation it would be returned to its proper place. David prepared a psalm for the occasion. Remember that psalms were the songs of the day. One verse of that song reads, "Remember His marvelous works which He has done, His wonders, and the judgments of His mouth..."~1 Chronicles 16:12 Here David is calling upon the hearers to remember who God really was. Not a god who could be kept in a box, but a God of renown!

The idea of remembering has three meanings. First, it means to mark so as to be easily recognized. Remembrances become like mileposts for us. They help us find our way back and forth through time. Second, remembering means to make mention of and so to talk about while in the present. Remembering what God had done in the past gives confidence for the present. Third, it means to be mindful of that which God had performed. These are the remembrances of the mind where we consider the deep things of God. It is in remembering God that we join David in our marvel and wonder of His judgments. God's handiwork becomes distinguished from the trivial. His mysterious actions become conspicuous. His judgments are perceived as righteous verdicts.

Take out the photo album of your walk with God today. Rejoice in His presence and take a moment to relish in His memorable majesty. You will join with David in singing a psalm of praise to Him who made you!

Lord, help me to remember to praise You always.

February 20

The Way of All the Earth

A dear friend of mine just went home to be with the Lord. I would have it no other way. Even though his wife, children, family, and friends will miss Bro. Gene dearly, they would not have this day be any different either. He has joined the chorus of saints who have also crossed the river into God's eternal presence.

Joshua is one of those saints and spoke of his own death in Joshua 24. "Behold, this day I am going the way of all the earth. And you know in all your hearts and in all your souls that not one thing has failed of all the good things which the Lord your God spoke concerning you. All have come to pass for you; not one word of them has failed."~Joshua 23:14 What a testimony! How many have joined Joshua in this same conclusion to life? You can join with him and a multitude of others who know in their hearts that God has been faithful.

Many struggle through life trying desperately to please God and somehow tilt the scales of eternity in their favor. My friend, there are no scales. The payment for your life was discharged on an old rugged cross. Your debt has been paid! He has declared it finished! Can you join Joshua this day in proclaiming the faithfulness of God? Not your faithfulness, but the fact that nary a word of God has ever failed. As Joshua put it, "I am going the way of all the earth." We all must come to such a day, but we need not fear it or doubt our readiness. He is faithful who has declared us righteous in Christ Jesus. He is faithful who promised to never leave us nor forsake us. He is faithful who has never left a promise unfulfilled.

I will leave this world one day with some unfinished tasks. Not so with my Lord. All that he has said has come to pass. As with your friends and loved ones who have already traversed the final day of their life, we will miss them. But be assured that the same God who walked with them through the door called death will do so with you if you have trusted His dear Son, Jesus.

Lord, help me to never forget those who walked with You.

February 21

The Great Multiplier

 If I had to choose a disciple that would best reflect my life it would be Peter. I am sure that many of you could relate. Peter always had his foot in his mouth. Peter is the kid who is always asking what you are doing or why you are doing it. He not only ask questions, he always had a ready answer--right or wrong!

In both of Peter's letters he uses the same word to describe the grace and peace of God. It is the word multiply. See it here in his second epistle, "Grace and peace be multiplied to you in the knowledge of God and of Jesus our Lord..."~2 Peter 1:2 This is so like Peter. It was not good enough to say as others like Paul simply "grace and peace." He added the modifier "multiply." Maybe Peter could not get the days he had walked with Jesus here on earth out of his mind.

Perhaps he could still see a lad giving away his lunch and watching it multiply to feed thousands. He might have remembered a man named Legion who was delivered from a multitude of demons. It may have been a misty morning on the Sea of Galilee that he remembered; a morning following a night of frustrating fishless work. He could still hear the Master's voice, "Cast your net on the other side!" He could still see the multitude of fish breaking the net.

Yes, Peter had every right to use the word multiply for he has seen firsthand the multiplying effect of grace and peace at work. He could not help but remember his own denial of Christ and the multiple times that Jesus asked, "Peter, do you love me?"

What is it that you need multiplied in your life? What situation will not pass with mere addition of grace and peace? Call on the great Multiplier today! He is ready to do some spiritual mathematics on your behalf. By the way, I'd get a bigger net!

Lord, help me always calculate my day as You do.

54

February 22

Catching a Heart Attack

I grew up in south Louisiana where a very strong Cajun culture exists. The area west of the Mississippi River over to the Texas line and south of Interstate 10 is called Acadiana. My first pastorate was there. These very loving folks have some very unique ways of saying things.

One Sunday morning I was picking up kids for Sunday School and a little girl climbed aboard our big blue bus. Before being seated she ask me to pray for her Pawpaw. I inquired as to the need for prayer and her response reflected the cultural setting. She said, "Pastor, please pray for my Pawpaw. He done caught a heart attack." I wasn't sure I heard correctly. But she repeated her request and assured me that her grandfather had CAUGHT a heart attack. I prayed, but part of me wanted to laugh also. I thought to myself if he had caught a heart attack, he only needed to turn it loose.

As Paul was ministering in Corinth, he too was experiencing culture shock. He responded to it in 2 Corinthians 4 this way, "Therefore, since we have this ministry, as we have received mercy, we do not lose heart. Therefore we do not lose heart, even though our outward man is perishing, yet the inward man is being renewed day by day."~2 Corinthians 4:1,16 Twice he used the phrase "we do not lose heart." The idea here is that of developing a bad heart or having a heart attack. Paul was declaring that even though his ministry was difficult (read for yourself the verses between verse 1 and 16) he was being renewed by the mercies of God.

He had caught a heart attack, but he made a decision to turn it loose. What troubles and trials are you facing today? Will you choose to lie around and bemoan the fact that you have caught a heart attack or will you get up and turn it loose? Never lose heart, just lose the heart attack!

Lord, help me to never lose heart.

February 23

My Daddy Can Whip Your Daddy

 When little boys get together they often like to brag. They will compare notes on all sorts of things. Eventually the discussion wears thin when they have just about matched up even. It's somewhere around this moment that one of the little fellows will say, "My daddy can whip your daddy!" How unfair! Bringing fathers into the affair!

As believers we can get into a few scrapes too. We will find ourselves in a battle with the devil as the tempter tries to drag us down. His attempts many times come as accusations against our Father. His methods have not changed since the Garden of Eden. He comes along with his twisted statement that questions God's truthfulness. It is always formed in a question like this: "Has God really said _____." Then he leaves room for us to fill in the blank.

God has a few questions of his own for times like these. "'To whom then will you liken Me, or to whom shall I be equal?' says the Holy One. 'Have you not known? Have you not heard? The everlasting God, the Lord, the Creator of the ends of the earth, neither faints nor is weary. His understanding is unsearchable.'"~Isaiah 40:25,28

In essence God gives us permission to say, "My daddy can whip your daddy!" Except in this case, we can say, "My daddy has ALREADY whipped you!" It does not matter how big your enemy seems to be, God has never seen his equal. It does not matter how long the attack lasts, God does not grow weary. He will never pass out from exhaustion.

Don't waste your energy trying to figure out how God does this. He clearly declares that understanding Him is beyond our search. Just poke your chest out and tell the devil, "My daddy's done whipped you and you're just too dumb to know it!" Whew! That felt good just writing that! Now go use it!

Lord, help me to act like the devil is already whipped.

February 24

No Fishing

We have a beautiful picture of God's compassion at work in His dealings with Israel. Time and again Israel turned her back on God and served idols in futility. When these times occurred, the enemies of Israel rose up to accuse. This would drive Israel back to God's arms of compassion.

Micah spoke of this in the seventh chapter of the book named for him. Israel's enemies had asked the accusing question, "Where is your God?" Those who claim they can sin and it not have any effect on others should take note here. Though it may seem that no one is affected, the name of God is always derided by those who are watching how His children are living.

But we serve a compassionate God. "Who is a God like You, pardoning iniquity and passing over the transgression of the remnant of His heritage? He does not retain His anger forever, because He delights in mercy. He will again have compassion on us, and will subdue our iniquities. You will cast all our sins into the depths of the sea."~Micah 7:18-19

The compassion of God works in several ways to restore His people. He pardons us. This is not parole, but a total removing of the sin. He covers our transgressions and sees them no more to the extent that His anger is soothed. His mercy pours forth as our sin is placed on the back of His own Son. That's mercy! Someone else pays the penalty due us.

If this was not enough, He subdues our iniquities and casts them forever into the depths of the sea. He, by Himself, conquers and brings our faults and failures into subjection. After binding them He sends them to the ocean's bottom. I like to add just a little note here to the text. God then puts up a *NO FISHING* sign so Satan will never be able to drag them to shore again!

Lord, help me to never go fishing for forgiven sin.

February 25

My Redeemer Lives

 Anytime we go through some degree of suffering that lasts for a very long time, we come to the conclusion that we are living the life of Job. Not to make light of anyone's predicament, but I wonder if any human being has ever suffered to the extent that Job did. Yet God recorded his story for us that we might take comfort in it. As a matter of fact, in the depths of his ordeal he cried out hoping that his story would be written down. "'Oh, that my words were written! Oh, that they were inscribed in a book! That they were engraved on a rock with an iron pen and lead, forever!'"~Job 19:23-24 He desired that all his woes be remembered by the generations that would follow and indeed they have.

The real story in Job's suffering was not the timeline of the events. It must have been a tragic day to hear that his flocks and herds had been destroyed. How he must have wept to hear that his children had all been taken in a violent whirlwind. None of us can imagine the painful boils on his body or the accusations of his wife and friends. Yet he responded, "'Naked I came from my mother's womb, And naked shall I return there. The Lord gave, and the Lord has taken away; blessed be the name of the Lord.'"~Job 1:21

No, the real story occurs after he has hit the bottom. His memories have lost touch with the good old days. He can only remember the bad, the ugly, the painful. He is on the verge of giving up and contemplating the advice of his wife to just curse God and die. But rising up from the ashes he brushes himself clean and lifts feeble hands to heaven while crying, "'I know that my Redeemer lives, and He shall stand at last on the earth; and after my skin is destroyed, this I know, that in my flesh I shall see God, whom I shall see for myself, and my eyes shall behold, and not another. How my heart yearns within me!'"~Job 19:25-27 This may be a deep dark day for you, but take heart with your friend Job and join him in declaring, "I KNOW THAT MY REDEEMER LIVES!"

Lord, help me to remember that today my Redeemer lives.

February 26

That Dog Won't Hunt

There are many distractions that can steal away our focus and our commitment to the Lord. These distractions are like the hunting dog the man bought with great promise. The dog was supposedly trained to track bear.

Sure enough the dog came upon a bear's scent on his first hunt. Soon, however, the bear's path crossed that of a deer and off he went after the deer. But then the deer's path intersected with a rabbit trail, so off went the dog toward the rabbit's lair.

Alas, before the dog could find the rabbit he came upon the tiny tracks of a field mouse. And the hunter found his bear tracking dog with his nose stuck firmly down a hole in the ground where the mouse lived.

The focus of the Psalmist is noted in these verses. "Whom have I in heaven but You? And there is none upon earth that I desire besides You. But it is good for me to draw near to God; I have put my trust in the Lord God, that I may declare all Your works."~Psalms 73:25,28

Make a decision today to join the writer of this Psalm in declaring that there is none to steal your attention while your desire is fixed on the Lord. Draw near to the God of the universe, trust in Him, and declare His mighty works. Leave the hunting dog to his distraction and stay on the path of Jesus.

Lord, help me to avoid the distractions of life today.

February 27

Bad Things Happen to Good People

 Have you ever noticed that bad things sometimes happen to good people? These are not people who are inherently good, but those who are good in the sense that their trust is in the Lord and they are living in obedience to the best of their ability.

Asa, king of Judah, was just such a man. Yet in the midst of his godly reign, the enemy rose against him and his people. They came at him with numbers that the Bible describes as thousands of thousands. At this point is where we see the real trust and character of Asa. He turned immediately to the Lord. "And Asa cried out to the Lord his God, and said, 'Lord, it is nothing for You to help, whether with many or with those who have no power; help us, O Lord our God, for we rest on You, and in Your name we go against this multitude. O Lord, You are our God; do not let man prevail against You!'"~2 Chronicles 14:11

Asa understood the size of his dilemma in relation to the God he called upon and determined that this situation was nothing for the Lord to handle. He concluded that God's readiness to help was not relative to the strength of those He helps. Asa declared that God helps whether there is a crowd or an individual. He helps whether there is great strength or minimal power. This king of Judah placed his total dependence on the God of heaven. Listen to his remarks. He rested on God. He relied upon and placed all of his weight on God's shoulders for support. He made the commitment to enter the battle, but to do so in the name of God. Finally, he surrendered all effort to God and asked God to defend Himself.

How many thousands are coming against you today? Maybe it only feels like thousands, but the battle is no less real. Let the words of Asa be your prayer today. "O Lord our God, I rest on You, and in Your name I go against this multitude."

Lord, help me rely upon You when bad things happen.

February 28

Way Down Deep

I was born in south Louisiana. This part of Louisiana differs markedly from the central and northern parts of the state. From food to dialect things can be drastically different. One of the things that stands in sharp contrast is the makeup of the soil. If I could choose just one word to describe south Louisiana it would be wet. Not just wet on the surface, but way down deep wet.

When anything is being built here it requires going all the way to bedrock to secure a good foundation. Without going deep the structure simply will not stand or at the least will soon start to tilt like the Tower of Pisa. To get down to bedrock pile drivers are used. These huge steam driven engines are used to force pilings of concrete one on top of another until solid ground is contacted. I can still remember as a child hearing these engines banging loudly as these support columns were driven to create a sure foundation. This process can take a lot of time and expense, but it cannot be circumvented without future consequences.

In our lives we must also secure a solid foundation if we are to stand the test of time. "Therefore thus says the Lord God: 'Behold, I lay in Zion a stone for a foundation, a tried stone, a precious cornerstone, a sure foundation; whoever believes will not act hastily.'"~Isaiah 28:16 God has set the stone of the foundation. The New Testament identifies this stone. "For no other foundation can anyone lay than that which is laid, which is Jesus Christ."~1 Corinthians 3:11

The verse from Isaiah tells us that those who believe will not act hastily. It is possible to build without a solid foundation. The cost will be reduced and a lot of time saved, but the consequences are tragic. It's either the banging noise of the pile driver preparing a sure foundation or the crashing sound of a building falling. If you do not have the foundation of Jesus supporting you then time will reveal this structural and spiritual deficiency. The consequences are eternal.

Lord, help me to build nothing without a sure foundation.

February 29

One More Day

 Today is defined as this present day in the *Merriam-Webster's Collegiate Dictionary (eleventh edition.)* I really expected a much deeper and dynamic definition. Especially, since I looked in a collegiate version dictionary. For comparison's sake I looked up the word *today* in a kid's dictionary and to my surprise it contained the exact same definition. Even in this technological age the best we can do in defining today is to see it in the context of the present.

Today is Leap Day. A necessary calendar adjustment that occurs every four years except on rare occasions. This allows us to "make up" for the one-quarter of a day extra that it takes the Earth to rotate around the Sun each year. On this special day, the best we can do is add a day and label it February 29. Soon it will be concluded like all other days and we will await its arrival again as we have all other Leap Days that we have lived.

Truthfully, we are not adding any time to the calendar or our lives. It really is just today. It will be exactly the same length for everyone who lives to its conclusion. Psalm 90:12 tells us to number our days–not years. "So teach us to number our days that we may gain a heart of wisdom."

We start out counting days. We make statements like, "Our baby is just six days old." Then somehow we transition quickly to counting months and then settle on years. Perhaps it is over confidence or maybe just hopeful thinking, but the Psalmist reminds us that it is days not years that we should learn to count.

Why days and not years? Because each day is a miniature life. Lose today: Lose a life. Waste today: Waste a life. We are to redeem the time given us and expend it for His glory–day by day.

Lord, help me make sure that every day counts for Your glory.

March 1

Pruning Time

It's time to get out the pruning shears. I've decided this year to allow the plants to prune themselves. My plan is to lean the pruning shears against the base of the plant and give it 24 hours to get the job done. If the plant doesn't do any cutting within that time I will assume that it has made a good decision and I will move the shears to the next plant. Sounds like a good plan don't you think?

Of course, you know that I'm kidding. My plants would never use the shears on themselves even if they had the ability to do so. Neither will you and I submit to the pruning process all on our own. That's the work of the husbandman. "'I am the true vine, and My Father is the vinedresser. Every branch in Me that does not bear fruit He takes away; and every branch that bears fruit He prunes, that it may bear more fruit. You are already clean because of the word which I have spoken to you.'"~John 15:1-3

Pruning my plants will remove all of the past winter's damage. To be healthy it must be cut away and dead branches removed. The process is not pretty. The plant will look worse for the wear, but it will be better for it in the long run. God has our best interest in mind also by pruning us. He reduces us to that which bears fruit and prunes that which does so we bear more fruit. He is not, however, waiting for your input in the process. He knows where the cuts should be made.

The words *prune* and *clean* in our scripture for today have the same root meaning. They mean to purify. Jesus told His disciples that they were clean (pruned) through His word. It is the word that acts as the pruning knife to cleanse us by cutting away the dead and damaged branches. Pruning will never take place if we just lean the Bible against the bark of our lives. Open the book. Get into its pages and be more fruitful for the Father.

Lord, help me to yield my life to Your pruning shear.

March 2

Refiner's Fire

 God's intent is that we be molded into the image of His Son. For some this will mean brokenness and complete re-molding. For others it will mean further etching and toning. But for all it will mean the fire.

"Take away the dross from the silver, and there shall come forth a vessel for the finer."~Proverbs 25:4

Only the refiner's fire can bring forth a vessel meant for honor in the hall of the King. The silversmith melts the silver and then time and again skims the surface of the molten metal. This process brings all of the impurities to the surface where the worker can slowly and meticulously remove them. There is a cost, however. Each passing of the sieve removes not only impurities, but also tiny amounts of the precious metal. There is a price to be paid for purity.

When will the silversmith know that his work is done? He skims the surface until he finally can see his own reflection therein. Only when that happens does he know that the highest degree of purity has been achieved.

Oh, for the day when we will finally look just like Jesus! The fires of purification may be painful to endure, but the reward will be out of this world. We will be a vessel fit for the finer upon His mantel!

Lord, take away everything that doesn't look like You.

March 3

God's GPS

I love shortcuts! The trouble is that so often what I thought would be a saving of travel time turns into just getting lost. Sometimes I find my way back to the main highway via my shortcut, but other times I just have to turn around and retrace my steps back to the point where I turned off the beaten path.

The Psalmist stated it this way, "I thought about my ways and turned my feet to Your testimonies."~Psalm 119:59

Life is a series of crossroads, blind turns, and forks in the road. Trust me. The old adage, if you come to a fork in the road, TAKE IT, just doesn't work in real life. Each turn in the road calls for a decision. You can make a choice in your own strength and wisdom most often with disastrous results or you can use a GPS (God's Plan = Success.)

I use a GPS in every vehicle I own. Two things hold true relative to my GPS. First, I have to keep the maps updated. That's the easy part. Second, I have to TRUST the GPS. There are times that I just don't believe the thing. It doesn't feel like it's taking me on the right course. This happens especially when the roads are curvy and unfamiliar.

To follow God's GPS you must keep the map up-to-date by staying in His word daily. He knows perfectly the map you need for this day. And you can always trust Him. Turn on God's GPS today and listen to the turn by turn directions. He will never send you down the wrong road!

Lord, guide me when I attempt to make a wrong turn.

March 4

Friends

 Someone said, "Friends come and go, but enemies accumulate." A man can count himself blessed in this life if he has only a handful of close friends. These close friends are the ones that neither time nor miles can bring about a reduction in the depth of relationship. I have always jokingly said that a close friend is one you could call from jail in the middle of the night and they would come to your rescue. More importantly, they wouldn't even ask why you were there!

As Jesus neared the end of His earthly ministry he prepared his disciples for His departure. Knowing that these first disciples would experience a great sense of disorientation at His crucifixion, burial, and resurrection, He told them in John 15:15, "I no longer call you servants, but friends."

The disciples would go through a season of faithlessness. His friendship for them was not based on their faithfulness, however, but His. His love for His friends led Him to tell them all that the Father had told Him. This transparency not only carried the disciples through difficult times, it gave the disciples a confidence to carry on as the founding fathers of the early church. Those who would write the gospels and epistles of the New Testament would recall that which Jesus told them as a friend.

Oh, to be the friend of Jesus! To have His confidence demonstrated by revealing all the Father's plan to our hearts. Are you the friend of Jesus? Can He trust you with the Father's plan and will for your life? Called to be His friend! What joy!

Lord, help me to be faithful because You have called me friend.

March 5

God's Choice

Jim Elliot was martyred while trying to reach the Auca Indians. Hear his words these many years later:

GOD ALWAYS GIVES HIS BEST TO THOSE WHO LEAVE THE CHOICE WITH HIM.

During David's reign as king of Israel, he made a poor decision when he decided to conduct a census of Israel. This may seem very insignificant, but the source of the decision was pride and arrogance on David's part.

David's trust of God's choice is clearly seen in these verses: "Now when David arose in the morning, the word of the LORD came to the prophet Gad, David's seer, saying, 'Go and tell David, Thus says the LORD: I offer you three things; choose one of them for yourself, that I may do it to you.' So Gad came to David and told him; and he said to him, 'Shall seven years of famine come to you in your land? Or shall you flee three months before your enemies, while they pursue you? Or shall there be three days' plague in your land? Now consider and see what answer I should take back to Him who sent me.' And David said to Gad, 'I am in great distress. Please let us fall into the hand of the LORD, for His mercies are great; but do not let me fall into the hand of man.'"~2 Samuel 24:11–14

When confronted with three choices that had been brought about by his own poor decisions, David did not make another bad decision. He decided that the safest place to be when under God's hand of judgment was in the hand of God.

Are you facing a difficult choice today? It is always a smart decision to leave the choice with God! Your best is always in His interest!

Lord, help me to leave all the choices up to You.

March 6

The Way

 I spend a lot of time on the highway as I minister to the churches in Northwest Baptist Association. On my way to preach in the very northwest corner of our county I came upon traffic at a standstill. Someone had left the road, broken a utility pole, and caused a complete shutdown of the highway.

We were barely a mile from the church. There we sat blocked and I was supposed to preach in 28 minutes. A man turned around ahead of us and headed in the opposite direction, so I flagged him down and explained my predicament. He told me to follow him and he would show me another road over the mountain that would lead to our destination. I followed a stranger off the beaten path...through the woods...over the mountain...and yes, to our destination! I am not sure that I would recommend this in every situation, but God was faithful in this situation.

Amazing how we use faith every day in so many ways. I thought about those who simply cannot trust Jesus as Savior. They have traveled and come just short of their destination. They do not know the way. Pride keeps them trapped on a dead end path. Others wait with them, but all will die on a road to nowhere. All the while a man has been sent to show the way to life. It only takes a turning around (repentance) and a following (faith). "Jesus said to him, 'I am the way, the truth, and the life. No one comes to the Father except through Me.'"~John 14:6

The result will be the same as it was for us. We arrived safely and on time. Are you stuck today on the road of life? Is your way blocked by sin and strife? Turn around and follow the Man with the nail-scarred hands! I promise a safe arrival!

Lord, help me see the hand of Your re-direction when my way is blocked.

March 7

Wait

Hurrying yet? The Prophet Daniel saw into our day and recorded the words of the Lord, "But you, Daniel, shut up the words, and seal the book until the time of the end; many shall run to and fro, and knowledge shall increase."~Daniel 12:4 Someone has said, the "hurrier" I go, the "behinder" I get!

As for the knowledge part of this prophecy, Martin Gover said in his *Ezine Article*, "Welcome to the information age." He quotes Eric Johnson, president of the US Chamber of Commerce. "...knowledge is doubling every ten years..." He then goes on to say, "That was before the Internet. With the advent of the web, knowledge was doubling approximately every eighteen months by 2004, according to the American Society of Training and Documentation. IBM predicts that in the next couple of years, information will double every 11 hours."

Even though we have more and more time saving devices invented by this ever increasing knowledge base, it seems that we just keep falling behind. Why not stop right now and get on God's timetable?

I have trained our little dog to sit on command and wait for a doggie treat. She knows that she must wait until I give her the command, "Now." At that point she takes the treat from my hand. When I first started training her I had to say over and over, "Wait, wait, waaiiitttt."

I know you have a boss, schedule, clock to beat, etc. God knew our times would be like this, yet He said, "Those who wait upon the Lord shall renew their strength."~Isaiah 40:31 Now either God lied or we need to learn how to wait.........................wwwaaaiiittt!!!

Lord, help me to wwwaaaiiittt!!!

March 8

Our Great Shepherd

We are privileged to reside as a sheep in the Great Shepherd's fold. Remember that sheep are dumb, dependent, and defenseless. Of course, our Great Shepherd is Christ Himself. As the Great Shepherd, He knows us by name. He knows that we are dumb, dependent, defenseless, and a few more descriptions that even we are not aware of at this time. Even with this keen insight into the characteristics of His sheep, He loves us and is at work in and through us.

"Now may the God of peace who brought up our Lord Jesus from the dead, that Great Shepherd of the sheep, through the blood of the everlasting covenant, make you complete in every good work to do His will, working in you what is well pleasing in His sight, through Jesus Christ, to whom be glory forever and ever. Amen."~Hebrews 13:20-21

As a sheep I never simply decide to get lost. I just put my head down, take my eyes off the Shepherd and eat my way into lostness. Not only does Jesus fill the role of protector of the sheep while in the sheepfold, and the door of the sheepfold to keep the enemy at bay, but He always comes looking for me when I've wandered away into lostness! He knows that we cannot fend for ourselves and that this is particularly true when we have wandered from the fold.

How long have you been wandering from the fold? Not only will the Great Shepherd come to rescue you, He knows where you are right now! Don't be dumb about this. Call out to the one who loves you as His sheep. Be totally dependent on Him. Soon you will be resting in His arms.

Lord, help me to always keep my eyes on You lest I become lost.

March 9

Awesome

Help me reclaim a lost descriptive of the God we serve. The word? *AWESOME!* We have allowed the world to steal this word and apply it to so many things temporal. You hear its use many times during the day as people describe the most menial experiences. I first became aware of the use of the word *awesome* for the strangest of things while at a craft fair. A child came out of a self-flushing portable toilet and said to a friend, "That was awesome!" I was speechless.

Compare the use of the word *awesome* in today's world to the words of Nehemiah, "Now therefore, our God, the great, the mighty, and awesome God, who keeps covenant and mercy..."~Nehemiah 9:32 In this verse Nehemiah bases his trust in God's covenant and mercy upon three descriptions of God. He describes God as great, mighty, and awesome. Each of these words holds a slightly differing nuance as to the character of God.

He is great in the sense of nobility. He rules as a King. He is mighty in the sense of championship. He has shown Himself as the victor in the battle. He is awesome in the sense of reverence due to the extent of fearfulness if reverence was not extended. It is this word *awesome* that should be set aside for God alone since He alone should be revered.

Use this word sparingly and remind others that the word *AWESOME* is reserved for the God of Glory. In it we are reminded that God can be trusted to keep His word both in covenant relationship and in mercy.

WHAT AN AWESOME GOD WE SERVE!

Lord, help me never forget how awesome You are!

March 10

Clay or Wax

 "But exhort one another daily, while it is called *'Today,'* lest any of you be hardened through the deceitfulness of sin."~Hebrews 3:13 There is no more dangerous position to find oneself than hardened by sin to the point that you no longer sense the word of conviction.

That word of conviction is to be delivered daily by believers to believers for the edification of all.

Consider the human heart. It can be likened to clay or wax as it is subjected to God's Word. The heart that yields and is transformed by His Word is like wax in the sun. It will be softened and shaped by its effect. The heart that rejects God's Word is like clay in the same sun. It just gets drier and harder each time the Word shines forth.

All of our hearts are made of the same stuff: wickedness. "The heart is deceitful above all things, and desperately wicked; who can know it?"~Jeremiah 17:9 How then can a heart be transformed from clay to wax? Of course, the greater answer is by the work of God's Holy Spirit in man, but there is another ingredient to this process.

God in His sovereignty has allowed the exhortation of fellow believers to be used to keep the heart pliable. This happens each time we come together as a body of believers, but we are instructed to do it *today*.

Hardening of the heart can slip up on us quickly. We need fellow believers applying God's word to their own lives and encouraging others to do the same. How about your heart: CLAY or WAX?

Lord, help me to always come before You for a heart check.

March 11

A Scarlet Cord

A few years ago, we were under the threat of tornadoes. I knew it was about to get bad quickly when we heard what we thought were horses running on the roof. It turned out to be softball size hail and the tornado following close behind. I still remember putting all of my family in the bathroom and piling a mattress on top of them. Thankfully, it missed our home. Is there anyone who would not with all diligence put your family in a safe place if you knew danger was coming? Sometimes with storms you have a little warning; sometimes there is none.

When the Hebrew spies went into Jericho, they were hidden by Rahab. She had heard that the storm of God was coming and asked that the life of her family be spared in return for her kindness. The spies told her, "We will be blameless of this oath of yours which you have made us swear, unless, when we come into the land, you bind this line of scarlet cord in the window through which you let us down, and unless you bring your father, your mother, your brothers, and all your father's household to your own home."~Joshua 2:17-18

Can you imagine the days that followed? The days before the storm of God leveled the city of Jericho. Rahab must have gathered every family member she could. All remained in safety behind a scarlet cord as they waited. Here they stayed as the children of Israel marched around the city. Here they stayed while trumpets sounded. Here they stayed as the people shouted. Here they stayed as the walls came tumbling down in a heap. And they were safe behind a scarlet cord of promise! The best I could do was put a mattress over my family in the face of a tornado. But you and I can still put our families behind a scarlet cord that extends all the way back to an old rugged cross. That cord is scarlet with the blood of Jesus and all who hide behind it are safe from the storm of God's wrath. Don't wait for the sirens. All the warning you need has already been given. Get your family to the place of safety under the scarlet cord of Jesus' blood!

Lord, help me to be prepared as I hide beneath Your scarlet cord.

73

March 12

With Jesus

 Compare these two accounts:

#1 Jesus is 12 years old and has gone to Jerusalem with Mary and Joseph. They left him behind and knew it not. (Luke 2:43)

#2 The people of Jerusalem noted upon hearing the disciples that they had been with Jesus. (Acts 4:13)

Have you ever left a child somewhere? I have and I can tell you it scared the living daylights out of me! You can imagine the fear that coursed through Mary and Joseph as they hurried back a day's journey out to seek Jesus. They found Him in the temple sitting with the teachers.

His answer to their question about His "disappearance" gives us great insight into finding Jesus if we have somehow left Him behind in our lives. "Did you not know that I would be about my Father's business?" And with that answer He was reunited with His earthly parents. You will find Him where God's business is being done!

So we see with the disciples in Acts 4 that because they had been engaged where God was working the people made public record that these men had been with Jesus. Which is your story today? Have you left Jesus behind or will others note that you have been with Jesus? It's up to you...

Lord, help me to never leave You behind.

Following Orders

Few of us really enjoy taking orders. I don't mean waiting tables, I'm speaking of someone telling us what to do or where to go. Several years ago I was visiting in the Chicago area. I came up with the idea that my kids needed to go to the top of the Sears Building, the tallest building in Chicago.

I will admit that I'm a country boy and I'm not apologizing for that, but country boys are quickly out of their element in really big cities like Chicago. I knew this, so I decided to go on Saturday. I figured nobody would be in downtown Chicago on a Saturday. Wrong! Not only do people still go into the downtown area on Saturday, I chose the one Saturday that the Blues Festival was being held. On top of this several candidates for the presidential race were scheduled to speak that day. It was mass confusion. Especially for a small town person like me.

Evidently, my out of town character showed in my driving. A police officer whistled me to a stop. I rolled down my window thinking she would offer me some help getting to the Sears Building. Wrong! First, she asked me what I was doing in downtown Chicago. Then she compelled me to leave. That's right! She told me to get out of there because I didn't belong in downtown Chicago! I left! Being compelled, I had no choice!

Paul told the Corinthians that he was compelled by the love of Christ to tell the news that Christ had died that man might live. "For the love of Christ compels us, because we judge thus: that if One died for all, then all died; and He died for all, that those who live should live no longer for themselves, but for Him who died for them and rose again."~2 Corinthians 5:14-15 Are you where you are supposed to be? Is the love of Christ compelling you to get up and tell someone today that Jesus loved them enough to die for them? That whistle you hear is the Holy Spirit compelling you to follow orders. Do it today!

Lord, help me to obey Your Spirit to share the gospel today.

March 14

Oil in the Lamp

 Growing up in south Louisiana you would find a hurricane lamp in nearly every home. These lamps would be invaluable during the power outages that often came along with the hurricanes that blew in from the Gulf of Mexico.

Sometimes after using the lamps you would forget to refill them and you could be caught off guard the next time a storm blew inland. Hurrying to the store to buy oil was a futile effort since the shelves would be empty. Keeping oil in your lamp is very important for the dark times.

Do you have oil in your lamp? Remember the parable of five foolish virgins that waited until it was too late and found the door shut! It was customary for the bridegroom to come at the midnight hour and light would be required to ready oneself. (Matthew 25) These ladies all knew that the bridegroom could come at any minute and it was their responsibility to keep oil in the lamp and the wicks trimmed.

Ask God today to refill your lamp. The oil is a picture of the Holy Spirit and the scripture tells us to be continually filled. "...be filled with the Spirit."~Ephesians 5:18 Just like those hurricane lamps that were used in the storm, we need to be refilled after our spiritual storms also.

Keep shining for Him! Ask Him to refill your lamp today. If you have never had the *oil* of His Spirit, then ask Him now. Give Him your emptiness and receive His filling! He has already paid for it all on an old rugged cross...ALL FOR YOU!!!

Lord, help me check the oil level in the lamp of my life today.

March 15

Responding to the Wilderness

I still remember as a child attending churches who had a portion of the worship service set aside for responsive reading. The pastor would read a portion of scripture and then the congregation would respond. Even though this is not very common today, it was a special time where scripture received an honored place in the worship time.

Psalm 136 could easily be read responsively. Each verse begins with a statement about God and His activity in the life of His chosen people Israel. Each verse of this psalm concludes with the phrase, "for His mercy endures forever."

As this Psalm progresses it recounts God's creative acts and His deliverance of Israel from Egypt. All of these are followed with the response, "for His mercy endures forever." But then this verse is written for us. "To Him who led His people through the wilderness, For His mercy endures forever."~Psalms 136:16

Now wait just a minute! I don't mind praising God for the sunshine, the plenteous harvest, or my healthy kids. I'm not sure I can or even want to praise Him for the wilderness, however. How about you? Can you praise Him when the journey is treacherous and tiring? How can we bring ourselves to this level of worship?

It begins long before we find ourselves in the wilderness. It begins like this Psalm does in verse one, "Oh, give thanks to the Lord, for He is good! For His mercy endures forever."~Psalms 136:1 It begins with thanksgiving from the very start. It is the realization that the wilderness will turn out okay because God is good. This attitude of gratitude will carry you through the wilderness because not only is God good; God is good all the time. God is good even in the wilderness. And for that we can say in response, "His mercy endures forever."

Lord, help me say that You are good all the time.

March 16

The Voice of God

 How many times have you ever heard a voice in a crowd and knew that an acquaintance was near? Indeed the human voice is very unique and even though there are similarities in the billions of voices that will speak today in this world some do stand out above others.

When you think of some prominent people, it is their voice that distinguishes them. For example, Jimmy Stewart, Kathryn Hepburn, John F. Kennedy, or Winston Churchill. These voices have left their indelible mark on our world.

But what of God's voice? Is it distinct enough in your life that you can hear it above the maddening crowd? For Adam and Eve it was the voice of God they waited for each day in the cool of the evening. "And they heard the sound of the Lord God walking in the garden in the cool of the day, and Adam and his wife hid themselves from the presence of the Lord God among the trees of the garden."~Genesis 3:8

This same voice came calling for them after they had sinned and hid themselves. Can't you hear the voice of God calling out, "Adam!, Adam! Where are you?" Is that God's voice you are hearing now? He is no longer calling for Adam, but sounding forth your name. Take time to answer Him today. He calls as your friend in the midst of your harried day.

It is His voice that sounds out above the clanging and clamor of the crowd. It is His voice that you strain to hear, yet it comes not with the shout, but in stillness. As Isaiah said, "For since the beginning of the world men have not heard nor perceived by the ear, nor has the eye seen any God besides You, who acts for the one who waits for Him."~Isaiah 64:4 So in the midst of your hurry, stop. Be still. Wait. You will hear the unmistakable voice of heaven, God Himself, calling your name.

Lord, help me hear Your voice above the maddening crowd.

March 17

High and Dry

A man was traveling along a country road one day and saw a strange sight. Suspended high on top of a fence post was a turtle. Its legs were extended and flailing as the poor creature sought for traction. Its neck was stretched as it strained to see some way out of its predicament.

Two things were evident to the traveler. The turtle did not get there all by itself and that turtle wasn't going anywhere in the position it now found itself. The traveler in mercy stopped and undid the work of a prankster. He lifted the creature from its perch and placed it safely on the ground where it slowly crawled away with no understanding as to what just took place.

In John 17 Jesus prays for us believers! He prays for our sanctification. "And for their sakes I sanctify Myself, that they also may be sanctified by the truth."~John 17:19 The word sanctify means to be set apart unto holiness. It is the same word from which we derive our word *saint*.

Now back to that turtle. We have a connection to this poor maltreated creature, but also a distinction. Jesus prayed that truth (that which is not hidden) would set us apart unto holiness. Like the turtle on the fence post, we didn't get here all by ourselves. It is His hands that lifted us to this position.

Unlike the turtle, however, sanctification occurs not to put us in a place where we are just treading air. We are set aside by Christ that we might be used to show others who it was that sanctified Himself for our sakes. That turtle couldn't tell the traveler one thing about how he got on that fence post. You and I on the other hand have a story to tell of how we discovered the truth and through truth we were lifted up by the love it uncovered. It's time to get off your fence post. Dig in. Stick out your neck and tell every passerby who put you where you are today.

Lord, help me get off the fence today.

March 18

He Lifted Me

 Most of my childhood I lived near some body of water be it lake, river, or canal. Of course, I grew up in Louisiana so being near water was no big deal. Nearness to water, however, always carried the possibility of flooding. I still remember waking up as a five year old and finding that my bed had been lifted during the night and placed on concrete blocks. At some point during the night water had intruded our home and my parents had placed me and my bed on higher ground all while I slept soundly.

God used a flood to destroy the earth in judgment, but like my parents lifting me to safety, He provided an ark of safety for Noah and his family. "Now the flood was on the earth forty days. The waters increased and lifted up the ark, and it rose high above the earth."~Genesis 7:17 The same waters which destroyed the unbelieving world lifted the ark to safety. All who were in the ark rode above the destructive waves in the protecting hands of the Lord. Can you imagine the intensity of the moment when the Noah's heard the first drops of rain on the roof of the ark? The horrors they endured as the crying and scratching started at the door, increased as the waters rose, and then ceased as the whole world drown. But God Himself had closed the door and it could not be opened by Noah.

Feel the groaning of the timbers as the floods which had drowned the outside inhabitants of the world began to lift those inside the ark to safety. I cannot help but think of the old gospel hymn, "Love Lifted Me." For I was sinking deep in sin, far from the peaceful shore, and love lifted me!

My bed of safety as a five year old was no ark. I had to wear rubber boots and wade out of our house. But I will never forget the strong arms of my father that had lifted me to safety. If you are not in the ark of salvation today, then come aboard while the door is still open. It's about to rain!

Lord, help me never forget how You lifted me by your love.

March 19

Big Rock on the Block

A museum in California recently spent 10 million dollars on a rock.
This huge two story high granite boulder was hauled by a special
truck at night on a circuitous route at an average speed of only five
miles per hour just to get it to the front door of the museum. All of
this is okay I guess, but it does seem a little over done for a rock.

This story reminds me of the pet rock phenomenon of a few years back. In this
case, the rock has grown up and the pet is much bigger than anyone ever thought
possible. Of course, all of this is so that museum goers can look at this rock as it
is cradled in place. Viewers can even walk under the rock. I suppose this gives
them a worms-eye view!

I could not help but think of several verses in scripture that describe either God
or Christ as the Rock. I don't know if the curators at the museum have ever read
this verse, but it sure puts their 10 million dollar rock into perspective. "No one
is holy like the LORD, for there is none besides You, nor is there any rock like
our God."~1 Samuel 2:2 The God of creation who placed the museum's rock in
the quarry has already declared Himself to be the Big Rock on the block! This
settles the issue of whether God could ever create a rock that He could not lift
since there is no rock like God the Rock.

In other scriptures we see rocks holding significant meaning. Moses was told to
strike the rock and water would flow for the children of Israel. Later he was
instructed to speak to the rock and the water would flow again, but in anger he
struck the rock again. Because of this he was forbidden to go into the Promised
Land. Why such penalty? The rock in this account was a type or picture of Christ.
Jesus was stricken once for our sins and the miracle of living water flowed out of
that act on the cross. Never again will He be struck. Now we need only call upon
Him and that same life giving force is ours. The rock in the wilderness was God's
picture to us of the salvation work of Jesus.

In the New Testament this Rock of the Old Testament was taken out of the city to Golgotha, the place of the skull. Here on a rocky hillside the Son of God was offered up as the Living Sacrifice. This Jesus, who was God in the flesh, described in 1 Samuel as being like no other rock, died on the rock of Calvary for me and for you. And this fact has become a rock of offense to many in this world today (Isaiah 8:14; Romans 9:33).

You can trust this Rock at this very moment. You can build upon this Rock and stand the tests and storms of time. This Rock will never be displayed in a museum with a DO NOT TOUCH! sign attached. This is a Rock you can put your arms around and hold as your own. But more than this, the Rock called Jesus will wrap His arms around you and love you forever! Sure beats a pet rock or even a big rock in a museum, don't you think?

Lord, help me to run to the Rock that is higher than I.

March 20

Recovery

Recovery is defined as the regaining of something lost. Most of us have at one time or another spent some time recovering either from an illness or a loss. Sometimes recovering is a very fast process and at other times recovery takes years.

As Hezekiah was lying on his death bed he sought the Lord in prayer. God's prophet was told: "Return and tell Hezekiah the leader of My people, thus says the LORD, the God of David your father: 'I have heard your prayer, I have seen your tears; surely I will heal you. On the third day you shall go up to the house of the LORD.'"~2 Kings 20:5

God in His mercy is ready to bring recovery to us. Our response should be the same as that of Hezekiah. "On the third day he went up to the house of the Lord." Our recovery should prompt worship of the One who has brought us back from the brink.

Our recovery always serves a purpose. Time and again we read of those who were touched by Jesus as He walked upon the earth. So often we see the result of recovery in these four words: THEY WERE MADE WHOLE! However, we sometimes see those healed who simply faded away into the crowd with no thanksgiving.

Oh, to be touched by Christ in our time of need! To know His recovering work of making us whole again is worth the time and extent of the loss! Be sure that you are found in the house of the Lord giving glory to Him alone for answered prayer.

Lord, help me worship you today for Your work of recovery in my life.

March 21

Like a Ragdoll

 Spring is a time of renewal. Our hope is renewed like the first leaves of tulips pushing up from bulbs that have lain dormant all winter. But spring is also a time of transition in the weather. As the temperatures change quickly over short times and distances, the chance of storms increases. Some of those storms turn violent and death and destruction result.

Tornadoes are a part of our spring time here in northwestern Arkansas. These destructive wind storms form as the last cold fronts of winter clash with the rising warm air of spring. As the air masses collide and twist upon themselves these cyclones are spawned and wreak havoc in their paths. Job must have felt like he had experienced a full-blown EF-5 tornado when he spoke these words. "I was at ease, but He has shattered me; He also has taken me by my neck, and shaken me to pieces; He has set me up for His target."~Job 16:12

Job's words can comfort us when troubles come our way. Job remained focused upon this one fact: GOD IS ALWAYS IN CONTROL! Job never let circumstance dictate the outcome. He admitted that he was shaken and shattered. He felt like a rag doll in the mouth of an angry dog. All that he had known had been blown to smithereens.

His conclusion though is where we can gather our confidence in the midst of the storm. He reasoned: It was okay to be the bull's eye of God's target as long as God was in control of the bow and the arrow! Remember this—the storm is coming, but God is in control!

Lord, help me remember that You are in control of this day.

March 22

What Do You See?

Flying at 33,000 feet can give you a real perspective on how God might see things. At that height you can see great distances and whole cities lie within your view. Holding your hand to the window of the airplane will allow you to block a city from your view. So height gives you both the ability to behold or to blot out of sight.

We serve a God who is not capricious in His dealings with man. He is long suffering in His loving kindness. Though He can contain us in one hand, He deals with us as dear children and reveals Himself in ways that we can comprehend.

In the days of King Ahab, Elijah was the prophet of God. He prayed that it would not rain and it did not for over three years. At the end of this time and after Elijah's contest on Mount Carmel with the prophets of Baal, he announced that rain was coming. He then sent his servant to go and look out over the Mediterranean Sea. Six times he looked and saw nothing, but the seventh time he reported a cloud. This cloud was the size of a man's hand.

Just like a hand at flight level covers an entire city, that hand would only appear to someone on the ground as a dot at best. Here, as Elijah's servant looked out over the sea the hand of God appeared as only a small cloud. We must never forget that what appears as an insignificant movement on heaven's part can bring blessings that cannot be contained. "Then Elijah said to Ahab, 'Go up, eat and drink; for there is the sound of abundance of rain.' Now it happened in the meantime that the sky became black with clouds and wind, and there was a heavy rain."~1 Kings 18:41,45 Get ready. Your blessing is on its way!

Lord, help me see life in Your perspective.

March 23

Words That Stick

 God has given us a wonderful healing instrument that we can use freely throughout the day and night. It is always at our disposal. We can use it privately or publicly. It is a one size fits all apparatus. The most wonderful thing is it doesn't take batteries nor does it have to be charged. The most dangerous thing about it is that the same operator of this item can use it for harm just as easily as good. What is it? Your tongue and the words that are formed and released by it.

The Bible tells us in Proverbs, "Pleasant words are like a honeycomb, sweetness to the soul and health to the bones."~Proverbs 16:24 Each part of this verse holds deep instruction for the use of this very powerful instrument called the tongue. The words that we use can be as sweet as honey if they are of the pleasant variety. This word *pleasant* means agreeable, beautiful, and yes, sweet. It always amazes me and sometimes disgusts me when I hear the tongue used for vile, filthy communication.

God intended our words to be overflowing with sweetness. As a matter of fact, that's exactly what the word *honeycomb* means in Hebrew. It means to drip with sweetness like syrup. It also has the concept of stickiness. You know the old adage about sticks and stones and words never hurting. It's not true! Words do hurt! But pleasant words are supposed to be sticky. They are supposed to last and continue their healing benefit. See in this verse, pleasant words *heal* bones instead of breaking them.

How sweet are these pleasant words? It takes 8.4 pounds of honey for a bee to make one pound of honeycomb. Wow! That's concentrated sweetness! So, go out today and say something sweet...

Lord, help me to speak words today that will sweet as honey.

March 24

The Colt and Me

Jesus sent His disciples on a mission to bring a colt for Him to ride into Jerusalem. He described in detail where they would find this colt and upon arriving they found it exactly as He had told them they would. Today, with cries of "Hosanna! Blessed is He who comes in the name of the Lord!" being shouted from the crowd, Jesus will ride into Jerusalem. (Mark 11:9) In a few days the same crowd will become a mob demanding that He be crucified.

The Holy Spirit in moving upon Mark to recount the details of this day includes for our benefit the particulars of gathering this transportation for Jesus' triumphal entry to Jerusalem. From this lowly colt's existence we can see a picture of our own spiritual journey.

The colt is identified in three ways: The colt was tied where two ways met. The colt had never been ridden. Taking the colt was contested.

So with us, Jesus found us at the point of decision. There were two ways for us to go and a choice to be made. We could choose the wide road to destruction or the narrow way to redemption.

We were unbroken. Our rebellious spirit ruled our lives. We needed the taming hand of Jesus and the weight of His being upon our lives.

There were many that challenged our going to be with Jesus. Satan, friends, and even family can challenge our decision to yield to Christ. Yes, it was I that Jesus rode into Jerusalem!

Lord, help me to yield my unbrokenness to You today.

March 25

Present

 Remember the weird kid in your class (maybe you were that kid) that always said *present* instead of *here* when the roll was called? One day the roll will be called in heaven and the weird kid will have been right all of these years, for the Bible tells us to be absent from the body is to be *present* with the Lord! (2 Cor. 4:8)

This thought of being present with the Lord was upon the mind of Paul after he had given an account of the many sufferings and trials he had experienced in his missionary journeys. In this accounting, he did not seek pity, but declared that through all of these struggles he was not cast down nor discouraged. "Therefore we do not lose heart. Even though our outward man is perishing, yet the inward man is being renewed day by day. For our light affliction, which is but for a moment, is working for us a far more exceeding and eternal weight of glory, while we do not look at the things which are seen, but at the things which are not seen. For the things which are seen are temporary, but the things which are not seen are eternal."~2 Corinthians 4:16–18

Out of this expression of confidence Paul concludes that no matter how difficult the circumstances, he has the hope of being with the Lord. Furthermore, he reasons that the only way to be with Lord is to be absent from this body. Therefore, if God chooses to use the sufferings to relieve him of this earthly body, then he has another awaiting him in the presence of the Lord. I believe Paul would have gladly sung this verse of a favorite old hymn as he raised his hand and said, "Present!"

When the trumpet of the Lord shall sound, and time shall be no more,
And the morning breaks, eternal, bright and fair;
When the saved of earth shall gather over on the other shore,
And the roll is called up yonder, I'll be there.

Lord, help me share Jesus with someone so they too can be present.

March 26

Moving in Day

I heard this morning that the price of homes fell another 3.1%. At this rate by the time my mortgage reaches zero so will the value of my home! I guess you could call that breaking even....???? Not only do homes cost a lot and carry the risk of devaluation, there is the constant upkeep. How can something that cost so much wear out so quickly? Paint chips, window seals dry out, plaster cracks, faucets drip, and on and on goes the list. It is a never ending process of maintenance, but considering the alternative of sleeping under a tree...

The good news is building permits are still being issued from the throne of heaven and the value of a home there is based on the relative value of paving material. Remember the streets in heaven are paved with gold! It is very simple to get one of these permits. You must surrender your life. All of it, and all that you have, to the authority of Jesus. Simply declare Him to be the Lord of your life. The reason for this action is just as simple. He died on the cross for your sins. He has paid the price in full to redeem you from this old broken down house you live in now. No, not the physical building where you sleep and get your mail. The house that is you.

Jesus promised, "'Let not your heart be troubled; you believe in God, believe also in Me. In My Father's house are many mansions; if it were not so I would have told you. I go to prepare a place for you. And if I go and prepare a place for you, I will come again and receive you to Myself; that where I am, there you may be also. And where I go you know, and the way you know.' Thomas said to Him, 'Lord, we do not know where You are going, and how can we know the way?' Jesus said to him, 'I am the way, the truth, and the life. No one comes to the Father except through Me.'"~John 14:1–6 Moving in day is coming soon! Are you ready?

Lord, help me be always ready to move in to my heavenly home.

March 27

Quit Flopping Around

 Little boys and girls love to walk in their parent's footsteps. Sometimes they will even put adult sized shoes on and flop around trying to make BIG steps just like mommy or daddy. First Peter 2:21 tells us, "For hereunto were you called: because Christ also suffered for you, leaving you an example, that you should follow his steps."

Imitation, they say, is the highest form of flattery. Jesus is not desiring our flattery, however. His example of suffering has left for us a track to follow. We are to be actively engaged in following His steps understanding that His steps sometimes lead to suffering. This runs starkly contrary to the present day mantra of health and wealth.

I still remember the gift my church gave me and other seniors as we graduated from high school. It was Charles Sheldon's book, *In His Steps*. In this fictionalized account, a pastor challenges his congregation to read and follow the directive of 1 Peter 2:21. He suggests that they stop before each decision in their lives and ask, "What would Jesus do?" Now you know where the bracelet with "WWJD" on it came from a few years back.

Some then said such a question was invalid, because we could never really know what Jesus would do, but why then do we have the words of Peter? Yes, we may have a hard time comprehending as mere mortals what Jesus would do in every case. But we do know what He has already done for us in the past. And I think that is enough!

So, follow in His steps! Jesus wears mighty BIG shoes, but He lives in the believer so we won't be just flopping around!

Lord, help me to keep in step with You today.

March 28

Smart or Wise

Michelangelo is noted for many works of art. One of his most famous is the marble statue, *David*. The statue is approximately seventeen feet tall and weighs over six tons. Michelangelo was commissioned to sculpt the statue from a stone that had basically been discarded. When he saw the granite block and understood the possibilities that lay within it, it had been laying in a heap of stones for over 25 years. It was brought to his studio where he worked on it for the next three years. *David* arose from a mess of rocks to become a masterpiece.

This story gives us a beautiful picture of David's condition in Psalm 51. He had just been confronted by the Prophet Nathan about his sin with Bathsheba and now David is offering his repentance to God. After concluding that all are born in sin he states, "Behold, You desire truth in the inward parts; and in the hidden part You shall make me to know wisdom."~Psalms 51:6

We live in a world that exalts knowledge as the answer to man's problems. Teach them and they will turn we are told! But head knowledge only puffs up a person. Wisdom is another matter altogether. Wisdom cannot be learned it must be earned. As David said, "You shall make me to know wisdom."

David had ended up on the rubbish pile and it took the Master's hand to reach down and in and bring out of him his renewed potential. The truth of his sin was painful to face, but he concludes that God desires us to be filled with truth on the inside. Truth (JESUS) in our hearts prepares us to receive the wisdom of God. Smart is not the answer. Wise is!

Lord, help me to know the wisdom of truth.

March 29

When the Sun Refused to Shine

 "Now it was about the sixth hour, and there was darkness over all the earth until the ninth hour. Then the sun was darkened, and the veil of the temple was torn in two. And when Jesus had cried out with a loud voice, He said, 'Father, into Your hands I commit My spirit.' Having said this, He breathed His last. So when the centurion saw what had happened, he glorified God, saying, 'Certainly this was a righteous Man!'"~Luke 23:44–47

What a scene! There had never been a day like this one and there would never be another like it. Evangelist Sonny Holland stated it well when preaching about this day, "When the Son of God went out on the cross and no longer shined, the sun in the sky refused to shine as well!"

Jesus finished his task of redemption by paying for the sins of the whole world with His own shed blood. And having done all, He commended His spirit unto God. As He had said in the days of His ministry, "No man takes my life. I lay it down freely." (John 10:17-18)

We need to take heed as we contemplate the Cross, lest we forget the importance of what Christ accomplished there. As Oswald Chambers said on this matter of Christ's suffering, "We are apt to think that Jesus Christ took all the bitterness and we get all the blessing. It is true that we get the blessing, but we must never forget that the wine of life is made out of crushed grapes; to follow Jesus will involve bruising in the lives of the disciples as the purpose of God did in His own life."

Lord, help me never forget what You did for me on the cross.

March 30

Sunday's Coming

Ah! The weekend! It seems that no matter what job people have they are always looking forward to the weekends. Whatever day of the week you are reading this, be it a weekday or part of the weekend, you are most likely one of these people. That's okay! Enjoy every weekend, but never forget one particular Saturday nearly 2000 years ago.

This would have been a miserable Saturday. Hidden away in the deep dark recesses of the city the disciples of Jesus hunkered down and waited for...for what? They had just witnessed the erasure of all their hopes and dreams. They had misunderstood the last words of their friend. "IT IS FINISHED!" What they did not know was that victory over death was being won even while they worried.

Minutes drifted by as discouragement mounted up to heaven and beyond. But heaven was not disinterested in earth's quandary. Jesus was at work on behalf of those fear-filled disciples. He is still t work on behalf of you and me. "Therefore He says: 'When He ascended on high, He led captivity captive, and gave gifts to men.' (Now this, He ascended—what does it mean but that He also first descended into the lower parts of the earth? He who descended is also the One who ascended far above all the heavens, that He might fill all things.)"~Ephesians 4:8–10

Yes, it was Saturday. It wasn't a very good Saturday for the disciples. But we know something they didn't know at the time. It might have been Saturday, but Sunday was coming!

Lord, help me look toward Sunday!

March 31

Questions

 Slipping away before dawn from their hiding place the women made their way through winding streets toward the burial place of their friend. They had been sure just a few days before. Sure that he was their Messiah; maybe even a king. But now, who could know? Their greater concern at this moment was who would roll away the stone? "And they said among themselves, 'Who will roll away the stone from the door of the tomb for us?'"~Mark 16:3 Would the soldiers guarding the tomb help them? Would they dare disturb the seal set to make sure the sentence passed on this one named THE KING OF THE JEWS? Will they be arrested? Will their mission to anoint his body be a success? Questions that filled their minds and could only be whispered in the early dawn.

Finally they came around the last bend in the lane and now the tomb filled their sight. Questions? NO MORE! In one brief moment all were answered! "But when they looked up, they saw that the stone had been rolled away—for it was very large."~Mark 16:4 The stone of doubt and unbelief had been rolled away! A gaping hole surrounded by no one now loomed before them for all the guards had fled.

Watch them draw nigh with bated breath. See them look with amazement at each other on an empty tomb. Hear with them the words of the man standing near the entrance, "Why do you seek the living among the dead? He is not here. HE IS RISEN!"~Luke 24:5

Who will answer your questions today? HE WILL! Rejoice today in a risen Savior! HE LIVES! So come out of the dark morning and run with the good news. HE'S ALIVE FOREVERMORE!

Lord, help me to celebrate everyday as Resurrection Day.

April 1

Out of the Darkness

Today the world celebrates Universal Atheists Day. Actually, it is April
Fool's Day. I just decided to rename it for atheists because Psalm 14:1
says, "The fool has said in his heart there is no God." Other holidays
have the modifier happy placed at the front of the day, but you can't
call it Happy Atheist Day. Atheist simply have nothing to be happy
about.

The good news is that they can be hopeful. Hopeful that God in His boundless
love and mercy will call them out of their darkness into the glorious light! This
hope is not just for those who would deny the existence of God, but for all who
will call upon His name.

The prophet Isaiah declared, "The people who walked in darkness have seen a
great light; those who dwelt in the land of the shadow of death, upon them a light
has shined."~Isaiah 9:2 This shining light is like the breaking of day. The darkest
hour occurs just before the dawn. The weariness of the long restless night is over
and the hope of a new day lies untouched before you. So with this light that God
pours out upon a people who have walked in darkness.

Darkness cannot exist where light is present. Truthfully, darkness cannot even
be defined without the contrast of light. Darkness is the absence of light. Those
who dwell there do so because they refuse the reality of the light. Make April
Fool's Day a day that you remember those who are in the dark. It is no foolish
matter to miss the light. To remain in the dark is to miss the reality of the true
Light that shines in the darkness even though the darkness comprehends it not.
(John 1:5)

Lord, help me to let Your light shine through me into the dark.

95

April 2

The Search

When I was a boy my daddy would sometimes send me to the shed to get some tool for him. He would with simple instruction give me the tool's name and in obedience off I would go.

The problem arose from the fact that I had no idea what I was looking for many times. Out of a healthy fear of my dad, I would never ask him to describe the tool. I would go to the shed and wait until I heard him coming across the yard. Then I would go into search mode. He would walk in, pick up the tool and show it to me. No yelling, no rebuke, just show me. Together we would walk back to the job. This scenario repeated itself time and again. I still don't know why he didn't give me more instructions or just go in the first place and get the tool himself except for this little fact. I never forgot what that tool was or its location in the shed!

God leads us in a similar way at times. He gives instructions that seem to us incomplete. We go on a search with no results. "And I set my heart to seek and search out by wisdom concerning all that is done under heaven; this burdensome task God has given to the sons of man, by which they may be exercised."~Ecclesiastes 1:13

These are strong words used by Solomon in this text. Solomon concluded that searching after the workings of this life can be a miserable task that just keeps us occupied with no answers. But like I was as a boy, I always knew my father would come to my rescue. God want us to find Him more than anything else. "And you will seek Me and find Me, when you search for Me with all your heart."~Jeremiah 29:13 More importantly, we will never forget the lesson of the search!

Lord, help me to find You with all my heart.

April 3

We Win!

Anyone who has watched little kids play baseball will agree that
some of the best sights are not seen in the infield, but in the outfield.
Little to no action takes place "way out there." Most hits never carry
beyond the baselines, so those who are destined to play the outfield
positions can become easily distracted. Small, seemingly
insignificant items draw fantastic attention. You will see players with their gloves
on the ground while sitting next to the unhanded mitt. They may be picking
clover or writing their names in the dirt. Any distraction will do until it is finally
time to be summoned in for their turn to bat.

It is amazing that these small time baseball players receive joy in the moment.
They are not concerned with all of the rules and rigor of the sport. They are just
enjoying their position on the team. I think we could learn a lot from watching
these children. We spend way too much time concerned about the latest call of
the umpire or who's scored the most runs or where our kid will "star" today.

This all reminds me of the story of just such a little boy. Put into right field with
little hope of ever seeing a ball come his way. A man watching the game from the
other side of the outfield fence strikes up a conversation with the young fellow.

"Having fun?" he asks.

With a smile the boy replies, "Yes sir, I'm playing baseball!" as he stealthily plucks
another 4-leaf clover.

The man looking at the scoreboard asks how the game is going after noticing that
the score was 29-0. "Oh, everything's goin' great!" the little boy says grinning
back his answer.

"Whose team has 29 runs?" asked the man.

"The other team," says the boy without even looking up at the scoreboard.

"Aren't you worried?" queried the outsider, thinking that the little boy must be greatly concerned with such a lopsided score.

"No!" said the little baseball player, "We haven't been up to bat yet!"

This little fellow could have written Romans 8:28. "And we know that all things work together for good to those who love God, to those who are the called according to His purpose." It's time to quit fretting over your position in life. It's time to stop looking at the score. It really is a matter of perspective. For you see...

WE HAVEN'T BEEN UP TO BAT YET!

And, oh, by the way...*our coach is Jesus and His Father is the umpire!*

WE WIN!!!

Lord, help me to never worry about the score.

April 4

Set Your Watch

Incredible is this thing called time. We must all live by its tick and tock, yet we function as if our life will be the one exception to it. Why not set your clock by God's time piece today? Where your watch has seconds and minutes and hours, God's timepiece has years. "But, beloved, do not forget this one thing, that with the Lord one day is as a thousand years, and a thousand years as one day."~2 Peter 3:8

In the two main divisions of the Bible, Old Testament and New Testament, we gain stark differences in the understanding of time. The Hebrew language really has no word for time as we conceive of it. For the modern mind time is an abstract. It passes and much of our attempt to control it has a future component. For the Hebrew, time was fixed by events and occurred at those moments.

The Greek mind of the New Testament had three words to denote time. The first is *chronos*. This was the term used for measuring a quantity of time. The second is *kairos*. This word measures the quality of time. The third is *aion*. From this we derive our word eon or eons. This term reflects the broad sweep of time.

Time was clearly God's idea and was given as a gift to man in Genesis. As humans we are intrinsically connected to time. So much so that we need to be reminded that our counting of time is not on the same scale as that of God. Don't miss fellowship in the present with the One who is eternally present while focusing on the tininess of your past or the fleeting of your future. SERVE HIM TODAY!

Lord, help me to every minute of this day as a gift from You.

April 5

A Bump in the Night

 Many years ago we had a Kenyan guest in our home. His name was Elijah Buconyori. I still have a photo of Elijah sitting on our couch with my daughters on each side of him. He told us many stories of his life in Kenya.

Years later I had the opportunity to visit Kenya with a mission team. I could still remember Elijah's story of walking in the dark of night from one village to another. He told us that when he would walk in the bush at night he would place his lantern on a pole and extend it before him to light his path. As the light drove away the darkness, he said that he could hear rustling in the bush. Not only was the darkness retreating, but night creatures were also pulling away from his path.

Is it dark for you today? Hear this word: "Indeed, the darkness shall not hide from You, but the night shines as the day; the darkness and the light are both alike to You."~Psalm 139:12 It is very interesting here that David used the word *hide* and then said that the darkness would *not* hide. This term could have been translated bruise. Like a bump in the night, darkness can sometimes trip us. As I write this I have a toenail that is still blackened from a bump in the night. I walked into an object in the dark six months ago. I still have the bruise. It hurt, but it did not kill me.

This is what David is saying here. We cannot remove the darkness. It returns every time the light is extinguished, but having God's presence with us can alleviate the bump in the night. Notice that he finishes this verse with the wonderful assessment that darkness and light are both the same for God. Like Elijah's lantern on a pole, let's keep God both with us and before us. Don't be afraid of the rustling in the bushes.

Lord, help to trust You when I must walk in the darkness.

April 6

Caught Speeding

My son-in-law is a police officer. He also pastors a church near my home. That may seem a strange combination, but the Lord has provided through his work as a police officer for him to also serve as a bi-vocational pastor. That means he has two full time jobs.

I called him one day with a "hypothetical" question. It went something like this. How would you handle a situation where you had stopped a driver who was speeding? Of course, being a diligent officer he needed some more details which I gave him to my fullest ability since this whole incident was purely "hypothetical" and I knew that the driver must have been "innocent."

The driver, I told him, was going 18 miles per hour over the speed limit; actually it was 53 miles per hour in a 35 miles per hour zone. I'm not sure what transpired, but his whole tone changed. He became all officer! His response was something to the order of, "I'd hook him up." This term meant that the offense was serious enough that this "hypothetical" person could have been arrested. Then he asked me, "Where did you get stopped?"

I confessed immediately. I took out the hypothetical parts and owned up to the offense. He then began to tell me how much the ticket was going to cost. It was my joy, and I do mean joy, to inform him that the officer who had stopped me gave me a choice. I could either receive a lecture or a ticket. I chose the lecture. By the way, that officer should receive some kind of award and go on a lecture circuit. He really did a masterful job!

"Now, wait a minute!" I can hear you thinking as you read this, "How can you justify getting away with such a serious driving offense?" I can't. It was pure mercy at work. The officer had every right to "hook me up." But he didn't and for that I'm grateful. I would have paid the ticket, but I was shown mercy. I became like one of the children of Israel. I knew better, yet I still broke the law. I chose to drive over the speed limit. I was guilty, but I experienced the manifold mercy of a stranger.

This is what God did for Israel time and again. After great disobedience and being driven from the land, God brings the people back and sends Nehemiah to rebuild the walls of Jerusalem. In Nehemiah 9 he recounts the history of Israel which included many violations. Then he reminds Israel of the manifold mercies of God. "Yet in Your manifold mercies You did not forsake them in the wilderness. The pillar of the cloud did not depart from them by day, to lead them on the road; nor the pillar of fire by night, to show them light, and the way they should go."~Nehemiah 9:19

Never forget the manifold mercies of God! They are beyond our comprehension to number. He could have left us to our error with no direction through our wilderness. He could have left us with the penalty intact and required payment at our hands. He could have "hooked us up." But He did not! Behold, the manifold mercies of God!

Lord, help me to remember and be thankful for Your mercy.

April 7

Doing Good

Do you have good things on your mind today? Not good food or good friends or even good health. I mean *doing* good things. Acts 10:38 tells us how God anointed Jesus with the Holy Spirit and with power, and He went about doing good. "The word which God sent to the children of Israel, preaching peace through Jesus Christ— He is Lord of all— that word you know, which was proclaimed throughout all Judea, and began from Galilee after the baptism which John preached: how God anointed Jesus of Nazareth with the Holy Spirit and with power, who went about doing good and healing all who were oppressed by the devil, for God was with Him."~Acts 10:36–38

Those things which Jesus did and were here chronicled by Peter as *doing good* are of the quality that they were of benefit to others. Where our translation gives us two words, there is only one word in the original. It is a compound word which means to be a benefactor. To work good would be an appropriate translation.

So much of what we do daily is just work. We work because we owe. We work for the pay we receive at the end of the work. It does not have the quality of doing good work. I am making the distinction for a reason. That reason lies in the fact that we have the testimony of Peter declaring that the Holy Spirit anointed Jesus to work good. We also know that Jesus instructed His disciples that this same Holy Spirit would reside with them after His death, burial, and resurrection (John 16.) What more then might we expect in and from our own lives? Jesus said we would do GREATER things than He had done (John 14:12).

May God anoint you today that you can greatly do GOOD things!

Lord, help me to work "good" today.

April 8

Bugs!

 Spring! Tulips are up and in full bloom. The trees are filling with leaves of various greens. The redbud trees are filled with their pink splashes while the dogwoods look like spots of fresh fallen snow on the hillside. The days are a little longer, the sun a little higher in the sky, and the temperature a little warmer.

Colors and warmth and I forgot to mention…BUGS! Personally, I don't like bugs. I treat them all like snakes…better off dead. I know. I can just hear the nature lovers complaining about my lack of compassion for these creatures. All I know is that even though some are supposedly harmless, I am not smart enough to know the difference and I'm not waiting for the bite or sting.

People are like this too. No, I don't believe that we should eradicate people just to be sure! I would be the first exterminated. I'm just stating the fact that sometimes we can be a bit "buggy". Paul said it in Philippians 2:15, "Do all things without complaining and disputing, that you may become blameless and harmless, children of God without fault in the midst of a crooked and perverse generation, among whom you shine as lights in the world…" These two words, *blameless* and *harmless*, mean without accusation and genuine. In other words, let it be known clearly that you are not dangerous.

Don't be a "buggy" Christian! How will you respond the next time someone picks on you? We're all bugs at heart. It's up to us whether we bite back…

Lord, help me not to bug anybody today.

April 9

Hyper-Christians

Do you happen to have one of those hyper kids? Maybe you are one of those hyper people. Most of us get a little frustrated at times with hyper activity and I'm pretty sure that hyper folks wish they could settle down a little bit too. I can only imagine what's going on inside a hyper mind, but it must be a little like me on a long flight. I get real "antsy." My legs become restless. I twist and turn. If I could, I think I would go ask the pilot to let me fly the plane. Did I mention that I *might* be a little hyper at times?

Did you know that the Bible speaks about being hyper? The word is found in the book of Romans. "Yet in all these things we are more than conquerors through Him who loved us."~Romans 8:37 The words *more than conquerors* are one word in the original. It could be translated hyper-victorious. Wow! What a relief! God intends for us as Christians to be hyper! Hyper-victorious that is.

The word for victory is played upon by one shoe company: *Nike.* The word they have chosen as the name of their company is the Greek word for victory. Remember their slogan, "Just Do It!" You see hyper people just do it. They don't always think before they act. They just...do...it!

Sometimes we need to *just do it* as believers. Just do it, because we have a hyper-victory in Christ!

Lord, help me live a hyper life for You today.

April 10

Poured Out

 Born into slavery, this poor man had never seen a day of freedom. His responsibility was to carry water from a mountain spring to his master's house. The work was never ending as the thirst of his master was unceasing. One day a traveler happened upon this man sitting beside the path sobbing as he rested his tired feet and aching shoulders. "Can I help you?" the traveler asked, but the weary slave only sighed.

"What is it that you do with these buckets?" asked the traveler with curiosity. "I must walk each day up this mountain and carry fresh water back down to my master," replied the slave. "But, he is a hard man. He not only requires the water, but refuses to give me new buckets."

"I have used these same buckets for many years and now they leak all the way back to the master's home. My work is made difficult as I can never get all of the water back to the master's table. I am only a poor slave. I have accomplished nothing with my life. When I die, there will be nothing left to show for all of my labor!"

"Oh, but you are mistaken," smiled the traveler. "Lift up your eyes from your labors and look along the trail you have walked these many years." "Don't you see what has happened?" he asked the slave. "As you have carried the water, the leaking buckets have brought life along the trail you have walked! None of these flowers would be here had you not traveled this way!"

Sometimes we are wearied by the work and the load given us to bear. We complain about the path laid before us. But God has put us on that certain path to spill His blessing along the way so that His flowers of mercy might spring up for some traveler that passes your way. (2 Timothy 4:6-8)

Lord, help me to spill my life out for You along the path I travel.

April 11

The Auction Block

As an associational missionary, I have the joy and privilege of preaching in many of the churches that make up our association. Recently, I preached in a church service that is held each week in a sale barn. You may not know what a sale barn is and I wouldn't expect you for not having such knowledge. A sale barn is where livestock auctions are held. It was a very unique experience to preach with cattle lowing in the background and the pungent smell of what cows leave behind filling the room.

We worshiped in the same room that the livestock auction takes place. I stood down on the auction floor and the congregation was seated up in stadium style seats that lined one side of the room. A couple of biblical stories came to mind in this setting. One of these comes from the Old Testament and one from the New Testament. Both accounts deal with the concept of an auction, but it was not cows being offered for sale. These were auctions where human beings were sold as slaves.

Hosea, the prophet took for himself a wife who later became unfaithful and left him to play the harlot. God instructed Hosea to go and purchase his wife and bring her back into his home. This was a beautiful picture of God redeeming Israel.

In the book of Titus we read, "[Jesus] who gave Himself for us, that He might redeem us from every lawless deed and purify for Himself His own special people, zealous for good works."~Titus 2:14 I can't help but think about the day Jesus visited the auction block and redeemed me from my sin and slavery. Oh, how high the price had become, but JESUS PAID IT ALL!

Lord, help me remember the great price You paid to save me.

April 12

Casual Christianity

 Most companies today have at least one day that is declared casual as for the dress code. Casual seems to be the thing today to the point that I would label it tacky. Everyone seems to be affected by this trend starting in the workplace down to our children. Presidents no longer wear suits and ties, preachers are wearing shorts and polos in the pulpit. Children wear clothes with holes in them and the hairstyle on some people looks like they have been in a wind tunnel.

I know there is a place for casual and everybody likes to be comfortable, but this "look" has spread through nearly every aspect of life. I am afraid it has severely affected our worship and diligence in studying God's word.

Timothy was a young preacher when Paul was mentoring him. He wrote Timothy two letters that we have as part of our Bibles. He instructed him daily as they traveled together. In his first letter Paul gave Timothy this instruction. "Meditate on these things; give yourself entirely to them, that your progress may be evident to all. Take heed to yourself and to the doctrine. Continue in them, for in doing this you will save both yourself and those who hear you."~1 Timothy 4:15–16

The word *meditate* means to look into with care and concern, to give serious consideration to, to ponder and dwell upon. This is the absolute opposite of casual. Paul advises Timothy that the evidence of his spiritual growth was dependent upon him giving himself entirely to the word of God, its doctrine, and the spiritual gifts that he had received at his salvation. Here's the real eye-opener of this verse. If he would refuse to be casual about the things of God, it would act as a proof of his own salvation and as a doorway for others to come to Christ. Be serious. Be a witness!

Lord, help me to never approach my life as a Christian in a casual way.

April 13

Defining Good

"Good" is a very small word, but have you ever looked it up in the dictionary? It has a very big definition. We use the word good all the time. We can have a good time, eat good food, see a good movie, or go to a good friend's home. What does God have to say about good?

The Psalmist stated it this way. "Oh, taste and see that the LORD is good; blessed is the man who trusts in Him! Oh, fear the LORD, you His saints! There is no want to those who fear Him. The young lions lack and suffer hunger; but those who seek the LORD shall not lack any good thing."~Psalm 34:8–10

Scripture makes a couple of interesting comparisons here as we think about what is good. First, finding the goodness of the Lord involves trust. The Psalmist tells us that we can show our trust by tasting. This is a great illustration. How many times has someone offered you a taste of something with the assurance of these words, "Go ahead, taste it...it's good!" No one has ever suggested that I should taste something because it tasted awful.

The second comparison has to do with the satisfaction that comes from having good things. Here the verse compares those who seek the Lord to the young lions. The young lions in the pride get the leftovers after the dominant males have had their fill. God says that those who seek the Lord shall lack no good thing. We are not subject to the rules of the pride. We do not find ourselves making do with leftovers.

What a promise! But here's the caution! Don't define good with a worldly definition. God's good for you may not always appear as such at the moment, but it never fails to reveal His eternal purpose for your life. Have a *good* day!

Lord, help me to define good by Your definition...not mine.

April 14

As a Child

 It has been a blessing for me to lead dozens of teams on short-term mission trips. Each of these journeys is unique in the fact that there is a moment that stands out above all others. In August 2002 our mission team had just finished feeding a large group of children. Each child had come to the little building with a container and a spoon in hand. As they passed along the feeding line our ladies would fill their bowls with some soup. The soup was made of restaurant leftovers and culled vegetables. I'll never forget one little fellow that had a small bucket in his hand. He asked for enough to take back to his family as well. We filled his bucket!

After the soup kitchen closed, I preached from John 3:16. Since very few of those in attendance had a Bible I used one of our team members as a Bible. All of us were wearing t-shirts that had John 3:16 printed on the backs in Portuguese. I had the team member stand on a chair facing backwards to the crowd and from his t-shirt I preached the gospel.

As the invitation was given to stand and receive Christ as Savior, many of the children came. But the moment that still stands out was when the big, burly six foot tall man stood with these children. There he stood with dozens of children accepting Jesus as his Lord and Savior. The only adult that made a decision that afternoon.

I can only imagine Jesus seeing this scene in Brazil and repeating as he said while walking this earth in the days of His ministry, "'He who humbles himself as a little child is greatest in the Kingdom of Heaven [and] assuredly, I say to you, whoever does not receive the kingdom of God as a little child will by no means enter it.'"~Matthew 18:4; Luke 18:17

Lord, help me be as a little child today in my walk.

April 15

The Tax Man Cometh

Jesus paid taxes! Somehow I wish He hadn't. There is an interesting account in Matthew 17. Jesus arrives in Capernaum and is questioned about paying taxes. He frames the question with a question as He so often did.

"...those who received the temple tax came to Peter and said, "Does your Teacher not pay the temple tax?" He said, "Yes." And when he had come into the house, Jesus anticipated him, saying, "What do you think, Simon? From whom do the kings of the earth take customs or taxes, from their sons or from strangers?" Peter said to Him, "From strangers." Jesus said to him, "Then the sons are free. Nevertheless, lest we offend them, go to the sea, cast in a hook, and take the fish that comes up first. And when you have opened its mouth, you will find a piece of money; take that and give it to them for Me and you."~Matthew 17:24–27

"Do sons pay taxes or strangers?" He asked. The answer from Peter was that strangers pay the taxes. He then sent Peter, the fisherman, fishing. The first fish caught had the exact amount due for His and Peter's tax bill. Now I know what you are thinking. Why doesn't God send me a windfall or should I say "fishfall" for my tax bill? I won't even attempt to answer that, but I have better news than a fish with a coin in its mouth!

We pay taxes because we are strangers in this world! This world is not our home the old song says. We are just a passin' thru! Our country is heaven and our King is JESUS! Heaven runs no deficit. Heaven has no pork barrel spending plan. Heaven has no government! Heaven has no taxes!

Certainly we should not want to go to heaven just to avoid paying taxes, but it sure will be a wonderful benefit. Just think...NO MORE TAXES!!!

Lord, help me trust You for the very basic provisions of life.

April 16

Priming Your Praise Pump

 The Psalms are full of reasons to praise God. They are the hymn book of Israel. Sometimes it is just not enough to say, "Praise the Lord!" If you are looking for a reason to praise the Lord today, these verses might just be the right words to prime your praise pump.

"Praise the LORD! I will praise the LORD with my whole heart, in the assembly of the upright and in the congregation. The works of the LORD are great, studied by all who have pleasure in them. His work is honorable and glorious, and His righteousness endures forever. He has made His wonderful works to be remembered; the LORD is gracious and full of compassion."~Psalm 111:1–4

Praise is best done in the presence of others for there it has a contagious effect. More than just generalities, praise is best when focused upon that which God has performed. The Psalmist said that God's works were great, but praise comes forth from those who *study* them. This word means to tread frequently. Rehearse regularly and remember what God has done and is doing in your life. Praise will be easier when you invest in it.

Made in God's image, man also has the ability to be compassionate, but not *full* of compassion. We are moved in the moment or by the scene until we witness the next tragedy. The word compassion means to be associated with love. Only a God who *is* love can truly be *full* of compassion.

Jesus loves me with *compassion* this I know, for the Bible tells me so! And that makes me want to praise His name. Hallelujah!

How about you?

Lord, help me to sing Your praises today!

 112

April 17

Stewards of His Grace

One of my favorite movie series is *Lord of the Rings*. In the last segment of the trilogy, Denethor is the Steward of Gondor. He comes to a tragic end when his perception of his rule as Steward becomes distorted. He begins to think of himself as a king instead of only being a steward. We, too, are stewards in the kingdom of God and we must always keep ourselves aware of this role and its limitations.

We do not understand very well this concept of stewardship in our world today. It is akin to being a manager or overseer, but its administration is much deeper than this. To minister effectively as stewards, God has given to believers spiritual gifts. "As each one has received a gift, minister it to one another, as good stewards of the manifold grace of God."~1 Peter 4:10 This verse instructs us to use our gifts as stewards according to the manifold grace of God.

Here is the wonder of the manifold grace of God. You and I both can have the same gift and can be faithful stewards in its use. Yet individually it is seen like the flash of light from a diamond by the multi-faceted grace of God!

These grace gifts are given by and directed by the Spirit of God. They are never ours. We are stewards of these gifts. They are not ours to hoard, but to minister to others in the name of the Lord. The word *minister* is the same word from which we derive the word deacon. We are stewards to serve; not to rule or reign.

Go out today and show off His grace!

Lord, help me be a faithful steward of Your grace.

April 18

Just a Pile of Dirt

 If there is one thing most of us have no problem with, it is not thinking of ourselves highly enough. I know that some people have self-esteem concerns and I do not take that condition lightly, but we live in a world that seems to pride itself on pumping self-esteem into every fiber of human existence. We indeed are riding on very high horses! Without harming anyone's healthy self-esteem let me take us down a notch.

Take one of us human beings and begin the process of extracting all of the chemical compounds from us and you would be surprised what you would end up with in your petri dish. The total value of the contents of your petri dish would be about one dollar. Not a trillion, billion, million, or even a thousand. Just one measly dollar.

The rest of what makes us, us, is just dirt. Just a pile of dirt. In five words I have just described me. Now lest you think I'm having a bad day, hear what God says in 2 Corinthians 4:7, "…we have this treasure in earthen vessels, that the excellency of the power may be of God, and not of us." We're clay pots! Like I already said, just a pile of dirt. Unattractive vases which display the glory of God!

Just a pile of dirt, but in me is the excellency of the power of God! That, my friend, can fix the lowest self-esteem. Since the power is not mine, it's not mine to maintain. God can use you today as a clay pot to display the bouquet of His beauty. May those around you sense the fragrance of the flowers and spend no time admiring the pot.

Lord, help me live that others see You and not me.

April 19

Heaven Bound

As I grow older, I join countless others who spend a little more time each day thinking about heaven. I guess it is as someone said, desiring heaven and going there is an easier proposition as more and more of our acquaintances depart this world. This is especially true of my loved ones and friends that have left this life to spend an eternity in the presence of the Father in a real place called heaven.

As the War Between the States began, families were ripped apart. Members of the same household found themselves on opposite sides in this great civil conflict. Stonewall Jackson and George Junkin, his father-in-law, were on opposing sides in the war. Even with the sharp differences that existed between these two men over the reasons for secession and the hostilities of war, they spoke as they parted of seeing each other in heaven, if not again in this world.

There is no better verse that I can think of to describe the desire of these two men to be in heaven together than the verse that holds the words of Jesus to the thief on the cross. "And Jesus said to him, "Assuredly, I say to you, today you will be with Me in Paradise.'"~Luke 23:43 No greater gulf could exist than that which was between the righteous Son of God and a common thief, yet Christ promised him heaven.

Three questions: Are you heaven-bound? Is there someone you would not see in heaven if they died today? Who are you looking forward to seeing again in Heaven one day? Spend a while today thinking about heaven. I sure hope to see you there!

Lord, help me think about heaven and tell others how to get there.

April 20

Spring City

 Thousands of towns and cities in the world have the word *spring* as part of their name. You can probably think of dozens without much difficulty. The reason for this is because these settlements developed around or very near a spring of water. If you have ever been in an area that has no ready source of water you can appreciate this so much the more.

I came to a deeper appreciation for water on a mission trip to Nigeria many years ago. Each day I watched as children carried heavy buckets and pans of water from a well over three miles away from where we were staying. Each night I bathed from one of those buckets of water. It changed my life forever as I thought of the labor of love that had brought to me that water of refreshing.

Jesus said, "He who believes in Me, as the Scripture has said, out of his heart will flow rivers of living water."~John 7:38 A spring is always in the process of giving. Pools on the other hand just receive. Put the word pool in any of the names of the cities you thought of and the whole concept changes.

Our lives should be overflowing springs that have their source in Jesus. These springs accumulate and form rivers of blessing. Unlike, the village where I stayed in Nigeria, we can be the source of refreshing to all whom we interact. It truly is more blessed to give than to receive, because giving is only possible if you have already received!

So, name a city for yourself today. _____ Springs. Put your name in the blank and watch people flock to you.

Lord, help me be a refreshing spring in someone's life today.

April 21

According to Purpose

Romans 8:28 is a favorite for many people. "And we know that all things work together for good to those who love God, to those who are the called according to His purpose." However, the "favoriteness" of this verse lies in the phrase *all things working for good*. What is missed is the fact that this promise is not general in its focus, but very specific. This promise of God is unto a certain group: THE CALLED. The verse is often quoted with the little article *the* left out of the recitation and therein lies a problem.

Believers are the called ones according to His purpose. The fact that things work together to produce good is not determined by our concept of goodness, but by His purpose being accomplished in the ones who are called. Therefore, the key to understanding this verse is not us passing judgment as to the good or bad that comes from a situation, but an acceptance of the fact of His purpose.

Purpose comes from the mind of the Creator. God does not simply wait for circumstances to unveil themselves and then make good things happen out of what chance has given Him. No, all things are already working according to the design He has created so that in the end His purpose is fulfilled.

When we finally understand that what we are experiencing in a moment is not the whole of the matter, then we can wait with patience until the purpose of God is revealed. After this, we can rejoice in our favorite part of this verse: *we know that all things work together for good to those who love God.*

Lord, help me understand all things work according to Your purpose.

April 22

Cushion of the Sea

 Let us go to the other side. So Jesus commanded his disciples and forthwith went fast asleep in the bow of the boat. A short time later in the journey across the Sea of Galilee a storm arose. The disciples were pummeled by wind and wave. With each blow their resolve diminished and soon they had forgotten the command of Jesus, "Let us go to the other side!" (Mark 4:35-41)

That command carried with it the promise of success. God cannot command that which He cannot perform. His intent in giving us the command to perform is to empower with the ability to complete the task. So, JESUS SLEPT! With the crash of the wave and the roll of the thunder, Jesus slept with a calm assurance of the spoken word.

When the disciples finally awoke the Master, their concern was of no little doubt. They voiced it loudly over the tumult, "Care you not that we die!" Having seen so much they believed so little! And would Jesus just let them die? Would the only lesson learned be a trip to the bottom of the sea? Oh, no! He is gentle with our unbelief. He knows that we are feeble and frail as dust. He is ready to show himself able in the midst of our doubt! With yet another spoken word Jesus spoke the wind out of existence and brought calm to a troubled sea.

If only the disciples would have trusted in the midst of the storm how much greater blessing would have been theirs. If only they had realized that just a little way beneath the surface of the water all was calm. Oceanographers call it the cushion of the sea. Undisturbed by the roiling surface the cushion of the sea is undisturbed by surface conditions. The deeper you go the calmer it gets. When you find your sea beset by a storm, GO DEEP! Remember, that God gives a peace that surpasses all understanding. Jesus promised a peace that the world didn't give and the world can't take away.

Lord, help me find Your peace in the midst of the storm.

April 23

The Friend of Jesus

A man can count himself blessed in this life to have friends. Of these whom he calls friends, he will have only a handful that can be considered close friends. I have defined a close friend as a person you can call from jail in the middle of the night, and he will not ask you why you are calling from there. A friend like this loves beyond error or failure.

The story is told of a man who was trying desperately to see President Abraham Lincoln, but could not gain access. The man's son had been falsely accused of desertion and the father wanted the president to pardon him. As he sat weeping at the gate of the White House, Lincoln's son passed by and inquired of his sorrow. After hearing the man's account, Mr. Lincoln's son brought him into his father's presence. After hearing the man's story, the president pardoned the man's son. The man did not gain access of his own accord, but because he was befriended by the son of the president. So it is with us who are friends of Jesus. By His friendship we have access to the Father.

Jesus said in John 15:15, "No longer do I call you servants, for a servant does not know what his master is doing; but I have called you friends, for all things that I heard from My Father I have made known to you." His friendship was not based on their faithfulness, but His. His love for His friends led Him to tell them all that the Father had told Him. Oh, to be the friend of Jesus and to be a friend like Jesus! To have His confidence demonstrated by revealing all of the Father's plan to my heart, is the pinnacle of trustworthy friendship. Are you the friend of Jesus? Can He trust you with the Father's plan for your life? Called His friend! What joy!

Lord, help me always remember that You call me your friend.

119

April 24

We Will Call Her "V"

 I met an interesting lady recently on a flight to Dallas. She was 81 years old. I was not supposed to be sitting next to her. Another person had taken my seat, so I just exchanged seats and settled in for the short flight. After we were airborne, we struck up a conversation.

When she discovered I was from northwest Arkansas she told me she had visited Eureka Springs. I asked what I thought was a perfectly logical question. Wondering if she had been to *The Great Passion Play*, an outdoor drama that takes place in a large amphitheater, I inquired about her attendance to the drama about the death, burial, and resurrection of Jesus. Wow! Did I ever push her button?

She quickly informed me that she was not religious and with a swipe of her hand told me that there was now a wall between us. We talked some more and I was able to bring the conversation back to her spiritual condition, but each time she would demonstrate with her hand that the wall was in place.

My final comment was that I knew someone that lives on the other side of her wall and that I would be praying for her. God can tear down her wall. "The fortress of the high fort of your walls He will bring down, lay low, and bring to the ground, down to the dust."~Isaiah 25:12

Would you join with me as we ask God to tear down the wall she has erected? At 81 time is of the essence. You can call her V. God knows her by name! I'm also sure that you know others who need a wall removed. Take time today to pray for God to send in a wrecking ball of mercy and grace.

Lord, help me to pray for "V" and others who need a Savior.

April 25

Museum or Hardware

The church is not a building with a sign above the doorway declaring it to be so. The church is not an organization; it is an organism. It is a living, ever growing, assembly of those who have trusted Christ as Lord and Savior. The church has always been in the mind of God since before eternity began and was founded by Christ Himself upon Himself. (Matthew 16:18)

It must be asked in this early part of the 21st century if the church is still fulfilling all that God intended for her. Especially in light of the fact that church can be so loosely defined. God's definition is much narrower. "For we are God's fellow workers; you are God's field, you are God's building."~1 Corinthians 3:9 It is very clear that you and I, as believers, are the church.

To what then shall I compare us as the church? Perhaps I will make a distinction between a museum and a hardware store! If the church is to be likened unto a museum then it becomes a place where relics are kept safe. The items, in this case, us who constitute the church are never intended to be used for fear they would disintegrate to dust. We are just icons of a time long past.

But the hardware store is a place where tools are purchased and put to use, each serving its individual purpose. This is a much better picture of the church and God's intent for the people who compose it. God has fully equipped the church to be at work outside of the hardware store shelves. Ask God how you can be used in His Kingdom. Don't worry! His answer will always be according to your design.

Lord, help me to be a part of Your Church alive in my world.

April 26

Lost in Space

 I have to admit that I am what is called a *trekkie*. I love to watch any of the *Star Trek* shows and movies. If I can't watch *Star Trek*, then *Star Wars* will do just fine. Truthfully though, my fascination for sci-fi goes back much further than these more modern examples. I can trace my fascination all the way back to *Flash Gordon* and *Lost in Space*.

Do you remember the robot from that old *Lost in Space* program? He had a design flaw; he had no elbows! On nearly every episode, Will Robinson would get into trouble with an alien or maybe through the shenanigans of Dr. Smith. The robot was a constant companion of Will Robinson, but the design flaw was always evident.

The robot's arms would flail about and he would exclaim with his warning subroutine, "Danger! Will Robinson, Danger! Now this was all just fine, but with no elbows he could never hug Will. There were times that Will needed more than a warning; he needed a hug. Even a hug from a robot is better than no hug at all.

Ephesians 2:12-13 says, "that at that time you were without Christ, being aliens from the commonwealth of Israel and strangers from the covenants of promise, having no hope and without God in the world. But now in Christ Jesus you who once were far off have been brought near by the blood of Christ." The word *near* in this verse means to place in the bend of the arm. Jesus' sacrifice put us within reach of God's hug. We are no longer lost in space!

Lord, help me hug someone today because I've been hugged by You.

April 27

Life's Puzzle

Imagine someone handing you a bag full of puzzle pieces and asking you to put them all together without the original box. Your ability to reassemble all of the puzzle pieces into their original form depends greatly on seeing the picture on the box top. We work towards the finished picture.

This is exactly how we function at times in our lives. We have a picture in our minds of what our life is supposed to look like when all the pieces have come together. Then we set out to make our life look like the box top picture. Usually this consists of sorting the pieces either by common colors or shapes. We especially like to find all of the edges of the puzzle and put them together. I think this does two things for us. It sets the boundaries of the puzzle and whether we will admit it or not we like boundaries. They make us feel safer. Second, we like to assemble the edges because it is the easiest part to do. We can achieve a measure of success early. Also the edge pieces stand out because one side of each piece is straight. Again, we like ruled edges in our life.

Now understand this: The puzzle called your life is not yours to assemble. God is working the pieces together according to the finished picture He has already planned for you! "For I know the thoughts that I think toward you, says the LORD, thoughts of peace and not of evil, to give you a future and a hope."~Jeremiah 29:11 We don't have the finished picture neatly airbrushed on a boxtop. The edge pieces of our life are the *last* pieces that are laid out for us because we don't know where the edge of our life exist. Our assurance is found in God's promise of a future and a hope. Our future is fixed in God's mind already and our hope is not wishful thinking, but the reality that life's puzzle is solvable.

Lord, help me realize that You already know what I'm supposed to be.

123

April 28

Amusing

 To what shall the world turn its attention now? More importantly what's grabbing your attention or should I say what's keeping you from thinking? The phrase *to not think* is the literal definition of the word *amuse*. This word has as its root the word *muse* which means to think, to dwell upon, or to consider. When the little letter "a" is placed in front of a word it negates it or makes it become the opposite. So, amuse means to not think, dwell upon, or consider.

We have amused ourselves into numbness. We even have entire acres set aside for the activity of amusement. These are places we can go and not think or at least that's what is supposed to happen. Now don't take this the wrong way. I love going to amusement parks as much as anyone, but I don't expect to spend my entire life being amused.

Be it drama, romance, or even tragedy, it seems that the average attention span grows shorter day by day. We move quickly from storyline to storyline and like the highest, fastest roller coaster you can only ride it so many times before it becomes boring. Then you are off to find one faster and higher. Hmmm...amusing!

Hear God's thoughts on this matter. "Finally, brethren, whatever things are true, whatever things are noble, whatever things are just, whatever things are pure, whatever things are lovely, whatever things are of good report, if there *is* any virtue and if there is anything praiseworthy—meditate on these things."~Philippians 4:8 Go on to the amusement park, but as you make that first climb on the roller coaster be thinking of a few of these things. It will sure make that first drop easier!

Lord, help me to only think on those things which are of good report.

124

April 29

Your Wedding Day

Weddings are always popular. Everyone attends with the best of wishes for the bride and groom. Some of course are more talked about than others, including those of royalty or celebrity. You and I have been invited to a wedding. If you are a believer you are the bride and Jesus is the groom. The next great event on heaven's calendar is Jesus coming for His Bride–the true Church of believers.

It is customary for a groom to present a gift soon after the wedding as a commemoration of the glad day. Never before has a groom given a bride such a gift as Jesus did in giving His own precious life. "Husbands, love your wives, just as Christ also loved the church and gave Himself for her, that He might sanctify and cleanse her with the washing of water by the word, that He might present her to Himself a glorious church, not having spot or wrinkle or any such thing, but that she should be holy and without blemish."~Ephesians 5:25–27

Our wedding day as believers will overshadow all previous weddings recorded here on earth. Our groom will come with the trumpet blast and the voice of the archangel. With veils upon our faces, we will leave a world of doubt and scorn behind. Our wedding supper will last for seven years as the celebration takes place in heaven. On earth a time of terrible tribulation will prevail. You can be a part of this wedding. You need only say yes to the proposal of Jesus.

If your delay is based on a lack of purity on your part, worry not! Jesus will sanctify and purify you by His word and His own shed blood. The invitations have been sent. Will you respond today?

Lord, help me deliver an invitation to someone today.

April 30

Welcome Home

 Cloth and carpet are discounted as remnants. Yet the Bible speaks with value about the remnant. From Joseph's ordeal in Egypt to Paul's passion for his brethren who would believe, we see this doctrine of the remnant. God always holds safely a remnant to continue His purpose.

When the children of Israel had returned from captivity they only found a speck of their former glory as a nation. Even the Temple had been destroyed. Much of what they knew about worshiping the one true God was linked to the function of the Temple. In the midst of this restoration, Ezra proclaimed to the people, "And now for a little while grace has been shown from the LORD our God, to leave us a remnant to escape, and to give us a peg in His holy place, that our God may enlighten our eyes and give us a measure of revival in our bondage."~Ezra 9:8

Remnants are often marked down from their original values and even discarded, but not so with God. God's remnants are of value, but not because of intrinsic worth. The remnant gains value because of God's grace at work. The remnant has value because it is given ground in God's holy place. Note that Ezra said God had given them a peg in His holy place. The idea here is of a nail driven in the wall of the Temple. Hence, our saying of having a place on which to hang your hat. In this case, the remnant was not the hat, only the nail on which the hat was hung.

Finally, the remnant's sight is restored and a measure of revival given to renew. If you are feeling left out today and a bit like a discarded remnant, it's going to be okay. God is in the remnant business. Let Him place you in His holy place. Though it be only as a nail in the wall...welcome home!

Lord, help me to remember that You use remnants.

May 1

May Day

May 1st is celebrated in many cultures as a special day. In some countries it is a national holiday which includes quite elaborate festivities. Like many of our holidays, May Day has a lot of pagan trappings that we would not participate in as Christians. It has, however, been observed over the years without the pagan influences.

I thought back this morning to my elementary days when we would go out on May 1st and wrap a maypole with bright crepe paper. Each child held a strip of crepe paper that was attached to the top of the pole and we would cris-cross each other as we marched around the pole until it was wrapped from top to bottom. I know this sounds weird to younger readers who cannot fathom anything that does not involve an electronic device, but it was a real fun day of celebration. And getting out of class is always fun, no matter the reason.

The book of Revelation tells of a day when a great multitude will stand before the throne of the Lamb having been wrapped in the white cloth of His righteousness. "After these things I looked, and behold, a great multitude which no one could number, of all nations, tribes, peoples, and tongues, standing before the throne and before the Lamb, clothed with white robes, with palm branches in their hands..."~Revelation 7:9

This day will make all May Day celebrations pale in comparison. Even though various people groups celebrate May Day in the context of their own cultures, on this day ALL people groups will be assembled in one place with a common connection. They will have all been made righteous by the shed blood of the Lamb before whom they stand. What a day this will be! Will you be one of the numberless multitude standing there?

Lord, help me to share Jesus so all might join in heaven's celebration.

May 2

Be Persistent

 There is surely no better example of persistence found in nature than that which can be seen in the life of a bee. We take for granted the sweetness of the honey that sets at our breakfast table. We pour it liberally and let it drip carelessly, but consider these bee facts:

One pound of honey is produced from a bee's visit to 56,000 flowers.
The worker can fly the equivalent of three times around the world to produce that pound of honey. A bee will fly up to eight miles if necessary to find a sufficient nectar flow to harvest.

Jesus gave several examples of being persistent in prayer. He would sometimes use parables. He told them, "'Which of you shall have a friend, and go to him at midnight and say to him, 'Friend, lend me three loaves; for a friend of mine has come to me on his journey, and I have nothing to set before him'; and he will answer from within and say, 'Do not trouble me; the door is now shut, and my children are with me in bed; I cannot rise and give to you'? I say to you, though he will not rise and give to him because he is his friend, yet because of his persistence he will rise and give him as many as he needs. So I say to you, ask, and it will be given to you; seek, and you will find; knock, and it will be opened to you. For everyone who asks receives, and he who seeks finds, and to him who knocks it will be opened."~Luke 11:5-10

Persistence in prayer is like a large ring of keys. One by one you try them in the lock until you have finished all on the ring. So often, we give up when the answer is to be found in the last key. DON'T GIVE UP! Keep knocking and trying each key that God has placed at your disposal!

Lord, help me never give up on prayer.

May 3

A New Recipe

Okay, I admit it. I watch *The Food Network*. Not all the time, but sometimes. It really is a bit silly when you come to think about it. You sit in front of a television screen and watch someone cook. They hold it up to camera and talk about how delicious it is and ooh and aah about how wonderful it tastes. You just sit there and get hungry. This drives you to the kitchen where you get something that is already prepared from a store as you hurry back to catch the next episode.

I would feel a bit strange about this, but their website says 99 million people in the United States can receive the same program and over eight million do so regularly. I guess the real attraction to this show is that you get to see new recipes that you would never have thought of on your own or have the courage to prepare.

Have you ever thought about how hard it must be to create a new recipe? Many failures must happen before it comes out just right. Not only must you try a lot of different variations of ingredients, but cooking times must be considered, size of the cookware, etc. I think I'll just watch television!

Here's a recipe that cannot fail. It's the recipe for knowing Jesus better: "But also for this very reason, giving all diligence, add to your faith virtue, to virtue knowledge, to knowledge self-control, to self-control perseverance, to perseverance godliness, to godliness brotherly kindness, and to brotherly kindness love. For if these things are yours and abound, you will be neither barren nor unfruitful in the knowledge of our Lord Jesus Christ."~2 Peter 1:5-8 I probably won't see you on *The Food Network*, but you will enjoy being filled up on the knowledge of Jesus.

Lord, help me to know You better today than ever before.

May 4

Buyer Beware

 Manufacturers have all caught on to a new packaging trend. To keep their pricing competitive they are reducing the size of the product and charging the same price. In some cases, they are reducing the packaging and charging more. For the consumer it's a lose-lose scenario. Some of the products look almost identical. So, *let the buyer beware* holds especially true today. An ounce here, an inch there, and soon the standard has changed.

The word of God has established the cost of sin. From the Garden of Eden until today, God has set forth the cost of sin. He told Adam and Eve that the day they ate of the fruit of the forbidden tree they would die (Genesis 2:17.) "For the wages of sin is death, but the gift of God is eternal life in Christ Jesus our Lord."~Romans 6:23 Paul in this verse from Romans reminds us that inflation or deflation has never affected the cost of sin.

Jesus promised us that He would send the Holy Spirit who would set the standard of righteousness that would expose sin. "And when He has come, He will convict the world of sin, and of righteousness, and of judgment..."~John 16:8

The work of the Holy Spirit then keeps sin from changing packaging and confusing us as to its real cost. The cost of sin will never change; it is always death. Beware when sin is revealed in your life that you do not try to reduce the standard of righteousness to compensate for the high cost. Remember, the cost of sin remains the same.

Lord, help me not to fall for the deception of sin.

Of Squirrels and Men

Why are mountains there? How come trees are as high as they are? On and on go the questions that children can ask. Once they grow up a little they may even attempt to answer a few of them. The thing about kids is that they are not afraid of getting the wrong answer and they will keep asking until they get it right.

My grandson decided to get an answer a few days ago. He's in his mid-teens. Answers from others are not enough anymore. He has entered the "I need to find out for myself" stage of development. The question was fairly simple. What happens when you climb up a 25 foot tall tree and strike a squirrel's nest?

The answer he discovered was found in the few seconds it took for him to fall that same 25 feet and hit very hard at the base of said tree. After achieving his goal of tapping the nest, the squirrel ejected rapidly from the nest and approached him at a high rate of speed. He then, turning loose of his grip, began a rapid descent at an even higher rate of speed. Some might say faster than the speed of sound, since he left his scream at the top of the tree and found his stomach in his throat at the bottom of it.

Today he is okay. Scratched, bruised, and quite sore, but alive and a lot smarter about trees and squirrels. For this I am very thankful to God. I could not help thinking of what Jesus said about God's care for us. "Are not two sparrows sold for a copper coin? And not one of them falls to the ground apart from your Father's will. But the very hairs of your head are all numbered. Do not fear therefore; you are of more value than many sparrows."~Matthew 10:29–31 All glory to the Father who cares for sparrows and grandchildren...and us!

Lord, help me rejoice in Your daily care.

May 6

Surprise!

 Everybody loves a surprise! Well, I'm sure there are a few exceptions, but for the most part people get a thrill out of a surprise. From birthdays to visits from unexpected guests, surprises can be a lot of fun. Most dictionaries begin their definitions of the word *surprise*, however, with a description of being attacked while unaware. That doesn't sound like fun to me! The fact that most began with attack instead of some happy occasion got me to thinking about how surprised the world is going to be when Christ returns.

Honestly, Christ's coming is going to be the biggest surprise this world has ever experienced. This should be no surprise though since unbelievers are simply not watching. Believers on the other hand should not be surprised at His coming. "But concerning the times and the seasons, brethren, you have no need that I should write to you. For you yourselves know perfectly that the day of the Lord so comes as a thief in the night. For when they say, "Peace and safety!" then sudden destruction comes upon them, as labor pains upon a pregnant woman. And they shall not escape. But you, brethren, are not in darkness, so that this Day should overtake you as a thief. You are all sons of light and sons of the day. We are not of the night nor of darkness. Therefore let us not sleep, as others do, but let us watch and be sober...For God did not appoint us to wrath, but to obtain salvation through our Lord Jesus Christ, who died for us, that whether we wake or sleep, we should live together with Him. Therefore comfort each other and edify one another, just as you also are doing."~1 Thessalonians 5:1–11

We are children of the day and the signs of that approaching Day abound. Don't let His appearing be a SURPRISE!!! Be ready! If I don't see you here or there will I meet you in the air?

Lord, help me be ready today for Your coming.

May 7

Paid To Be Wrong

Weather has always been a hobby for me. I think if I would have had the opportunity I would have been a meteorologist. That's a fancy term for a weather man. A meteorologist is a person that gets paid to be wrong most of the time. After all, how many people do you know that get to go to work every day, make one mistake after another on that job, and never risk losing their position. As a matter of fact, when they are wrong everybody blames it on some lady named Mother Nature.

It does seem with all of the weird weather happening everywhere that all of creation is groaning louder than ever (Romans 8:22.) We have seen the power of God's creation as storms have raced across the country. Tornado outbreaks, hurricanes, and massive lightning strikes to name just a few, have become very commonplace it seems.

Usually in the spring with snow melting and heavy rains, many will face impending flood waters. The Psalmist seemed to have also encountered such times. Psalms 69:1-3 says, "Save me, O God! For the waters have come up to my neck. I sink in deep mire, where there is no standing; I have come into deep waters, where the floods overflow me. I am weary with my crying; my throat is dry; my eyes fail while I wait for my God."

Many people know they are in a flood plain. Others watch while the waters rise and all escape routes are closed. Others suffer a flood and move right back into harm's way. Why do we wait until we are neck deep and slipping to cry out to God? Call on Him today! He's always ready to rescue us! Don't wait for the sirens to sound!

Lord, help me show others the way to safety in Christ.

May 8

Where's My Privacy

 The world is getting smaller every day. This digital world has brought us into such close proximity that the issue of privacy is no longer whether you have the right to privacy, but how much privacy do you actually expect to keep intact. I can only think of one place that is really private and everyone is dying to get there. You guessed it—a coffin. Once that coffin is sealed hopefully you'll never be bothered again.

So how are we to function in a world that is ever encroaching into our lives both private and public? The answer really lies in my thoughts from the previous paragraph. It's going to take a death.

Now wait a minute you may be thinking, I like my privacy, but aren't you taking this a little too far? Not really! The possibility of us living like a dead person does exist. Paul gives us the method in his letter to the Colossians. "Set your mind on things above, not on things on the earth. For you died, and your life is hidden with Christ in God. When Christ who is our life appears, then you also will appear with Him in glory."~Colossians 3:2-3

When you have trouble with this world re-read the obituary column. Look for your name. FOR YOU HAVE DIED! Dead men are not affected by this world. In essence, we can climb inside a spiritual coffin and escape all those who are encroaching upon our privacy.

I'm not advocating a life of solitude in a monastery. We need to interact with the world around us if we are going to tell them about Jesus. However, everyone has to have a place to themselves and that place is found when our lives are hidden in Christ. So, when's the funeral?

Lord, help me to keep my mind focused on things above.

May 9

Mother on a Mission

God knew what he was doing when He made mothers. In the heart of a mother beats a love that cannot be squashed. A mother always sees the best in her children and will lay her life down for them. We would be hard pressed to find a better demonstration of First Corinthians 13 love than in our mothers.

The Shunnamite woman was just such a mother. Childless, she had received a miracle from God by the word of Elisha the prophet. But in the course of time the child fell ill and ultimately died. "And the child grew. Now it happened one day that he went out to his father, to the reapers. And he said to his father, 'My head, my head!' So he said to a servant, 'Carry him to his mother.' When he had taken him and brought him to his mother, he sat on her knees till noon, and then died."~2 Kings 4:18–20

One thing about us dads, we know when it's time to call for mama. Because the woman knew that her son had been a gift from God, she did not hesitate to seek out the man of God. Her husband questioned the decision to seek out Elisha, but the mother would not be deterred. So he said, 'Why are you going to him today? It is neither the New Moon nor the Sabbath.' And she said, 'It is well.' Then she saddled a donkey, and said to her servant, 'Drive, and go forward; do not slacken the pace for me unless I tell you.' And so she departed, and went to the man of God at Mount Carmel."~2 Kings 4:23–25

The child's life was restored and a mother's faith rewarded. Moral: Never get in the way of a mother on a mission in defense of a child.

Lord, help me to prayer for mothers everywhere today.

May 10

Who's Your Hero?

There has been an abundance of movies about super heroes that have been produced lately. The characters I used to read about in comic books while waiting in the barber shop are now living, breathing, and BIG! My childhood heroes are in HD quality and sometimes in 3-D reality.

In every case there is a villain. This character is holding some grudge about being treated unfairly or overlooked in some long ago time. Usually, they are scripted as having a warm spot, but it got all glossed over with hatred. Then there is the hero. Excuse me, SUPER hero! Somewhere in his past he was a nerd. At least, he played the part of a nerd, but he gets called into active service and saves the damsel in distress.

No matter the movie's name, that is always the plot. Sorry I ruined it for you! Save your money and read the story of Job. Satan's complaint about Job was that God had hedged him about for protection. The villain, Satan, couldn't touch him. God the super hero takes down the hedge and proves Satan's accusations against Job wrong. Satan loses. Job wins. God remains the real super hero.

Paul put it this way in Ephesians 1:13 for us believers who live today. "When you heard the message of truth, the gospel of your salvation, and when you believed in Him, you were also sealed with the promised Holy Spirit." Being sealed is like being fenced in and secure. We are guarded by the Holy Spirit, our super hero! Nothing can approach us without His express permission. So relax and enjoy the movie!

Lord, help me remember that Your Holy Spirit stands guard in my life.

May 11

Believe It or Not

Ripley made a fortune with his *Believe It or Not Exposition*. He gathered all sorts of oddities and displayed them in various forms. He began showing his display of these rarities in cartoon books. Soon newspapers carried his items of curiosity. His collection has been talked about on radio, shown on television, and is now housed as attractions in museums around the world.

Here's an item from the Bible that Ripley would have had in one of his museums. Problem is it wouldn't have fit unless it was a very big building. The item of interest: the ark. "And God said to Noah, 'The end of all flesh has come before Me, for the earth is filled with violence through them; and behold, I will destroy them with the earth. Make yourself an ark of gopherwood; make rooms in the ark, and cover it inside and outside with pitch.'" ~Genesis 6:13–14

You might think that the *believe it or not* part has to do with the size of the ark or the fact that God sent animals of all sorts to dwell in the safety of the ark. Perhaps the length of time Noah took to build the ark would be an odd thing. After all, he worked non-stop for 120 years to complete it!

No, the one thing that makes the ark such an item of interest for me is that God told Noah to build an ark and *pitch* it within and without. The word *pitch* is the same word in Hebrew that is translated cover or atone. Amazing! God was demonstrating His grace as he gave instructions for building the ark! In the ark, all were safe under the pitch. In Christ, we are covered from the penalty of our sin as we dwell under His blood.

Believe it or not? BELIEVE IT!

Lord, help me see Your amazing grace at work in my life.

May 12

Faith Is

 Charles Haddon Spurgeon said that any man can sing in the daytime, but that only the man of faith can sing in the night. But what exactly is faith? It is best defined by the text of scripture. One such verse that gives us a good definition is Hebrews 11:1, "Now faith is the substance of things hoped for, the evidence of things not seen." Here we clearly see that faith is not some mystical state of belief, but it is tangible. It is the substance that makes up the basis of our hope and the proof of unseen things.

Further, we see in Hebrews 11 that faith is not optional. It is a requirement to pleasing God. "But without faith it is impossible to please Him, for he who comes to God must believe that He is, and that He is a rewarder of those who diligently seek Him."~Hebrews 11:6

Polls of Americans continue to reveal a disconnect between the biblical definition of faith and a more theoretical view of the concept. The polls reveal that a very high percentage of people claim to believe in God, but an ever growing percentage answer "no" when asked if faith plays a part in their everyday lives apart from religion. Notice that Hebrews 11:6 connects faith and believing that God exist.

Consider these elements of faith: the gift; the growing; the gain; the glory. The gift is from God not ourselves. The growing comes by testing not by resting. The gain is victory as we overcome. The glory is God's for without faith it is impossible to please Him who *gives* that we might *grow* and *gain* victory unto His *glory*.

Lord, help me live a life of ever increasing faith.

 138

May 13

Kicked While You're Down

Bad days are inevitable. I know that sounds a bit fatalistic, however, this does not mean that you have a right to find a corner to crawl into and wait for a good day. God knows *exactly* where you are and what's nipping at your heels today.

David had a few bad days too, and he is described as a man after God's own heart. You would think that if anyone could avoid bad days, it would be David. He not only had a bad day, he had a whole string of them. David had become the enemy of Saul. None of this was of his making. Saul just had it out for David. You know—all the makings of a really bad day! But God is faithful and He delivered David from all of his enemies.

"They confronted me in the day of my calamity, but the LORD was my support. He also brought me out into a broad place; He delivered me because He delighted in me."~2 Samuel 22:19–20 These verses are part of a song David sang after his enemies were crushed. This was a pattern in David's life. Before, during, and after the storms of life, we find him singing. No pills, no psychiatrist's couch, no corners...just God and David!

How could David trust God like this? Two words in these verses give us a hint: *calamity* and *delighted*. These words seem dissimilar, but they are the key to understanding God's care for us on bad days. The word *calamity* means to bend down and rake over as in the poking of a fire. It's like being kicked when you're already down. *Delighted* means to incline toward, bend over as in care, to come near. Now you can see why David was singing. In the day that he was bent down and being raked over the coals, God bent down and came near to his side in care and concern. That is a God of compassion! That is the way out of your corner!

Lord, help me look to You as my Deliverer.

139

May 14

Impossible? Never!

 IMPOSSIBILITY: Up against it; not going to happen; never occurring; an unbelievable situation. All of these are fair definitions of impossibility. But I like to think when I see words like *impossibility* that the word is not *possible* without knowing that there has been a *possibility* at some point in time.

Confused? Don't be! It's very much like trying to define hunger if you've never been full. Poor means nothing without having some idea of rich. Darkness can only be understood as the absence of light. So, impossible can only mean the lack of possibility, but with God nothing is impossible. Consider when Mary was told that she would be the mother of Jesus. She did not say this was impossible. She asked how it was possible. The angel responded, "'For with God nothing will be impossible.'"~Luke 1:37 This is the use of a double negative. The angel was saying that there is not a thing that God cannot do.

Impossible is the door to God's provision. Avoid this door and experience the poverty of need; pass through this door and experience the provision of His abundant supply!

After the disciples had failed to cast a demon from a boy they asked Jesus why it had not been possible for them to do so. "So Jesus said to them, 'Because of your unbelief; for assuredly, I say to you, if you have faith as a mustard seed, you will say to this mountain, 'Move from here to there,' and it will move; and nothing will be impossible for you.'"~Matthew 17:20

Truly, there is *not* a thing that God *cannot* do!

Lord, help me remember that there is nothing that is impossible for You.

May 15

Looking Busy

There are very few people who do not have to work. Come to think
of it, those who don't have to work probably have to work very hard
at not working. Sometimes it is just easier to work than to avoid it. I
can still remember the days that I worked in supermarkets as a stock
clerk. Sometimes I would find myself finishing a task and having a bit
of time left before I could go home. Those minutes were the most tedious as I
would try to "look" busy. It was just easier to be busy!

Most of us will report on time for work, do what we are instructed according to
someone else's plan, punch out, and go home. Few of us will enter a day's labor
with the mindset that our work is to be a witness of our walk with Christ.

Jesus was being questioned about His authority to do the things He was doing
during His ministry. He said that there were several things that testified of His
authority, such as the witness of John the Baptist, but the greater witness was the
works that He did. "But I have a greater witness than John's; for the works which
the Father has given Me to finish—the very works that I do—bear witness of
Me, that the Father has sent Me."~John 5:36 Jesus completed all that the Father
had sent Him to do and He declared so from the cross when He said, "It is
finished!"

Are you working because you have to work or because you are sent to work?
Making this distinction will keep you from "looking" busy. Instead, you will be
busy for the Kingdom until it is time to go home.

Lord, help me to be really busy for You—not just busy.

May 16

Full of Holes

 Imagine a rusty old bucket with holes in the bottom and sides. Like your life it's the only bucket you've got. Now, imagine it all cleaned up on the inside like the day you accepted Christ. You may have noticed though that the holes are still there: YOU LEAK!

How can you keep this bucket filled? You can try running back and forth to the well, but with so many holes you can never keep the bucket full. But wait! Keep the bucket immersed in the water source and the holes don't matter!

This is a picture of what the Apostle Paul was teaching the church at Ephesus. He begins his letter talking about the sealing of the Holy Spirit and then near the end of the letter tells them that they need to be filled with the Spirit. "See then that you walk circumspectly, not as fools but as wise, redeeming the time, because the days are evil. Therefore do not be unwise, but understand what the will of the Lord is. And do not be drunk with wine, in which is dissipation; but be filled with the Spirit, speaking to one another in psalms and hymns and spiritual songs, singing and making melody in your heart to the Lord, giving thanks always for all things to God the Father in the name of our Lord Jesus Christ, submitting to one another in the fear of God."~Ephesians 5:15–21

The phrase *be filled* could best be translated as *be being filled*. It is an ongoing process of being filled made necessary by our leaking buckets. As long as we are in these bodies, we will need regular refreshing and refilling of God's Spirit. Remember, keep your life immersed in Christ and you will always be full of His Spirit.

Lord, help me keep my bucket filled with You.

May 17

A Song in the Night

During my teenage years most of the radio stations I listened to were on the AM frequencies. These AM stations were restricted during the daylight hours as to the amount of power they could use to project their signals. I remember waiting each night for KAAY out of Little Rock, Arkansas to boost their signal. It came in clear as a bell way down in south Louisiana. I could only tune in because of the station's power increase. In the light of day only static came from that frequency, but each night there it was.

Listening to a nighttime radio broadcast is a picture of what it is like to hear God. His word comes in clearly when we get quiet enough to hear Him. The night times are when He boosts His word into our hearts. "I rise before the dawning of the morning, and cry for help; I hope in Your word. My eyes are awake through the night watches, that I may meditate on Your word."~Psalm 119:147–148

The psalmist made it a purposeful act to tune into what God was saying. He rose early in the morning before the busyness and noise of the day began to drown out the reception. I had to tune my radio to 1090 on my radio dial to receive the station out of Little Rock. No other spot on the dial would pick up that signal. God speaks on His frequency. We must dial Him in at that point or we miss Him entirely.

Then the psalmist said, "That I may meditate on Your word." The idea here is not casual listening, but to ponder and converse with oneself. Sometimes when I would hear a song that I knew well, I would sing along. It wasn't pretty, but I was communing with the signal. This is a little like meditating on God's word. We rehearse it until we can sing along with God's word in harmony with the signal. In your dark times, tune in to God and His word!

Lord, help me spend time today meditating on Your Word.

143

May 18

In the Shadow of Victory

 Epic battles take place rarely. The contest between Elijah and the false prophets of Baal would qualify as one of those battles. As the opposing sides gather on Mount Carmel, the challenge was clearly defined. Let the one true God answer with fire and consume the sacrifice.

Elijah allowed the Baal worshipers to proceed in their rituals first. All day long they tried to entice an answer from their gods, but to no avail. As the time of the evening sacrifice approached Elijah put all in order on the altar. Then adding the extra step of soaking everything with water, he simply asked God to respond. "And it came to pass, at the time of the offering of the evening sacrifice, that Elijah the prophet came near and said, 'LORD God of Abraham, Isaac, and Israel, let it be known this day that You are God in Israel and I am Your servant, and that I have done all these things at Your word. Hear me, O LORD, hear me, that this people may know that You are the LORD God, and that You have turned their hearts back to You again.'"~1 Kings 18:36–37

Elijah must have been filled with awe as fire fell consuming everything: sacrifice, stones, dust, and water. But shortly thereafter we find him under a juniper bush asking God to take his life. (1 Kings 19:4) God graciously refreshed and restored Elijah, but also sent him to anoint Elisha to take his place. My pastor, Paul Jones, told me early in my ministry if I ever came to the place where I could not serve the Lord, I should step aside–there is always an Elisha waiting in the wings.

Beware the victories! They take place in the shadow of the juniper.

Lord, help me serve you even in the time of victory.

May 19

Time to Move

After my first short-term mission trip, I said that I would never go back again. It was a rough trip which ended with a flight that had to turn around midway across the Atlantic and return to Brussels. The entire east coast of the U.S. had been closed by a gigantic snow storm. I finally got home nearly 40 hours later.

God had a different agenda. As of today, I have made dozens of mission adventures that are mine to remember. These trips have changed my life and the lives of many who have traveled with me. Because many of those who traveled with me were pastors, they have in turn led additional teams from their churches. I said, "I'm done!" God said, "You've just begun!"

Why do I go back again and again? For the same reason the children of Israel moved when the cloud moved. "And when the cloud was taken up from the tabernacle, then after that the sons of Israel pulled up stakes."~Numbers 9:17 Is it time for you to get moving? Is it time for you to ask God where He would have you go? It may be for the first time or it may be that you need to go again, but you need to move when God moves.

Someone asked me once if I was ever afraid to go to some of the places I have been. One of those places was Bosnia not long after the attack of September 11, 2001. The Lord gave me an answer to that question that I have often used. Now I always say that I have used a mapping program to determine the distance from Bentonville, Arkansas to Heaven and I found that it was exactly the same distance from Bosnia to Heaven! The safest place to be is in the center of God's will!

Watch the cloud and never, never plant your stakes too deep!

Lord, help me to always be ready to move.

May 20

Confidence in Asking

R.A. Torrey, American evangelist, pastor, teacher and writer (1856-1928) tells this story about having strong confidence in God answering prayer. A day of fasting and prayer had been called for in Dundee, Scotland. We were planning for a meeting at two o'clock in the afternoon in the open air. One of the brethren as he led in prayer, offered a very earnest and confident prayer that it would clear off for the open air meeting, and as he closed his prayer expressed the utmost confidence that the prayer would be heard.

A good many that listened to the prayer were uneasy at the man's confidence and feared that God would be dishonored by the prayer not being answered. One of the ministers said to Mr. Alexander, "That man ought not to have prayed that way. The barometer is going down all the time and there is no chance whatever of its clearing up."

I went to my room and began to pray alone to God about the various interests of the work. Before I finished the prayer, it was nearly two o'clock. I was led to pray that it would clear up and the sun shine during the afternoon meeting. As I opened my eyes, the sun burst through the clouds and streamed into my room. There was a great gathering for the open air meeting and God's Spirit was present in power, but no sooner had the open air meeting closed than the rain began again and poured incessantly.

"Now this is the confidence that we have in Him, that if we ask anything according to His will, He hears us. And if we know that He hears us, whatever we ask, we know that we have the petitions that we have asked of Him."~1 John 5:14-15 Ask in confidence with boldness, courage, and out-spoken bluntness. Ask in His will and count it as done!

Lord, help me to ask.

May 21

Like a Security Blanket

If there is one thing most of us enjoy it is our comfort. We develop this need for comfort from our childhood. It may be a parent that the child seeks out for comfort. Sometimes the object of comfort becomes a special toy or a blanket. Remember Linus and his blanket from the *Charlie Brown* cartoon strip.

As we grow older our comfort takes on different forms. We take comfort in such things as our favorite chair, our bed, or even some food that we turn to in time of stress. We quickly get used to these comfortable objects and soon we live only in our comfort zone.

Whatever you do, don't try to move someone out of their comfort zone! Comfort zones can numb us to the truth of our own condition, but our comforting needs to come from the God of all comfort. "Blessed be the God and Father of our Lord Jesus Christ, the Father of mercies and God of all comfort, who comforts us in all our tribulation that we may be able to comfort those who are in any trouble, with the comfort with which we ourselves are comforted by God."~2 Corinthians 1:3-4

As important as our own personal comfort is, we should understand that God does not comfort us just so we can be comfortable. Our comforting is to be used as a comfort to others who are uncomforted in their trouble. We become the conduit of comfort. Like an aqueduct channels water from a faraway spring to satisfy thirst, we can be the source of comfort to those who think God is far away from them. The key to this spiritual undertaking is for us at some point to be forced out of our comfort zone. Then and only then can we experience the comforting of God ourselves. When this occurs, then we can become someone else's security blanket. Somewhere out there is a Linus waiting for comfort from God and God is waiting on you to deliver a blanket.

Lord, help me to be a comfort to others as I have been comforted.

May 22

Storms in the Night

 Weather alarms are wonderful instruments that can warn us of impending storms coming our way. They are so area specific that you can put codes in that will only notify you if the storm is in your county. I have been awakened many times from a deep sleep with the scream of the alarm on my radio. Shocking, but very effective. I know that soon the storm will be here. Some storms come with much warning; others spring upon us.

The disciples were told by Jesus to get in a boat and go to the other side of the lake, but they were caught by a sudden storm. "Now when He got into a boat, His disciples followed Him. And suddenly a great tempest arose on the sea, so that the boat was covered with the waves. But He was asleep. Then His disciples came to Him and awoke Him, saying, 'Lord, save us! We are perishing!'" ~Matthew 8:23–25

The word *tempest* found in these verses comes from the Greek word *seismos*. You have heard this word before as part of a larger word. When an earthquake strikes some professor from a department of *seismology* will give an assessment. We normally would not think about seismic activity when a storm on the sea is being discussed, but Matthew used this word to better describe the predicament the disciples were in as they tried to negotiate the wind and waves. The word can mean either a shaking of the earth or a commotion of the air.

Storms can be earth-shaking, but remember that Jesus is in the boat. He has given command to go to the other side. He may be asleep, but He is ready to respond to the alarms of our life even in the night hour. Most important of all—He rules the storm!

Lord, help me remember today that You rule the storms of life.

May 23

The Deceit of Deception

Martin Luther in his work *Treatise on Christian Liberty* said, "He who would gain righteousness by faith and works is as the dog who runs along a stream with a piece of meat in his mouth, and, deceived by the reflection of the meat in the water, opens his mouth to snap at it, and so loses both the meat and the reflection."

Like the dog in Luther's illustration, we discover too late that deception is such a cruel master. It deceives to the point that the person deceived no longer comprehends the deception. So Jesus warned in Matthew 4:4, "Take heed that no one deceives you." Once begun deception develops rapidly and soon the truth can no longer be discerned. This is the strength of sin in our life. Left to itself, it quickly disarms us to its inherent danger.

We must also be on the watch for those who would deceive us and never fall under the deceitful notion that we cannot be deceived. I believe that many, thinking that they have risen above the danger of deceit, are already deceived as to their standing. Paul speaks of those who would deceive us in his book to the Romans. "For those who are such do not serve our Lord Jesus Christ, but their own belly, and by smooth words and flattering speech deceive the hearts of the simple."~Romans 16:18

To deceive is to seduce wholly to the point that one develops erroneous views of the truth. Therein, lies the danger. The deception of deceit is that it holds elements of the truth. Removal of deception is like peeling away an onion one layer at a time. The problem is that the top layers are truth. Therefore, we may think that we are discarding truth and stop the correction before reaching that which is really true. Be not deceived and join me in praying today for thousands caught in the deceit of deception.

Lord, help me to be watchful for deception.

May 24

Falling Isn't Fun

 No one could fake a fall as well as Dick Van Dyke. I always enjoyed watching the opening of the show that bears his name. His character Rob Petrie would come home and tumble over an ottoman, bounce up, and act like nothing had happened. The man was jointed in the middle of his bones!

People usually don't fall on purpose. That's why we call falls an accident. I remember falling at a carwash many years ago. I had walked away from the auto to get change for the machine. As I stepped on the soapy, wet concrete my feet went out from under me. One moment I was upright and the next I was picking myself up from the concrete. I don't think I ever knew concrete was so hard until that day. Not only do I remember falling, but I also remember how I hurt the next day. More than my soreness from the fall, I remember my two oldest girls laughing! When I asked them why they were laughing at my catastrophe their response was, "We've never seen an ADULT fall!"

The older we are in Christ the further we have to fall and the more it hurts. Jude in his letter to the Church was warning about apostasy or falling away from the faith. Here he said, "Now to Him who is able to keep you from stumbling, and to present you faultless before the presence of His glory with exceeding joy, to God our Savior, who alone is wise, be glory and majesty, dominion and power, both now and forever. Amen."~Jude 24

Thank God there is recovery from falling, but the better position to be in is one where you have never had to get up from a fall. Jude tells us that God has all ability to *keep* us from falling. God *keeps* us close to Himself and thereby guards against a tragic fall.

Lord, help me not to fall.

May 25

In a Fog

I'd rather work than pray, because prayer is a LOT of work! The religious folks of Jesus' day prayed pompous, proud, protracted prayers in public forums. They were known for their loudness, but they did not know the Lord who answered prayer! Here is some prayer instruction: "But you, when you pray, go into your room, and when you have shut your door; pray to your Father who is in the secret place; and your Father who sees in secret will reward you openly."~Matthew 6:6

George Mueller was a prayer warrior extraordinaire. This story tells just one of the testimonies of his prayer life. Mueller was traveling across the Atlantic in a steamer when a very dense fog forbade all progress. Mr. Mueller approached the captain and said, "I have come to tell you that I must be in Quebec on Saturday afternoon." "It is impossible," the captain replied.

"Very well, if your ship can't take me God will find some other means of locomotion to take me. I have never broken an engagement in fifty-seven years," was the calm response of Mueller. "Let us go down to the chart room and pray," he said. "Mr. Mueller," said the captain, "do you know how dense this fog is?" "No," he replied, "my eye is not on the density of the fog, but on the living God, who controls every circumstance of my life." George Mueller then prayed a simple prayer asking God to remove the fog in five minutes. The captain started to pray, but Mueller stopped him with these words, "You need not pray because you do not believe that God will remove the fog and I believe that he already has. Get up, Captain and open the door, and you will find the fog is gone." The fog had lifted and on Saturday afternoon George Mueller was in Quebec.

Lord, help me to pray with my eye upon You.

May 26

Buried Treasure

 When I was a little boy a few of my friends and I formed a club. It wasn't exactly a pirate's club, but we did have some buried treasure. With great care we measured distances from fixed objects and drew a map to the exact spot of our treasure's burial location. We put our money in an empty prescription bottle and safely placed it in the ground. You have probably already determined that it wasn't a great amount of money if it fit in a prescription bottle. If I remember correctly, it was somewhere around 14¢. All went well, until my mother overheard us talking about our treasure. She promptly made us go dig it up. She said that was too much money to leave in the ground!

Oh, for the days when 14¢ would make a difference in our survival. The disciples had concerns over the everyday needs of their lives just like you and I do. Jesus had just told them the parable of the rich fool and instructed them about laying up treasures here on earth. He then said, "Therefore I say to you, do not worry about your life, what you will eat; nor about the body, what you will put on. Life is more than food, and the body is more than clothing."~Luke 12:22–23

After making comparison of God's provision to everyday items like birds and lilies or to physical characteristics like growth and food, Jesus summarized His thoughts on treasures like this: "But seek the kingdom of God, and all these things shall be added to you. For where your treasure is, there your heart will be also."~Luke 12:31,34 And what is God's response to our surrender of all our treasure? Here's what He will do–"...it is your Father's good pleasure to give you the kingdom." Luke 12:32

Lord, help me to seek Your Kingdom and place my treasure there.

May 27

Don't Be a Carrier

If you have ever walked in a field in the southeast you most likely have fallen victim to beggar's lice. I can remember walking in the woods and getting covered with it. It sounds like a living creature, but it is actually the prickly seed pods of a plant that cling onto a person or animal and get rubbed off down the road thereby replicating itself. Whether it can be proven or not, I do not know, but some believe this little seed was the idea behind the invention of Velcro. It works exactly like Velcro as it attaches itself with a tiny burr that can only be removed by scraping it away or picking each seed pod off individually. The best remedy against getting beggar's lice on you is to not get near it. There is no other safeguard!

There is a warning in scripture about what might be labeled *beggar's lice of the mind*! Peter warned us to gird up the loins of our mind. "Therefore gird up the loins of your mind, be sober, and rest your hope fully upon the grace that is to be brought to you at the revelation of Jesus Christ; as obedient children, not conforming yourselves to the former lusts, as in your ignorance; but as He who called you is holy, you also be holy in all your conduct, because it is written, 'Be holy, for I am holy.'"~1 Peter 1:13-16

Peter was describing the gathering up of a robe before work or running when he used the phrase, *gird up your loins*. The idea is to keep yourself from tripping or being entangled as most people of his day wore loose fitting, flowing robes. We are to tie up the loose ends of our minds with sound thoughts and grace-filled holy living. There will always be a patch of beggar's lice just waiting for you to pass by and take away a load of seed pods. There is danger in our own contraction of the seed and in us helping to spread its infection on down the road. Don't be a carrier!

Lord, help me be holy in my conduct.

153

May 28

Escaping the Rage

 We live in a very rage-filled society. Road rage, domestic disputes, school shootings; the list goes on and on. I'm not sure of all the reasons for this. The fact that so much of our world is without Christ certainly is the main reason, but to act out in rage is becoming somewhat a norm. We have lost our moral bearings and foundation. Maybe we have so much interaction in solitude via electronics that when we do have to interact in real time and with real people, we just do not know how. The video game lets us restart or use extra lives. Real life doesn't work that way!

Since we as believers have the answers that can be found in scripture and we know the author of those scriptures personally, it only makes sense that the weight of bringing tension down a notch is ours to bear. For example, the Psalmist might have been in some traffic in my city lately. It seems so as he penned these words, "Cease from anger, and forsake wrath; do not fret—it only causes harm."~Psalms 37:8

So, take a slow deep breath...now do it three more times...SLOWLY! Now clearly hear the Psalmist as I define the main verbs in this verse.

Here's the progression: ANGER—to breathe hard; WRATH—to become hot; FRET—to glow as in a fire. Do you see how rage develops?

Here's the prescription: CEASE—to let alone; FORSAKE—to refuse; DO NOT—to never even once do.

Do you have a fire escape plan?

Don't be a firebug! You'll be the first victim and others will surely suffer the harm! TAKE A DEEP BREATH!

Lord, help me keep my anger in check.

May 29

See You in the Light

Oswald Chambers said in his book *Workmen of God* that "[w]hen you come to God's way, you will find something very different; immediately a soul gets introduced into the kingdom of God, it has got to do something, but it is something along the line of the new life it has received, obedience and walking in the light, until it is consolidated in the ways of God."

Chambers included two elements that are apparent when a person comes to know Christ as Savior. These two elements set the parameters for the desire to do something for the Lord. Not something to do for salvation, but something that must be done because of salvation.

These two elements are obedience and walking in the light. John stated it this way, "If we say that we have fellowship with Him, and walk in darkness, we lie and do not practice the truth. But if we walk in the light as He is in the light, we have fellowship with one another, and the blood of Jesus Christ His Son cleanses us from all sin." ~1 John 1:6–7

Practicing the truth is obedience. Jesus declared that we were His friends if we kept His commands (John 15:14.) By keeping His commands we walk in the light and from that light we gain two additional benefits. First, we have fellowship with one another. There is a sense of honesty and openness that happens in the light. This in turn brings us into mutual association, participation, and communication with each other.

Second, we are cleansed by His shed blood. Only in the Light will we truly see ourselves, confess our sin, and be cleansed. This second benefit keeps us in fellowship with heaven which keeps us in fellowship here.

Lord, help me to walk in the light of obedience.

May 30

Remembering

 Memorials come in many forms. For those who are familiar with the work of the Gideon's International group, you will know about their Memorial Bible program. Sometimes statues are erected as memorials. Nearly every city has something that is built to memorialize someone or some occasion. We have a need to remember the lessons learned from significant moments of history.

God instructed the children of Israel to build a memorial after they crossed the Jordan River on their way into the Promised Land. The stones for the memorial were to come from the river bottom. To gather these stones would take a miracle and that is exactly what God provided.

"...and Joshua said to them: 'Cross over before the ark of the LORD your God into the midst of the Jordan, and each one of you take up a stone on his shoulder, according to the number of the tribes of the children of Israel, that this may be a sign among you when your children ask in time to come, saying, 'What do these stones mean to you?' Then you shall answer them that the waters of the Jordan were cut off before the ark of the covenant of the LORD; when it crossed over the Jordan, the waters of the Jordan were cut off. And these stones shall be for a memorial to the children of Israel forever."~Joshua 4:5–7

Has there been a miracle moment in your life? Maybe it wasn't as dramatic as the dividing of a river, but nonetheless, it was clearly the hand of God at work in your life. Then take a stone of memory and erect it to the glory of God in your life. The day will come that someone will ask you, "What do these stones mean?" On that day you can recount the blessings of God. That will be good for them and you!

Lord, help me leave a memorial of Your great work for all to see.

May 31

Like Sheep Gone Astray

Sheep don't just decide to get lost. They wander...they will put their head down and nibble their way into lostness. One sweet morsel more; one sweet blade of grass just off the path; one luscious leaf pulling them away; and then the shepherd is out of sight.

So with our walk as Christians. A misstep here, a stumble there, and the Shepherd of our souls is nowhere to be seen. "For you were like sheep going astray, but have now returned to the Shepherd and Overseer of your souls."~1 Peter 2:25 The word *astray* means to roam from safety and truth. This verse paints a picture of a sheep that is going astray and then returns. You must understand that the return or repentance from straying is impossible apart from the convicting work of the Holy Spirit. So the words of Paul ring true in Romans 3:11, "There is none who understands; there is none who seeks after God." We returned because the Shepherd came looking for us. We are after all just dumb sheep.

We see this heart of compassion in the Shepherd, as Jesus spoke to His disciples in Matthew. "But when He saw the multitudes, He was moved with compassion for them, because they were weary and scattered, like sheep having no shepherd."~Matthew 9:36 Jesus saw the people like sheep who have been broken to the point of no strength. It was beyond their ability to come to Him. Not only were they broken, but they were driven away as by force. The word *scattered* means to hurl or throw with force. Like a glass crashing to the floor the pieces fly in every direction.

The Great Shepherd alone can gather all the pieces and reassemble the flock. Lost? Call out for Him! He will leave the ninety-nine to rescue you!

Lord, help me to be used by You to reach the ninety-nine.

June 1

For Better or Worse

 It can't get any worse! Have you ever made a comment like this? Maybe you woke up to a flat tire, then ran out of gas on the way to work, and discovered after finally getting there that you had been passed over for a promotion. I guess you are right. It can't get any worse. Sorry to break in on your pity party, but it can!

Consider this little piece of history from Israel's past. Jerusalem had been besieged by the Syrians. It was so bad in the city that people were eating donkey heads and using dove droppings for fuel. At the gate of the city are four lepers. No one will let them into the city because they have leprosy and they have the Syrians at their backs blocking any retreat from the death that was rampant in the city. For these men it got desperate enough that they said to one another, "Why are we sitting here until we die?"~2 Kings 7:3 So these four lepers decide to throw themselves on the mercy of the Syrians. Can it get any worse than this?

As the lepers made their way to the Syrian camp, God made their footsteps sound like approaching chariots. The Syrians fled in a mad rush and left everything. When the lepers entered the camp they found themselves suddenly rich men. Gold, new clothes, and all the food they could eat. Can it get any *better* than this? These men who owed nothing to a city that had left them to die realized that it may not be possible for it to get better, but it could get worse real fast. So they said to one another, "We are not doing right. This day is a day of good news, and we remain silent. If we wait until morning light, some punishment will come upon us. Now therefore, come, let us go and tell the king's household."~2 Kings 7:9

Has it been a can't-get-any worse time for you? Get up! Don't sit there until you die! And if it can't get any better for you right now, get up and share the blessing you have received at the hand of God, lest you come quickly to the place that it can't get any worse!

Lord, help me to trust You when it seems like it can't get any worse.

June 2

No Words

I had only been in Nigeria a few days when we made a trek to a neighboring village. It was a hot Tuesday evening as we met under a mango tree for services. A good size crowd had gathered to hear this white man speak of Jesus. That night an elderly man gave his life to Christ and was gloriously saved.

Peter described this work of salvation as indescribable! "...whom having not seen you love. Though now you do not see Him, yet believing, you rejoice with joy inexpressible and full of glory, receiving the end of your faith—the salvation of your souls."~1 Peter 1:8–9 He simply ran out of words to tell of such a marvelous gift from God, so he used the term *inexpressible*. Salvation sometimes just cannot be put into words which can be uttered.

The old hymn says, "...it is joy unspeakable and full of glory..." The prophets of old sought to understand it, but could not. The angels of heaven cannot fathom its depths. It just does not make sense that God would offer grace to a sinner such as I. My response? "................." SPEECHLESSNESS! It matters not since I have no words to speak anyway!

Now, as Paul Harvey would say, "Here's the rest of the story!" The old man in Nigeria died two days later. The people of the village contacted the pastor where I was staying and asked us to perform a Christian funeral for him. After we walked back to the village, we were surprised beyond words. Where there had been a crowd on Tuesday night, now the entire village had turned out to see this Christian funeral service. People were in the trees, on the rooftops, and standing around the grave. That old Christian man without words in his death told of a salvation that is simply inexpressible!

Lord, help me to never lose my amazement of the majesty of salvation.

June 3

Impersonation

 Some folks just have the gift of gab. Somewhere along life's journey they learned how to talk their way into and out of a myriad of situations. This was the story of Frank Abagnale, Jr. A movie was produced about his life in 2002. *Catch Me If You Can*, chronicles the exploits of Abagnale who began a life of impersonation at the age of 16, and by his 19th birthday had successfully posed as an airline pilot, a doctor, and a prosecuting attorney. He became so adept at check fraud that after his arrest, he was hired by the FBI to help crack other fraud cases involving check forgers.

His life certainly does not need to be emulated. It does, however, paint a picture of how many people live their religious lives as impersonators. Charles Banning said, "Too many of us have a Christian vocabulary rather than a Christian experience. We think we are doing our duty when we are only talking about it."

Jesus said that many would live their entire lives believing that they were doing God's will, but in reality it was just all words. "Not everyone who says to Me, 'Lord, Lord,' shall enter the kingdom of heaven, but he who does the will of My Father in heaven. Many will say to Me in that day, 'Lord, Lord, have we not prophesied in Your name, cast out demons in Your name, and done many wonders in Your name?'And then I will declare to them, 'I never knew you; depart from Me, you who practice lawlessness!'"~Matthew 7:21–23

Impersonation as a Christian is not enough. It took the FBI years to catch Frank Abagnale—God knows who you really are now. Call on Him and turn yourself in; He will always show you mercy.

Lord, help me to truly and openly be Your follower today.

June 4

Well, Throw Me Away!

I'm about to be in trouble. I'M NOT GREEN! There. I've said it. I'm not into green energy, recycling, renewables, or anything close. It's perfectly fine with me if you are green. I will sort through some things and put it in the correct container, but I'm just not ready to start walking everywhere or giving up my lightweight plastic doo-dads. Hopefully, you have already forgiven me!

I really do understand the whole conservation thing. I know that we need to take care of God's creation. I'm not a litter bug, I don't drive a huge vehicle, and I'm old enough to have a thing about turning off lights. I think the reason I'm not as green as I maybe should be is that I'm dying. Don't worry, it's been going on a long time now. As a matter of fact, ever since I was born.

I'm being used up day by day. I'm not recyclable. Everything in me is winding down and my battery takes longer and longer to recharge. But, not so with my God! "Have you not known nor heard, that the everlasting God, the Lord, the Creator of the ends of the earth, faints not, neither is weary?"~Isaiah 40:28 God never needs to find a power source and He can't be recycled!

Here's the great news though. He's ready to lend some power to you. Call unto Him in your weakened condition for "He gives power to the weak, and to those who have no might He increases strength. Even the youths shall faint and be weary, and the young men shall utterly fall, but those who wait on the LORD shall renew their strength; they shall mount up with wings like eagles, they shall run and not be weary, they shall walk and not faint."~Isaiah 40:29–31

Lord, help me to be renewed by You today.

June 5

The Perfect Measure

 In Washington, D.C. resides the Bureau of Standards, where is kept a perfect inch, perfect foot, perfect yard, perfect ounce, perfect quart, perfect gallon, etc. If a question ever arises relative to measurement, the Bureau of Standards can settle the issue because they hold the perfect measure for comparison.

What is the perfect measure of our love for Christ? It is determined in one word: OBEDIENCE. Our love is not measured by ever-changing words nor by fickle emotion. Obedience is the standard! Jesus said, "He who has my commandments and keeps them; he it is that loves me."~John 14:21

During the Cold War days the arms race caused both our country and the Soviet Union to build up vast arsenals. At the end of this time of escalation, both sides began to disarm by dismantling and destroying thousands of weapons. President Ronald Reagan made famous the phrase, *Trust, but Verify*, during the negotiations with the Russians over disarmament. After Reagan used the phrase at the signing of the INF Treaty, his counterpart Mikhail Gorbachev responded, "You repeat that at every meeting," to which Reagan answered, "I like it."

I like another phrase, *Trust and Obey*. The chorus of the old hymn by the same title says,

Trust and obey, for there's no other way
To be happy in Jesus, but to trust and obey.

Obedience is the standard. It demonstrates our love for Him who died for us and it results in our happiness. *Trust and Obey.*

Lord, help me to demonstrate my love for You as I trust and obey.

June 6

Singing in the Rain

Long periods of clouds and rain can sure spoil one's attitude. Hope
seems to ebb low and our outlooks dim. Israel had come through such
a time. Some of it had been of their own making and they found
themselves under the corrective hand of God. But God is always ready
to reach out to the repentant heart and restore the days of glory. Hang
on! The sun will shine again!

The prophet Zephaniah spoke of this time in Israel's life and the time of
restoration. "God in your midst is mighty; he will save, he will rejoice over you
with joy; he will rest in his love, he will joy over you with singing."~Zephaniah
3:17 It is one thing to know that we serve a mighty God and quite another to
know that He displays His power in our presence as a warrior/defender. You
never have to go looking for God...He's here now!

Note that it's not us who breaks forth in praise but God Himself! There is joy in
the presence of the angels (Luke 15:10); it's not the angels rejoicing, but God
rejoicing in their presence! God gets excited about folks getting saved! And what
is God's confidence in our salvation? How can God rest after delivering us?
God's confidence rests in His own unchanging love for us! It's not in our
performance! God is love (1 John 4:8) and He changes not! (Malachi 3:6) He
cannot stop loving the believer!

God expresses His joy over us in singing. Have you ever imagined God's singing
voice? Like many waters falling and booming throughout the universe, He sings
about you and me! We are His joy! This little word *joy* means to spin about with
rejoicing. God is twirling about in joy over us...now that will make your day!

Lord, help me to hear You singing over me today.

June 7

Measuring Sin

 A caliper is a handy tool for measuring distance across odd shaped items. People in many professions use calipers to take critical measurements because they provide high levels of precision. A caliper is especially useful in measuring items of odd shape where a standard measuring tool would not be effective.

Sin is one of those odd shaped things. It takes all sorts of forms and as humans, we love to measure sin...especially in other folks. God, however, does not take such measurements. Sin is sin! The smallest in our estimation is enough to destroy fellowship. The largest can bring us to think it unforgivable.

Go with me to a dry dusty morning in Judea. See Jesus kneel before a woman caught in the very act of sin and her accusers railing against her. The guilt of the woman is not in question. The scribes and Pharisees are waiting to see how Jesus will measure her sin. "'Now Moses, in the law, commanded us that such should be stoned. But what do You say?' This they said, testing Him, that they might have something of which to accuse Him. But Jesus stooped down and wrote on the ground with His finger, as though He did not hear."~John 8:5–6

Instead of passing judgment, He stoops and writes in the dust. This is the only recorded time that Jesus ever wrote. Conjecture runs wild about what he wrote, but this I know, the next refreshing rain washed it all away. We are blessed that all our sins are washed away!

Lord, help me to rejoice in the fact that my sins are washed away.

June 8

Speed Limit

It is interesting to see the various ways the word slow is used. Of course, we think of the command to slow down, especially when we see a speed limit sign. But slow is used in other instances also. I remember a candy I used to buy as a kid for a nickel. It was called a Slo Poke. It was hard caramel plastered on a stick and it would last a long time. You couldn't bite it or chew it; you just licked it until it melted away. A good choice when you only had one nickel and a lot of time!

You have seen signs that warn drivers of children in the area. It says SLOW, CHILDREN! That's an oxymoron since I've never seen a slow child. Another sign says SLOW, WORKERS! This is usually posted at highway construction sites. I don't think I should comment here...

The Bible says we should be slow to speak. "So then, my beloved brethren, let every man be swift to hear, slow to speak, slow to wrath."~James 1:19 Now that's good advice considering the fact that nearly 100% of my problems can be traced to a *quick* tongue attached to a *slow* brain!

Make every effort today to slow down your tongue. Consider in our world of fast communication, how easy it is to hit the send button on an email or text. There was a time when we wrote letters and then carried them to the post office. It gave us time to think and maybe *not speak*. Now our speech is delivery almost instantly around the world with the touch of a button. Why not substitute the word SLOW for the word SEND? It could save you a lot of trouble.

Think before you speak and when you lie down to sleep tonight you will have much less to regret!

Lord, help me slow down before I react.

165

June 9

What Are You Wearing?

 A young couple came to know Christ as Savior and joined a local church. The husband attended a men's meeting at the church, but came home sad and downhearted. His wife wanted to know what had happened. He explained that all of the men at the meeting had on shirts with writing on the back and he felt out of place. Since neither of them could read, he could not tell his wife what words were on the shirt.

His wife sought to remedy the situation by buying him a shirt of the same color and decided to write some words on the back that she had copied from a store across the street from their home. After the next men's meeting, her husband came home beaming with pride. Everyone was talking about his shirt and thought it was wonderful. The words on the shirt read, "Under New Management!"

How often do you stand before a closet full of clothes and ask, "What shall I put on?" Romans 13:14 tells us that we are to put on the Lord Jesus. The phrase *put on* means to sink down in to; to invest in; to dress. We are to be so clothed with Jesus that those looking at us only see Him. We have sunk down into Jesus. We are *under new management!*

You may stand at your closet and wonder what to wear, but let Him be what folks see first in your life as they stand before you. You will be well dressed for any occasion.

Lord, help me to dress like a believer today.

 166

June 10

Bigger than McDonald's

While traveling in Orlando, Florida once, I heard that our hotel was very close to the world's largest McDonald's. I drove a few extra miles to get breakfast there. The building is shaped like a bag of french fries. I'm not sure what I expected, but this is what I found. The menu was exactly the same and the food tasted the same! Even though the building was of a unique architecture, McDonald's was still McDonald's.

Soon I will walk through the largest gate ever created. It has for a door a single pearl. I will not see golden arches, but instead I will walk on streets made of pure gold. The wait time there does not exist, because this is a place where there are no clocks; time doesn't matter there. No artificial lighting will guide me to this door. There is no sun, moon, or stars, but instead a light that is; it just is! As I enter through the door, I discover that many others have found their way here. Unlike my visit to the McDonald's in Orlando where I did not know anyone inside the restaurant.

There is nothing being prepared here for all has been finished long before my arrival. There are no workers, because this is a place where work has ceased. No manager can be found. Instead there is a throne, and He that sits upon it has the appearance of a Lamb, but the power of a Lion. In his hand is a scepter, won by the shedding of His own blood and a book upon whose pages is written my name in reservation. And I join those already there in a hallelujah chorus. He is Jesus! He is King of Kings and Lord of Lords!

"After these things I looked, and behold, a door standing open in heaven."~Revelation 4:1 On my way to heaven...are you going?

Lord, help me to make sure I share Your name with someone today.

June 11

Ivory Christians

 Purity is not an ideal that is easily obtainable. We tend to settle for that which is almost pure. We prefer to leave room for the assumption that pure equals perfect and since no one is perfect, then no one can be pure. The term Ivory Christian would be a good moniker since we are happy with 99 $^{44}/_{100}$ % pure.

Jesus in His sermon on the mount spoke of the pure in heart. "Blessed are the pure in heart, for they shall see God."~Matthew 5:8 David said basically the same thing in Psalm 24, "Who may ascend into the hill of the Lord? Or who may stand in His holy place? He who has clean hands and a pure heart, who has not lifted up his soul to an idol, nor sworn deceitfully."~Psalms 24:3-4

Is purity of heart possible? It must be or we will not be able to ascend to God's presence. But what of our sin nature and the fact that we cannot be perfect? Purity is not just an internal work of the Spirit as the blood of Jesus cleanses us, though this is vital to us being pure. We also have a responsibility in the process of being pure. It is best understood by comparing innocence and purity.

Children are born innocent not pure. They are conceived in sin and thereby not pure (Psalm 51:5.) They have not sinned in their innocence, but the potential is there. They are sinners. Purity comes by trial of fire in the life of the spiritually mature. We are tested and we overcome the temptation by the work of God's Spirit in our lives. Through this we are proven 100% pure and the pure in heart will see God.

Lord, help me to have a pure heart today.

June 12

The Grit of Irritation

What's irritating you today? Nothing? Well, have a blessed day while the rest of us mull over that one little thing that bothers us so badly. I think that most everybody has an irritation to deal with from time to time. We can't prevent most of them, but we can learn to deal with them in a godly manner.

Very few of us, at least at this present time, will endure great persecution. I hesitate, therefore, to refer to Paul's words to young Timothy, but I believe they can relate to everyday irritations as well. Paul spoke of his sufferings for the gospel. "Therefore do not be ashamed of the testimony of our Lord, nor of me His prisoner, but share with me in the sufferings for the gospel according to the power of God..."~2 Timothy 1:8 In the book of Romans, Paul encourages us not to return evil for evil, but instead to return good when people do evil toward us (Romans 12:21).

We can deal with irritation like the oyster does. When an oyster gets a grain of sand or other irritant inside its shell it secretes a substance that begins to coat the irritant. Layer by layer the irritation is coated until it is all smoothed over into a shiny pearl. Harvesters have discovered that they can force an oyster to produce a pearl by causing an irritation, but the most valuable pearls are those produced naturally, because they are the rarest.

It is a rare thing to find the person who can deal well with irritation. Remember inside every pearl is the grit of irritation!

NOW, GO MAKE A PEARL OUT OF YOUR DAY!

Lord, help me to respond correctly to today's irritations.

June 13

Walk Your Talk

 Are you a person that lives up to your testimony? "But whoever keeps His word, truly the love of God is perfected in him. By this we know that we are in Him. He who says he abides in Him ought himself also to walk just as He walked."~(1 John 2:5-6)

This is no casual relationship. Abides means to stay, dwell, or be present. It is continual. This is not just a Sunday visit. This verse tells us that we have an obligation to walk our talk. That's exactly what the word *ought* means in these verses. It carries the same weight as a debt that is accruing interest. It must be repaid with due diligence.

Our testimony is not based on our character, but His. We know the pace of our walk by His word. We are to keep His word. This little word *keep* means to guard. Here's the first hint at trouble. If we must guard it, then evidently someone is trying to steal it from us. If we depart from the truth of His word then our walk stops lining up with our talk. Jerry White in *The Power of Commitment* said, "No one is so empty as the man who has stopped walking with God and doesn't know it." A secondary meaning is to mature or reach consummation. As we keep God's word, our walk becomes more and more stable. We also as a mature Christian will more quickly recognize when we have stopped walking with Jesus.

The life of Jesus is the path we walk. When we stay within its parameters, our testimonies prove us to be true and this gives us the right to testify! Before you talk, check your walk!

Lord, help me to walk my talk today.

June 14

Help! I'm Lost!

You will never hear this news story. "A man went to the deepest part of the forest today and declared that he knew where he was and the way back to his home." On the other hand, it would be news if this same man were totally lost deep in the forest. Heaven waits not for our declaration of "foundness," but our confession of lostness.

Zacchaeus was a man that sensed his lostness. In Luke 19, you can read the account of this tax collector who sought to see Jesus. Zacchaeus, as the children's song so aptly says, "Was a wee little man; a wee little man was he." Luke's account says that Zacchaeus had heard that Jesus was passing very near to where he was, but because of his stature, it would be impossible for him to see over the heads of those in the crowd.

Like anyone who is truly lost, he tried desperately to find a way out of his lostness. Embarrassment is no longer considered when desperation sets in fully. This man, an officer of the Roman tax system, ran ahead of the crowd and climbed up in a sycamore tree. This sycamore tree of the Middle East grows with low arching limbs that would provide a perfect perch for him to get a view of Jesus.

To his amazement when Jesus came to that tree, he looked up and called Zacchaeus down from his vantage point. Jesus declared that he was going to the home of Zacchaeus that day. The little man was found in a tree and his lostness was remedied as He trusted Jesus as his Lord and Savior. Jesus proclaimed for all to hear, "...the Son of Man has come to seek and to save that which was lost."~Luke 19:10 Are you lost? Don't be embarrassed! Call on Him today and be found!

Lord, help me find someone today that needs to be found.

June 15

Break the Bank

 Most everyone has had (or still has) a piggy bank. The bank itself is of little value. Someday it will be broken to reveal the treasure inside. So with these bodies of flesh, for they too must be crushed to reveal the true value of life: the soul. Our true value is the in-breathed soul—not the shape, size, or color of the piggy bank that holds the soul for a few short days!

We place so much value on the outside that we lose any concept of what is really valuable. It would be like placing our life savings into a huge ceramic piggy bank and then refusing to damage the surface to redeem the treasure. So it will be for many when Christ comes to claim His own. Too many have placed a high value on these bodies that are only like piggy banks holding the true treasure of Jesus Christ. Paul reminds us, "If then you were raised with Christ, seek those things which are above, where Christ is, sitting at the right hand of God. Set your mind on things above, not on things on the earth. For you died, and your life is hidden with Christ in God. When Christ who is our life appears, then you also will appear with Him in glory."~Colossians 3:1–4

How are we to realign our values, so that, we see ourselves as Paul described? We die. It's really that simple. When you die you take no treasure with you. No matter how ornate the piggy bank was, it is of no value after death. The reality of this happens when we set our minds on heavenly things, not earthly. And how are we to die to self? Accept the reality of Christ's crucifixion and our resurrection in Him. "I have been crucified with Christ; it is no longer I who live, but Christ lives in me; and the life which I now live in the flesh I live by faith in the Son of God, who loved me and gave Himself for me."~Galatians 2:20

Lord, help me break the bank today.

June 16

Victory in Jesus

Few folks would consider preaching to be a battle, but as a preacher,
I can tell you that there are times that a real struggle takes place. From
time to time I need to remember the encouraging words of that old
hymn which repeats, "Oh, victory in Jesus!"

My battle took place once in a little church on the bayou. I had been asked to
preach there even though I was already a pastor at another church. These folks
needed someone to preach so the doors of the church would remain open. So, I
went for several Sunday afternoons in August in south Louisiana. In other words,
it was hot! There was no air-conditioning; only an attic fan to stir a little air. On
the fourth or fifth Sunday I had preached, no one came to the service. I was there
all alone; well, God was there. I was angry. I had prepared a great message and
no one came to hear it.

The Lord impressed on me that I should preach anyway and after a time of
arguing with Him, I did. (I know you never do this!) I finished the message and
drove home. On the way, God impressed on my heart to preach that same
message at the evening service where I was pastor. I did and seven people came
to know Christ as Savior! "Oh, victory in Jesus!"

I needed to learn what King Jehoshaphat had to learn that, "the battle is not
mine, but God's."~2 Chronicles 20:15 Don't look for the victory of the moment
as if that would end the war. Look to the battle of this particular hour and know
that it is His! One day the banner of Christ will fly over the high wall and then
we will really sing,

"OH, VICTORY IN JESUS, MY SAVIOR FOREVER!!!"

Lord, help me remember that the battle is not mine, but Yours.

June 17

Our Heritage

 Years sure have a way of piling up before you have noticed their passing. It seems sometimes a long, long time ago since I was a boy, but with only a pause those childhood memories come flooding back to the forefront of my mind. I always remember my father. Now that's a little formal...I remember my daddy!

My dad was 45 years old when I was born and I was his firstborn. This was no disadvantage. I had a dad who had accrued a lot of wisdom by this juncture in his life and he freely passed it on to me. He was always passing along bits of information that included everything from how to repair an old car to casting with an open-faced reel to caring for my mama.

I was 10 years old when my daddy became a believer. He had his first heart attack when I was only 12 and he went home to glory just ten years later. I'm sure that he had no expectancy of dying at a relatively young age, but he had prepared me for the occasion. Even now he speaks at times from the grave with words of advice that I cherish. He left a great heritage.

We all desire to leave such a heritage. But even the best of people with the most shining examples of living well and dying well have no hope of leaving a lasting impact, unless they begin with a focus on the eternal.

You can't expect a heritage that will last long without having this this key ingredient in your life. "For no other foundation can anyone lay than that which is laid, which is Jesus Christ. Now if anyone builds on this foundation with gold, silver, precious stones, wood, hay, straw, each one's work will become clear; for the Day will declare it, because it will be revealed by fire; and the fire will test each one's work, of what sort it is. If anyone's work which he has built on it endures, he will receive a reward."~1 Corinthians 3:11-14

Lord, help me to leave an eternal heritage.

Fly to Jesus

Noah's ark is a picture of Christ protecting and preserving through the judgment of the flood. Near the end of its journey Noah released two birds. "Then he sent out a raven, which kept going to and fro until the waters had dried up from the earth. He also sent out from himself a dove, to see if the waters had receded from the face of the ground. But the dove found no resting place for the sole of her foot, and she returned into the ark to him, for the waters were on the face of the whole earth. So he put out his hand and took her, and drew her into the ark to himself."~Genesis 8:7–9

First, a raven which did not return. This bird is a symbol of those who are glad to ride through the storm, but not endure to the end. The second was a dove that did not rest until it found safety back on the ark. This dove is a picture of the weary Christian who can always find a place of rest in the Ark of Jesus. The words of a song written by Christian recording artist, Chris Rice, give great insight into the safety and rest that is found in Christ.

> *Weak and wounded sinner, lost and left to die, O, raise your head, for love is passing by. Now your burden's lifted and carried far away and precious blood has washed away the stain. And like a newborn baby don't be afraid to crawl. And remember when you walk sometimes we fall. Sometimes the way is lonely and steep and filled with pain so if your sky is dark and pours the rain, then...fly to Jesus, fly to Jesus, fly to Jesus and live!*

So weary Christian, fly to the Ark! Jesus is the Ark of safety and life. He awaits you with outstretched hand. Let your faith rest fully in Him today!

Lord, help me to fly to You today.

June 19

To the Point

Disappointment comes when our hopes or expectations are not fulfilled. The root of this word is *appoint* and that word has in its meaning simply, a *point*. We place our hopes and dreams on one precise moment or person. All must take place as we have planned or the result is "dis" appointment. That is, loss of the point and/or place in time.

Results: disorientation and confusion

If you live long enough you will be disappointed. I will disappoint you given enough time and space! As you have read the pages of this book there have been days that the material has been disappointing to you. It does not mean that the scripture for that day has no power. It does not mean that another person reading the same day's devotional did not find strength and comfort. It just means that you were disappointed at that point.

But hear the words of Romans 5:1-5, "Therefore, having been justified by faith, we have peace with God through our Lord Jesus Christ, through whom also we have access by faith into this grace in which we stand, and rejoice in hope of the glory of God. And not only that, but we also glory in tribulations, knowing that tribulation produces perseverance; and perseverance, character; and character, hope. Now hope does not *disappoint*, because the love of God has been poured out in our hearts by the Holy Spirit who was given to us."

I want to challenge you today to place your hope in the finished work of Christ. Only there will you be able to lay down your disappointments and walk away assured that He alone never disappoints!

Lord, help me to have hope—not disappointment.

June 20

Following Daily

The preaching of God's word is the vehicle God has chosen to deliver His message to the heart of all mankind. "For since, in the wisdom of God, the world through wisdom did not know God, it pleased God through the foolishness of the message preached to save those who believe."~1 Corinthians 1:21 The world hears it as foolishness, but to those who believe it has the power to bring salvation to the soul and light to a darkened heart.

It is not only the message of salvation that comes by preaching. Recently I came under the conviction of God's Holy Spirit as I heard the preaching of the word. I was the preacher! The text was Luke 9:23. "Then He said to them all, 'If anyone wants to come with Me, he must deny himself, take up his cross daily, and follow Me.'"

One single word was implanted into my heart from my message. The word for me: FOLLOW! My business is to follow; not plan; not worry; not second guess. I was convicted of all my schemes. I was convicted of the wasted hours of worry I have been engaged in when my plans did not come to fruition. I could count the times that I had second guessed what God was clearly instructing me to do. And I repented of my sin and found Him faithful to forgive and cleanse me of them all.

Do I expect this to be the end of this matter? Not at all. Following is preceded with denying self and taking up a cross—daily. To follow Jesus I must go to the cross every day. Crosses are a place to die and dying takes care of self. Remember now, this was my message to myself, but you are welcome to get in on the following.

Lord, help me to take up my cross daily and follow You.

177

June 21

Releasing the Power

 Great insight can be gained from the prayers that are recorded in the Bible. Spending some time studying the content of these prayers can help you understand how to better pray. You will find that prayer covers a myriad of subjects and situations.

Paul was always praying for the church, that is, for us. "For this reason I bow my knees to the Father of our Lord Jesus Christ from whom the whole family in heaven and earth is named, that He would grant you, according to the riches of His glory, to be strengthened with might through His Spirit in the inner man, that Christ may dwell in your hearts through faith; that you, being rooted and grounded in love, may be able to comprehend with all the saints what is the width and length and depth and height—to know the love of Christ which passes knowledge; that you may be filled with all the fullness of God. Now to Him who is able to do exceedingly abundantly above all that we ask or think, according to the power that works in us, to Him be glory in the church by Christ Jesus to all generations, forever and ever. Amen."~Ephesians 3:14-21

This prayer for us is still valid today and I believe that God is still answering it for all believers. Paul prayed for our inner strength, a filling of God's presence, that we know His love and love as He loves. He concluded by proclaiming all of this possible because God is able to do more than we can ask or think according to (in agreement with) the power that is already in us!

Do you hear that ticking noise? Like a time bomb, it's the power of God in you waiting to be released! You've been prayed for today!

Lord, help me to pray for my church today.

June 22

According to Scale

Isaiah asked, "To whom then will you liken God or what likeness will
you compare to Him?"~Isaiah 40:18 His question followed this
declaration, "Behold, the nations are as a drop in a bucket, and are
counted as the small dust on the scales; look, He lifts up the isles as a
very little thing."~Isaiah 40:15

Look closely at most packaging and you will see that it says somewhere on the
package, "Sold by weight; not volume." I never paid much attention to this until
my son-in-law became a scale technician. It was a surprise to me how many places
he had to go to install or service a scale. Scales are everywhere as product is
weighed and analyzed. He showed me a scale once that was so sensitive it could
measure a breath of air that was passed over its deck.

Now imagine the set of scales that God uses to measure things. They are so large
that entire nations can be placed upon them, yet they move the scale like particles
of dust. He lifts entire islands like small pebbles. This really puts everything into
perspective. Those who think themselves to be very important are only micro-
particles of dust. Distilled droplets and dry dust describe the nations who think
they can decide their own fate or fame! Put them all together on God's scale and
there is no comparison!

Calibrating the accuracy of a scale is vital to businesses. Even a small discrepancy
when volume is considered can make a huge difference in a day's profit or loss.
God's scale never needs to be calibrated. It is based on His own righteousness
and justice. You and I will never be weighed on God's scale to determine our
salvation, however, because the full weight of our sin was placed on Jesus. No
scale at the gate of heaven; just a pair of nail-scarred hands waiting to welcome
you.

Lord, help me to see myself relative to Your scale of measurement.

June 23

Holy Ground

 I have had the privilege to visit many places that have been deemed hallowed ground. These include sites like Gettysburg and Pearl Harbor. It seems that most places that we declare as hallowed ground have been made so by the shedding of blood. When you walk through these places there is a real sense of supreme sacrifice. Though the word hallowed carries at least some connotation of holy, I try to make a clear distinction between the two. Where hallowed ground usually was made so through conflict and victory, holy ground is made so by the very presence of God.

When Moses stood before the burning bush in Exodus 3 he heard God say, "'Do not draw near this place. Take your sandals off your feet, for the place where you stand is holy ground.' Moreover He said, 'I am the God of your father—the God of Abraham, the God of Isaac, and the God of Jacob.' And Moses hid his face, for he was afraid to look upon God."~Exodus 3:5-6 In Joshua 5, Joshua was confronted by Jesus, the captain of the Lord's host, and he also found himself on holy ground. "Then the Commander of the Lord's army said to Joshua, 'Take your sandal off your foot, for the place where you stand is holy.' And Joshua did so."~Joshua 5:15

In both of these cases it was the presence of the Lord in a common place that made it uncommon. God instructed both Moses and Joshua to remove their sandals so that the soles of their feet were in contact with ground that was now holy. There could not be even a thin leather sandal bottom between God and these men. What is it that is preventing you from being on holy ground? Any place can become holy ground for you. Make sure that there is nothing between you and God hindering this. Like standing on some battlefield that has been declared hallowed, when your piece of ground turns holy, you too will want to remove your shoes.

Lord, help me to understand that anywhere You are is holy ground.

June 24

Spiritually Sensitive

We connect to the world we live in through five senses. Without those we may as well be a machine. We are handicapped if even one of our senses is deficient. Try wearing a patch over just one eye and you quickly get the idea of the necessity of sight. Lose both eyes and your ability to interact in this physical world becomes very difficult and that is just the loss of one of our five senses.

We are more than just physical, however. We also interact with a spiritual world in which our five senses are useless. How then do we function in the spiritual realm? How can we even know that there is a spiritual world? The Bible tells us in 1 John, "By this we know that we abide in Him, and He in us, because He has given us of His Spirit. And we have seen and testify that the Father has sent the Son as Savior of the world. Whoever confesses that Jesus is the Son of God, God abides in him, and he in God. And we have known and believed the love that God has for us. God is love, and he who abides in love abides in God, and God in him."~1 John 4:13–16

The Holy Spirit is our sense of God's presence. He connects us to the spiritual world. Having the Spirit of God dwelling in you is the only real difference between you and a non-believer. Both the believer and non-believer have their full faculties and can interact and communicate with the physical world. But without the Spirit of God, a person is dead spiritually. "And you He made alive, who were dead in trespasses and sins, in which you once walked according to the course of this world, according to the prince of the power of the air, the spirit who now works in the sons of disobedience..."~Ephesians 2:1–2 As a believer you have your full spiritual faculties. Ask God to sharpen your sense of Himself today!

Lord, help me to remain sensitive to things that are spiritual.

June 25

Fill in the Blank

 R.A. Torrey tells the following account of a note he was handed one evening just before he was to preach at Christ Church in New Zealand. It read, "Is there any place where I can find satisfaction for my soul? I have been looking for it everywhere. I have sought it in wealth, but have not found it; I have sought it in society, but have not found it; I have sought it in the pleasures of this world, but have not found it; I have sought it in study, but have not found it; I have sought it in art, but have not found it; I have been seeking it in travel, I have just returned from a tour around the world seeking for satisfaction for my heart, but have not found it. Can you tell me where I can find it?" The note was unsigned.

There are many who find themselves today in the same search for satisfaction. We live in a time when dissatisfaction is marketed. We think that satisfaction will be ours if we can just possess _____. You fill in the blank. But real satisfaction will come when we behold Jesus! Note the Psalmist, "As for me, I shall behold Your face in righteousness; I will be satisfied with Your likeness when I awake."~Psalms 17:15

Dr. Torrey read the note he had received that night as he introduced his text from John 4. He preached about the woman at the well who had met Jesus. In this encounter Jesus told her, "Whoever drinks of this water will thirst again, but whoever drinks of the water that I shall give him will never thirst. But the water that I shall give him will become in him a fountain of water springing up into everlasting life."~John 4:13–14

At the close of the meeting a lady came to Torrey and said, "It was I who wrote that note." With an open Bible, he showed her the way of life and she accepted Jesus. Her blank had been filled!

Lord, help me to be satisfied totally with You.

June 26

Sufficient Grace

Imagine receiving a vast inheritance consisting of a country manor, several automobiles, stables full of horses, and servants to tend it all. How long could you maintain this new possession? It would not be long for me. I would soon have to sell autos and horses. The day would come for staff layoffs. Soon property would be sold, until I reached a position that matched my resources.

Now, imagine the same inheritance, but with the promise that all expenses to operate such a manor would be paid for the rest of your life with this condition: The cost of operating the manor would be paid in full each day, but on any day that the funds were not expended there would be a reduction of the next day's funds in the same amount not spent. If you were smart you would empty the account daily lest the day came where frugality had depleted tomorrow of its supply.

Are you emptying your account daily? Your grace account that is! It is not possible to keep grace stored up as if in a bank vault. Attempting to do so will only rob you of tomorrow's supply. God's daily grace deposit is always sufficient for each new day of our lives. Nothing more—nothing less! "And He said to me, 'My grace is sufficient for you, for My strength is made perfect in weakness.' Therefore most gladly I will rather boast in my infirmities, that the power of Christ may rest upon me. Therefore I take pleasure in infirmities, in reproaches, in needs, in persecutions, in distresses, for Christ's sake. For when I am weak, then I am strong."~2 Corinthians 12:9–10

Go ahead! Try to use grace up. Like manna in the wilderness those who gathered much had no surplus and those who gathered little had no need. Tomorrow may have its troubles, but your grace account will be renewed for the cause!

Lord, help me to spend all the grace You give me daily.

June 27

Could This Day Be That Day?

 Growing up in the South and being named after my father gave me three possibilities for a name. I could have been called Junior. I could have been labeled with my initials—which I was. Or I could have been called Bubba!

Bubba's sort of take it on the chin when it comes to jokes. For example, Bubba was asked once how many seconds there are in a year. He responded, "Twelve!" When asked to explain he said, "January 2nd, February 2nd..." When he was asked another calendar question his answer was just as profound. What are the names of the week that start with the letter "T"? Bubba did not have to think long or hard. With deep sincerity he responded, "Today and tomorrow!"

The calendar seems to rule a lot of my life. Some dates necessary...others NOT! One date needs to be on all of our calendars: HIS COMING! Martin Luther said he only had two dates on his calendar: Today and That Day! That day being the day that Jesus comes again for the church.

We need to mark each day of our lives as that day and be ready for His appearing. In Malachi 3:2 we read, "But who can endure the day of His coming? And who can stand when He appears? For He is like a refiner's fire and like launderers' soap."

Only the redeemed will stand on that day for He will separate the impure from the pure as fire purifies gold and as soap takes away filth. Be ready! It could be today that is *that day*!

Lord, help me be ready for that great day of your coming!

June 28

Got Jesus?

GOT MILK? Remember when having a white mustache made you a super star? Now the question is: GOT GOLD? Everyone's clamoring to protect against the collapse of the dollar by hoarding what is considered a precious metal. What does the Bible say about gold?

Peter tells us that we were not redeemed with corruptible things like silver or gold. "...knowing that you were not redeemed with corruptible things, like silver or gold, from your aimless conduct received by tradition from your fathers, but with the precious blood of Christ, as of a lamb without blemish and without spot."~1 Peter 1:18-19 Our redemption has been made with that which is not perishable or temporary. Gold is not the answer to our problems, nor can it buy for us eternal life. Gold is so disregarded in heaven that it is used as paving material on the streets! "...and the street of the city was pure gold, like transparent glass."~Revelation 21:21

Matthew 13 contains several parables that Jesus told to illustrate the kingdom of heaven. In one of these parables He said, "Again, the kingdom of heaven is like treasure hidden in a field, which a man found and hid; and for joy over it he goes and sells all that he has and buys that field."~Matthew 13:44 There is so much more to be gained than securing the riches of this world. Jesus said that this man upon finding that a possession of the kingdom of heaven was possible, went and sold all to buy it. Of course, the kingdom of heaven is not for sale, but its value can only begin to be recognized when we are willing to forego all to obtain it.

GOT JESUS? Now that's the real question!

Lord, help me to keep my investments secure by having only You.

June 29

Highly Exalted

 Exaltation of self is rampant today in every arena of life. It has affected our homes and our churches. In 1544, Philip the Prudent sailed to England to take Mary Tudor as his wife. His father ordered him to go with a "minimum of display." So he took only 9,000 nobles and servants, 1,000 horses and mules, three million ducats in gold, and 125 ships. So much for a minimum of display! There is only One who deserves the honor of exaltation and that is God Himself. In three verses from Psalms His exaltation is declared and the parameters of His exaltation defined.

"Be still, and know that I am God; I will be exalted among the nations, I will be exalted in the earth!"~Psalms 46:10

"Be exalted, O God, above the heavens; Let Your glory be above all the earth."~Psalms 57:5

"Let them praise the name of the Lord, for His name alone is exalted; His glory is above the earth and heaven."~Psalms 148:13

The word *exalt* means to lift up, to promote, to extol. In Psalm 46 God Himself declares that He will be exalted. It will happen whether we participate or not. Then the Psalmist confesses God's exaltation as fact in Psalm 57 with a simple "be exalted." Finally, the command for God's exaltation is sounded forth, "Let them praise...for His name alone is exalted." God is to be exalted in the earth among all nations until His exaltation rises above the earth to the heavens. Then it is to reach the farthest extremes of God's creative ability. If God could ever reach the end of Himself, there at the edge of infinity, He would find His own exaltation ever expanding. This leaves no room for the words self and exaltation to be connected in all of creation, much less in me or you. His exaltation will not diminish your value to Him. It will only serve to make you more aware of the magnificent step God took to come down to man and deliver us from self.

Lord, help me to exalt Your name all the day long.

June 30

His Face I'll See

Fanny Crosby wrote over nine thousand hymns during her life, many of which we love to sing on any given Sunday in worship. She was blinded at six weeks of age after developing an infection in her eyes. When asked if she had ever wished that she had not been blinded she replied with calm assurance, "It seemed intended by the blessed providence of God that I should be blind all my life, and I thank him for the dispensation. If perfect earthly sight were offered me tomorrow I would not accept it. I might not have sung hymns to the praise of God if I had been distracted by the beautiful and interesting things about me." She later added to this sentiment, "When I get to heaven, the first face that shall ever gladden my sight will be that of my Savior."

A common saying is *seeing is believing* but, Jesus stated it differently. After Nicodemus had come seeking Him in the night Jesus said, "Most assuredly, I say to you, unless one is born again, he cannot see the kingdom of God."~John 3:3. It is not seeing in order to believe; it is not really believing to see, though that does play a part. The only real way to see is to be! BEING IS SEEING! That's the way sight comes. We are born again! Made alive! The dead can't see, but all who are made alive by faith can see and do see!

Those with physical sight so casually view this temporal world that surrounds them. But for those who have received eternal life from Christ, there is the vision that comes at the moment of salvation. It is the sight which Fanny Crosby beheld on February 12, 1915. On that day she stepped from this life into the glorious presence of her Savior whom she had written of in her hymns for decades. Her faith became sight.

Lord, help me to look forward to that day I will see You face to face.

July 1

Shine On!

 Jesus uses 3 verbs to describe us as light in Matthew 5:14-16. "You are the light of the world. A city that is set on a hill cannot be hidden. Nor do they light a lamp and put it under a basket, but on a lamp stand, and it gives light to all who are in the house. Let your light so shine before men, that they may see your good works and glorify your Father in heaven."

First, we *are* light. It is not artificial light, but the real thing. Because Jesus lives in us as believers, we become the light that He is described as in John's gospel. "In Him was life, and the life was the light of men / the true Light which gives light to every man coming into the world." (John 1:4,9)

Second, we *give* light. Light is not meant to be hidden. It simply shines to all without prejudice. Our light giving can be the beacon of hope in the fallen world which we reside. So the Apostle Paul says, "that you may become blameless and harmless, children of God without fault in the midst of a crooked and perverse generation, among whom you shine as lights in the world..."~Philippians 2:15

Third, we are to *let* our light shine not to bring glory to the light, but to the one who brought us into the light in the first place. Remember, light makes no noise! It just silently shines as it pierces the darkness. The reward that light receives is not when someone says, "What a magnificent light!" The reward instead is fully realized when someone says because of the light, "Now, I can see!" This is what Peter meant as he wrote, "having your conduct honorable among the Gentiles, that when they speak against you as evildoers, they may, by your good works which they observe, glorify God in the day of visitation."~1 Peter 2:12

Lord, help me let my light shine for You today.

July 2

Moving Day

As the children of Israel left Egypt by way of the wilderness, God was with them every step of the way. He demonstrated His presence in a pillar of cloud by day and a pillar of fire by night. Not only were these visible signs given to the Hebrew children to encourage them for the trials of the wilderness, they were also given for protection and guidance.

"Whenever the cloud was taken up from above the tabernacle, after that the children of Israel would journey; and in the place where the cloud settled, there the children of Israel would pitch their tents. At the command of the LORD the children of Israel would journey, and at the command of the LORD they would camp; as long as the cloud stayed above the tabernacle they remained encamped."~Numbers 9:17-18 The instructions were very clear: IF THE CLOUD MOVES YOU MOVE; IF NOT...STAY PUT!!! Never go ahead of God. You will regret it every time. Move when God moves and you will receive the blessing of divine appointment.

The Wesleyan missionary Barnabas Shaw had been forbidden to preach in Cape Town, South Africa. Where others would have forsaken the mission, he decided not to leave Africa, but to push into the interior. He bought a yoke of oxen and a wagon. With his wife and meager goods he moved, determined to settle wherever he would be allowed to preach. Three hundred grueling miles later as he and his wife were camped one night they discovered that a band of Hottentots were also camping nearby. Meeting with the tribal leaders, Shaw learned that the travelers were on their way to Cape Town to find a missionary to come to their village. In that moment he realized that God had been leading him where He wanted him to go. Stopping or going is the Lord's business. Follow Him!

Lord, help me stop and go at Your command.

July 3

Too Many Funerals

 The first funeral I can remember was that of my grandfather. I was about eight years old and an honorary pall bearer. I still remember walking alongside the casket with my hand resting on one of the handles. Since that day long ago, I have been involved in many funerals both personally and as a pastor.

Funerals are as varied and unique as the folks for whom they are conducted and I speak not of the dead, but the living. At the end of the day, no matter the background of the person being honored at the funeral, we all must walk away from the cemetery with a sense of unfinished duty. I believe even the hardest heart knows in that brief grave side moment that this is not the end of the story.

The book of Lamentations is a funeral message. It was written to help Israel through a time of trial and sorrow. Jeremiah who authored this book writes, "Through the LORD's mercies we are not consumed, because His compassions fail not."~Lamentations 3:22 It is a funeral message, but hope abounds in the midst of it.

The word compassion in Hebrew has the connotation of an unborn child in its mother's womb. Fragile, defenseless, yet protected and nourished. God's heart breaks for us in times of tragedy and heartache. God demonstrates the pity He has for us. He does so by putting a limit to our grief, hence, we are not consumed by it. Also, He promises that His compassion has no end. No matter how deep, how wide, or how high the suffering, His compassion for us will never fail. You may feel like you've been to a funeral today. As an unborn child in your mother's womb, curl up and let God love you through it all today.

Lord, help me to show compassion on Your name today.

July 4

Let Freedom Ring

Thank God for men and women who bore the cost of a vision that could have only been birthed in heaven. Some today would sell out for cheap peace, but our founders could face all the perils of a war for independence because they had real peace in their hearts through the cross of Calvary. Only men set free from sin will gladly die to set others free.

Being an American—even a proud American will not get you into heaven. Citizenship in heaven comes only to those who have trusted Christ's great sacrifice in payment for their sin debt. No passport or visa is needed at the gate of heaven! Only a living relationship with King Jesus will give you full and everlasting access to that fair land!

Anticipation must have been present on this day back in 1776, as our founding fathers signed the document disavowing allegiance to England and becoming Americans. Some of you are on the edge of freedom today. God signed your declaration of independence 2000 years ago on Calvary. Don't wait another day to declare your independence! No one is asking you to give your life for the cause, because One already has.

That One is Jesus and he has declared, "The Spirit of the LORD is upon Me, because He has anointed Me to preach the gospel to the poor; He has sent Me to heal the brokenhearted, to proclaim liberty to the captives and recovery of sight to the blind, to set at liberty those who are oppressed; to proclaim the acceptable year of the LORD."~Luke 4:18–19

From one captive set free to another: Have a Happy 4th of July!

Lord, help me to pray every day for my country.

July 5

Smile! You're On Candid Camera!

 All of us are movie stars! You cannot move anymore without a video camera recording every step you make. Cameras are watching each traffic light and regulating who gets the next green signal. Go to the bank and you are on candid camera. Some of this is good for personal safety, but you have to wonder where the fine line of personal liberty is crossed. In the meantime, I hope to see you on the big screen somewhere today!

You are being watched in another way also, but not with cameras. Now before you develop a phobia about all this picture taking and video recording going on, I can tell you that this watchfulness is actually good. It is God's eyes that are upon you, but not you alone. "For the eyes of the Lord run to and fro throughout the whole earth, to show Himself strong on behalf of those whose heart is loyal to Him."~2 Chronicles 16:9

Asa, king of Judah, was actually rebuked by these words from God after he had sought the help of the Syrian king. He forgot that God was His strength and help. God had already helped Asa defeat greater enemies, but now when a weaker challenge had arisen he turned to the king of Syria for help. The Lord is standing ready to help those who are totally dependent on Him, but he will withdraw that support if we trust the arm of flesh.

This good news for us is that God is always watching. He wants to show His strength to those who are loyal to Him. The word *loyal* means whole or complete. We cannot let fear rule our decisions and divide our loyalties. God's eye is not only watching us He is constantly watching the enemy as well. Trust in the Lord with all your heart and lean not on your own understanding. (Proverbs 3:5) You never want to be out of God's sight. It's the safest place to be!

Lord, help me trust You as You watch over me today.

July 6

I Don't See It

I am a man. My statement is in defense and in excuse for the fact that no matter what shelf you tell me I can find the item, I will not be able to find it. Truthfully, I can't even see it! I am a man! Certainly there are some who do not fit this mold, but I think that the majority of us men can claim this defense or at least use this excuse. It is genetic because other males of my family seem to have it also.

When Jesus was speaking publicly in His ministry here on earth, He would speak in parables. His disciples asked Him privately why he did this and His answer exposed the hardened hearts of most of the hearers. "Therefore I speak to them in parables, because seeing they do not see, and hearing they do not hear, nor do they understand. / But blessed are your eyes for they see, and your ears for they hear; for assuredly, I say to you that many prophets and righteous men desired to see what you see, and did not see it, and to hear what you hear, and did not hear it."~Matthew 13:13;16-17

Jesus declared of those hearing Him speak that they could not really hear nor see. Why not? Vision comes by faith and faith is the gift of God. Faith comes by hearing and hearing by the word of God (Romans 10:17.) It was clearly not that He did not want them to hear, but that they would not. They were given the privilege of hearing and seeing what prophets of old had only dreamed about knowing. Yet in their day of revelation they turned away to their own destruction. Without vision we perish (Proverbs 29:18.)

Oswald Chambers said, "God gives us the vision, then He takes us down to the valley to batter us into the shape of the vision, and it is in the valley that so many of us faint and give way." Blessed are your eyes for they see, and your ears for they hear!

Lord, help me to see with a heavenly vision.

July 7

My Testimony

 Religion has never been a problem for mankind. In the absence of any formal religious exercise, people have always been able to create a god in their own image and worship that god very well. This desire to worship is generated by a God-shaped void in the human heart.

Nothing will fill that emptiness except a relationship with the God of this universe, but people try everything but God.

I was one of those people. My first experience at making a religious decision came when I was nine years old. My mother had me sit with the pastor who with the best of intentions on both their parts asked me some questions about Jesus and my life. I had been in church long enough that I had learned the answers. I passed the test and the next Sunday was baptized. I had a form of godliness, but no power (2 Timothy 3:5.) I was, still lost in my sin.

Fast forward sixteen years. I had been faithful most of those years to attend church. I taught the adult men's Sunday School class as a 19 year old. Knowing the content of the Bible was not a problem for me. I loved to study and prepare a lesson. I led the youth department at my church. All of these religious activities were to my credit, but to no avail. I still had that void in my heart that could not be filled.

I began to ask myself and others why I was alive; why was I born here; what was my purpose in life? At this time in my life, I had stopped attending church, but I was still searching. It was during this search that a dear friend asked if she could take my children to Vacation Bible School. That one act broke my heart! I never thought I would be at the place that someone else would have to bring my children to church.

My children did attend V.B.S. that week. My wife and I went to the commencement activities and the next Sunday we were in church as a family. But the emptiness only grew larger. My questions could not be answered through religious activity. Each sermon seemed aimed directly at me and when an invitation was given to receive Christ as Savior, I would go back to that experience as a nine year old boy. In my heart, though, I knew that all I had done then was seek to please my mother and my pastor. My emptiness loomed more real than ever, but God was at work in my life.

I owned a grocery business at this time. On a Monday morning in October 1979, I opened my store early as usual and began to prepare for the first customers of the day. All alone in that empty grocery store building, God spoke to my heart. It was not audible, but it may as well have been. "Trust me today. My Son has paid the price for your sin. Come to me."

I knelt behind the deli case of my grocery store and gave my heart and life to Christ that morning. I was gloriously born again. Everything was new and my questions no longer mattered. There were no bright shining lights. There was no angelic choir singing—only me and God on a grocery store floor. When I raised my head from praying, I was looking into the back of my deli case. There staring me in the face was a large stick of bologna. I have never forgotten that scene. It was as if God was saying, "R.E., no more bologna for you."

I had lived the life of religious bologna. It did not hold the answer to life's greatest questions. It could not fill the void of my life. Only Jesus could do that...and He did! That's my testimony—what's yours?

"Whoever calls on the name of the Lord shall be saved."~Romans 10:13

Lord, help me to never live a life filled with bologna.

July 8

Growing in Grace

 Someone has said that anything that is not growing is dead. This is a true statement for the most part, but it is possible for a period of dormancy to exist. Life is still there, but it is no longer evident. It has become static, but with the right conditions will blossom into vivid growth once more.

This holds true for the subject of grace as well. There are two primary truths about grace: It is always sufficient and it is never static. You will have enough grace for today, but you should be growing in grace as well. The sufficiency of grace prevents a static grace from existing!

"Therefore, beloved, looking forward to these things, be diligent to be found by Him in peace, without spot and blameless; but grow in the grace and knowledge of our Lord and Savior Jesus Christ. To Him be the glory both now and forever. Amen."~2 Peter 3:14;18

Growing in grace is preventative. It keeps us pure; it protects us from falling into the trap of deception; it keeps us on the path. Peter used the phrase *grow in the grace* to communicate the process of an expanding and increasing grace that is necessary for an active and vibrant faith. Grace should be ever flowing like electricity through a wire. It is not for us to store and use like static electricity which produces a spark and then is gone.

Be filled with dynamic grace today and watch the power of faith flow in your life. When you sense a time of dormancy, then saturate the soil of your life with the word of God and prayer until the bloom of grace unfolds in its beauty.

Lord, help me to grow in Your grace today.

July 9

Jesus, Others, Yourself

Joy is the privilege of the believer. Not because the believer is somehow special or endowed with the ability to be joyful. It is because the believer knows the Master of the circumstance. Knowing who holds the issue you face will always result in joy. William Barclay said, "Men need to discover the lost radiance of the Christian faith. In a worried world, the Christian should be the only man who remains serene. In a depressed world, the Christian should be the only man who remains full of the joy of life."

The Christian does not have the option of being joyful; it is a requirement. Joy should be evident in the believer's life because it is listed as one of the fruit of the Spirit. "But the fruit of the Spirit is love, joy, peace, longsuffering, kindness, goodness, faithfulness, gentleness, self-control. Against such there is no law. And those who are Christ's have crucified the flesh with its passions and desires. If we live in the Spirit, let us also walk in the Spirit."~Galatians 5:22–25 There nestled between love and peace is the little word *joy*. Its location is not by accident in this list of the fruit of the Spirit. No joy is possible without the love of Christ in one's heart and the love of God being lived out of our lives. No peace is possible in a joyless heart or mind. J-O-Y can be described as: Jesus–Others–Yourself!

R.A. Torrey told of a man who was always the merriest at every gathering. This man came to one of Torrey's meetings and after the services the two of them walked home together. When the man was asked about his spiritual condition he revealed his heart to Mr. Torrey. Torrey said, "I found that the merriest of all men I had ever known, underneath all this gaiety, was one of the saddest of men. He had not found the true secret of joy, the joy that goes down to the deepest depths of the heart and that never fails...which Jesus alone can give.

Lord, help me live a life of J.O.Y. today!

July 10

Wish You Had Been There

 What happens when you attend worship? You may think that I would like to know an order of your services. For most folks it follows generally along the lines of a song or two; welcome and prayer; a couple of more songs; an offering; preaching; invitation; AMEN! Variations occur, but for the most part it's all the same. We could do it with our eyes closed, but most of us do it instead with our hearts closed! Worship has become more for us than for God's glory. What's really sad about it all is that we can have our "worship" with or without God! The little boy's prayer on Sunday night tells the story well. "Dear God, we had a good time at church today, but I wish You had been there."

Psalms 73:28 says, "But it is good for me to draw near to God; I have put my trust in the Lord GOD, that I may declare all Your works." There is a communion that deepens when we draw near to God. The word *draw* means to approach and the Psalmist says that this is a good thing to do. The idea of it being good to the Hebrew mind was that it was pleasant, sweet, bountiful, and one filled with ease. We draw near as one would get close enough to hug a friend. This only occurs when there is a high level of trust. He then draws near to us and in that closeness we experience His great works.

Do you depart from a time of worship marveling at the works of God? Do you come away bragging on Him? We need to draw near in worship and spend enough time there that we have an awareness of what God is doing and wants to do in your life.

Only after we have worshiped will we have a story to tell!

Lord, help me to worship You and then tell the story to others.

July 11

Happy Sailing!

Fellowship has often been described as two fellows on one ship. But this definition leaves open the possibility that either one or both may be there against their wills. Our fellowship with Christ is based on love, trust, and obedience. It is founded in His love for us. It is based upon our trust in His word. It is maintained by our obedience. There is no room on the ship for your own will to function. He is the Captain of our souls!

We are on the ship by God's call upon our life. He has placed us into fellowship with His own Son. "God *is* faithful, by whom you were called into the fellowship of His Son, Jesus Christ our Lord."~1 Corinthians 1:9 The basis of this call is the love of God which he bestowed on us by giving His only Son to redeem us from the stormy sea of life.

If you have ever read much about sea captains you will know that they rule their ships with an iron fist. If you do not live up to the standards of the deck, you could find yourself walking the plank. Not so with our Captain. He who called us also promises that we will succeed on board His ship. The Apostle Paul in praying for believers at Philippi thanked God, "...for your fellowship in the gospel from the first day until now, being confident of this very thing, that He who has begun a good work in you will complete it until the day of Jesus Christ..."~Philippians 1:5–6

Our obedience comes as we walk in the light of His fellowship. If we fail, He is ready to forgive and cleanse as we confess our sin to Him (1 John 1:3-7.) Happy sailing on the good ship, *Fellowship.*

Lord, help me to walk in the light of Your fellowship today.

July 12

Dressing Up

 Some my age will remember the guy that would bring his pony around the neighborhood. You could dress up, put on a holster and a gun, and sit on the pony while you got your picture taken. That picture of me on the pony stayed up around our home for years. I have seen a similar picture in other homes where I have visited. It still amazes me how far that man and his pony traveled!

Now I travel about in lots of churches and meetings. I am finding new pictures scattered about the country. These are not pictures of little boys and girls dressed up sitting on a pony. The picture is of folks who are dressing up like Christians. The pictures are all the same. They show folks sitting in a pew and getting their picture taken like real Christians, but they are not.

First Peter 4:1 says "Therefore, since Christ suffered for us in the flesh, arm yourselves also with the same mind, for he who has suffered in the flesh has ceased from sin, that he no longer should live the rest of his time in the flesh for the lusts of men, but for the will of God."

The word *arm* means to equip oneself with weapons fit for offensive battle. The battle that we are in determines whether we fulfil the lusts of the flesh or the will of God in our lives. God's preparation for us is the boot camp of suffering. We have as our example, Christ, who suffered the agony of the cross and its ridicule and came forth victorious. We must and can have the same mind set of Jesus. He determined before the battle ensued that He would be yielded to His Father's will. Don't wait for hell's first blast before you make this decision. This is no photo-op! It is war! Arm yourself!

Lord, help me to have Your mind so I can be prepared to fight.

July 13

Walking with God

How would you like for God to hold your hand and walk along with you today? He will! Psalm 37:23 tells us, "The steps of a good man are ordered by the Lord, And He delights in his way." There is here the unseen hand of Providence at work. As one anonymous writer stated it, "Providence: The Hand behind the headlines."

Several years ago I was driving in a terrible storm. Tornadoes had touched down in several places. Hail broke the windshield of the van I was driving. As I made my way cautiously along, I suddenly came upon a large tree that had blown across the highway. I braced myself and leaned over as I careened through the top of the downed tree. When I rose back to an upright position, I was in the middle of the road on the other side of the tree. I had plowed a huge square hole with my van and I had survived.

Later that day one of my customers came by my business. He drove a small auto and told me of a harrowing drive he had that morning on his way to work. He told me that he came upon a tree blown across the highway. It happened so suddenly that he had no way to stop, but to his amazement someone had cut a nice size square hole in the top of the tree. He simply drove through the treetop safely.

I took him out to my damaged vehicle and showed him what had cut the hole. Then I explained to him the providential hand of God at work. When we make our schedule line up with His, then He is delighted to walk with us. He literally bends down and takes note of our steps! The same God that led me through the tree delivered that young man along the same path moments later. Now, whose hand are you holding? The more we trust the sovereignty of heaven, the less we fear the calamities of earth.

Lord, help me align my schedule to Your will for me.

July 14

The Ultimate Makeover

 One of my favorite fairy tales is *Beauty and the Beast*. The story line is simple and predictable, but I still like it. A beautiful maiden is entrapped by an ugly beast. The beast, who really is a prince, was turned into an ugly creature many years before for not helping a passerby. The spell can only be broken if someone falls in love with him and a tear from her face falls upon his. By the end of the tale, the beautiful maiden does love him, spills a tear, and the spell is broken. And as always in these tales, "They lived happily ever after." The End.

Beauty is only skin deep, but in this fairy tale so is ugly. Unfortunately, in our world today it seems that only the beautiful get a chance to prove themselves. How many beautiful people have you seen come to a tragic end, because their beauty was really only skin deep. Our outward appearance means nothing to God. It is His salvation that brings the real beauty to our lives.

All of us, no matter our outward appearance, have hearts that are desperately wicked. "The heart is deceitful above all things, and desperately wicked; who can know it? I, the LORD, search the heart, I test the mind, even to give every man according to his ways, according to the fruit of his doings."~Jeremiah 17:9–10 But God wants to give to us an inward beauty. This beauty is much more than just skin deep and can pierce the ugliness of our souls. "For the Lord takes pleasure in His people; He will beautify the humble with salvation."~Psalms 149:4 The word beautify means to make gleaming; to embellish.

God's mercy is not available for only saving the beautiful...He makes all the saved shine with beauty!

Lord, help me to do a regular self-check on my heart.

July 15

Report Card

Do kids still get a grade in conduct? We did when I was in school! It was an important indicator of why the rest of the report card looked as it did. Conduct is central to the Christian life. It matters how we live out our life in Christ! Timothy was a young man in the ministry. He had been taught by Paul and faced many challenges.

One of those challenges was his youth. Paul encouraged him not to let others judge his character by his age. Character is who we are. Conduct is what we do. But our conduct will reveal our true character. "Let no one despise your youth, but be an example to the believers in word, in conduct, in love, in spirit, in faith, in purity."~1 Timothy 4:12

Paul's instruction to Timothy about being an example through his conduct came from his own personal experience. Paul's conduct in the days before he met Christ on the Damascus Road was in stark contrast to his life as a believer. He had to address his former conduct so that others might know his new character. "For you have heard of my former conduct in Judaism, how I persecuted the church of God beyond measure and tried to destroy it."~Galatians 1:13 The report on Paul was greatly affected by his former conduct and this was important for him to correct.

When a person decides to correct their conduct, there will always be those who will challenge it. They are like the wicked of Psalm 37:14. "The wicked have drawn the sword and have bent their bow, to cast down the poor and needy, to slay those who are of upright conduct." Prayer governs our conduct. Through prayer who we are changes, i.e., our character, and our conduct will follow suit.

Lord, help me be a godly example today.

July 16

I Am Resolved

 I can still hear our music director (these were the days before we had worship leaders) call out number 105. We sang it out of the old *Broadman Hymnal*. Probably some of you are humming the tune already. This was over forty years ago! How you might ask can I still remember this number? We sang it *every* Sunday night! At the time, it seemed a little redundant. There were over 300 hymns in that old book, yet we sang 105 *every* Sunday evening. The song: *I Am Resolved*.

Now, more than forty years later, I can still sing most of the tune from memory. I guess that old music director knew something I didn't way back then. Resolve is not redundancy, yet we reach a point of resolution by repeating over and over the same truths. Resolve means to decide, determine, to distinguish. Redundant means repetition, but it also means duplication so as to prevent from ultimate failure. For example, in a space craft there are multiple redundant systems which serve as backup if one fails. This redundancy builds the resolve of the astronaut to complete the mission. That's what happened in me as we sang number 105 *every* Sunday night. I became more and more resolved to complete this mission God has given me.

Only resolve could bring the Apostle Paul to the place where he could write with strong assurance, "I have fought the good fight, I have finished the race, I have kept the faith."~2 Timothy 4:7 So, let's turn to number 105 and stand as we sing. *I am resolved no longer to linger, charmed by the world's delight, things that are higher, things that are nobler, these have allured my sight. / I am resolved to go to the Savior, leaving my sin and strife; He is the true One, He is the just One, He hath the words of life. / I will hasten to Him, hasten so glad and free; Jesus, Greatest, Highest, I will come to Thee.* (words by Palmer Hartsough)

Lord, help me fight the good fight until the end.

July 17

Don't You Know

There are a lot of things that I don't understand. One in particular comes to mind when I consider my lack of understanding. I don't understand gravity. I just don't get it. How can I be standing upright at the North Pole while another person at the South Pole is standing upright also? Logic tells me that one of us should be falling and since I'm at the North Pole I think it ought to be the other fellow! Since I can't understand gravity, I am not responsible for its consequences, right? I should be able to leap tall buildings in a single bound or walk up the side of a building if I so desired. We both know better! I may not grasp the concept of gravity fully, but I'm still very glad that it has its grasp on me!

Paul uses the phrase *don't you know* 10 times in First Corinthians. Each time there is an understood answer of positive acknowledgment. Paul would not let the Corinthians off the hook by feigning ignorance. Warren Wiersbe said in his book, *Be Determined*, "Some people prefer not to know what's going on, because information might bring obligation. 'What you don't know can't hurt you,' says the old adage; but is it true?" Indeed, I wouldn't apply that adage to the law of gravity!

One instance where Paul uses the *don't you know* phrase is in First Corinthians 3:16, "Do you not know that you are the temple of God and that the Spirit of God dwells in you?" God dwells in believers and makes us His temple, thereby making the temple holy. Ignorance of this will not avoid the consequences of the next verse. "If anyone defiles the temple of God, God will destroy him. For the temple of God is holy, which temple you are."~1 Corinthians 3:17 What hope have we then? The key is found in the verses which precede our text. Our foundation is Christ! The building is secure not because of our righteousness, BUT HIS! Don't you know?

Lord, help me to never forget that my body is Your temple.

July 18

Delivered

 Many people are upset when the scales of justice tilt in what they perceive to be the wrong direction. More than a few times the facts don't seem to line up with the charges brought against someone or the penalty received. It appears too harsh at times and at other times too lenient. When these judgments are doled out and we make our analysis, we can sometimes be very passionate about our opinion.

Let me help you redirect that passion. Be angry at me! I KILLED JESUS! Or at least my sins did. I should have been imprisoned, but I walked free. Jesus paid the entire price of my debt. He paid the penalty for the crime committed against Himself! So, cry injustice towards me for I am truly guilty, yet totally free!

Paul wrestled with this concept of right and wrong even as a believer. Romans 7 deals with this extensively. In verse 18, Paul declares himself guilty, "For I know that in me (that is, in my flesh) nothing good dwells; for to will is present with me, but how to perform what is good I do not find." Paul's guilt as a sinner was based on his very nature, yet he did not use this as a defense as some would today.

His conclusion about his condition was that he was a wretched man. The idea is that of being miserable because a person is unable to be released from certain consequences. He cries out, "O wretched man that I am! Who will deliver me from this body of death?"~Romans 7:24 In Paul's day when a man was convicted of murder, the body of the person killed would be strapped to the murderer and allowed to decay, slowly killing the convict. Thank God for the "who" not the "what" of this verse. Jesus is the One who has delivered us!

Lord, help me to thank You daily for my deliverance.

July 19

Rain Down

A lady approached me in my early days as a pastor with the following story. She told me that a friend of hers had died. She had attended the funeral which happened to take place on a rainy day. Nothing about this was unusual since it occurred in Louisiana where it rains most every day at two o'clock whether you want it to or not. Her last comment as she recounted the day's activity is what really shocked me. She said, "I comforted the family at the grave side with this verse: Blessed are they who are buried in the rain."

I didn't know what to say. She was so convinced by her recitation of this verse that I was sure that I had overlooked this verse. The truth is this verse is not in the Bible. She had quoted it with the best of intentions, but it simply was not scripture. I suppose the family was comforted by the sentiment, but I do hope they never tried to look it up in the Bible!

Another statement often attributed to the Bible is: God helps those who help themselves. Again, like being buried in the rain, this sounds right. It even sounds like something David or Solomon would say in the Psalms or Proverbs, but there is not a verse that even resembles this!

On the contrary Psalm 143:6 tells us, "I spread out my hands to You; my soul longs for You like a thirsty land." We come to the Lord in our deep time of need. The spreading out of the hands is a picture of surrender and agreement as to our emptiness and His endless supply. We can no more provide the answer to our own need than dry ground can rain upon itself. Open your emptiness before Him. Watch Him rain down into your dryness and you will be truly blessed!

Lord, help me to always look to You for my needs to be met.

July 20

Clamoring for Peace

 The world is clamoring to find peace. That's what you call an oxymoron. The word *clamor* means a loud and confused noise. The word *peace* means the freedom from disturbance; tranquility. But the statement is still true: the world is clamoring for peace. Most people are even willing to pay for peace in some form even though it may be temporary.

One entrepreneur has developed a recording of what he calls an album of peace. Each side of the disk has twenty minutes of absolute silence followed by thirty seconds of thunderous applause. The CD sells for five dollars. Imagine people are willing to pay for forty minutes of silence and one minute of applause. Why didn't I think of this?

Peace is such a fragile thing. Even when we are alone it can be difficult to secure peace. But Jesus said, "Peace I leave with you, My peace I give to you; not as the world gives do I give to you. Let not your heart be troubled, neither let it be afraid."~John 14:27 Several truths can be gleaned from this one statement on peace.

First, true peace is not fleeting. Jesus told His disciples I am *leaving* my peace with you. This is a wonderful aspect of this promise of peace. It is always available. Second, this peace is a gift to us. It is not a CD of silence nor do we have to struggle to claim it. God has given it to us deep within our very souls. Finally, Jesus clearly defined His gift of peace as being not of this world. This is important when you consider how easily peace evaporates in our world. Peace accords are always dependent on the parties all keeping their end of the bargain. The world didn't give us this peace and the world can't take it away!

Lord, help me seek true peace from You.

July 21

Feet Planted in Mid-air

So, what's bugging you already today? What worry has crept in or rebounded to bring its cloud to your day? Worry is like fog. It creeps in and reduces visibility. It disrupts normal routine. Planes, cars, and people are affected. Did you know that a fog covering seven blocks if condensed, would not fill an eight ounce glass? Now, would you like to tell me about your worry again?

You may think this too simplistic or that I am making light of your situation. That is not my intent, but I know how much damage worry can do. Someone has said that worry is a canal dug through the mind into which all of our hopes and dreams are drained. When speaking of worry, the Bible uses a strong word, *anxious*. It means to be distracted with care. This word is used in two places: Philippians 4:6 and Luke 12:26.

In Philippians 4:6, Paul says, "Be anxious for nothing, but in everything by prayer and supplication, with thanksgiving, let your requests be made known to God." In Luke's account he records the words of Jesus to his disciples, "If you then are not able to do the least, why are you anxious for the rest?"~Luke 12:26 Jesus' question was relative to the discussion about everyday needs like food and clothing. God feeds the birds and we are of more value than they, so why worry about these things?

It is difficult to accept, but God leaves us no room for worry. As a matter of fact, Jesus continued in His response to the disciples about worry and said, "And do not seek what you should eat or what you should drink, nor have an anxious mind."~Luke 12:29 The phrase *have an anxious mind* in the original language means to be left suspended in mid-air. If you choose to worry the result will be an unsure footing in the midst of your day.

Lord, help me not to worry.

July 22

Just Words

 How many times have I used the wrong words? You don't want to know! Solomon said, "A word fitly spoken is like apples of gold in settings of silver."~Proverbs 25:11 Such words should be spoken in season. Far too many times, we not only use the wrong words, but we miss an opportunity to say the right ones.

Words like these are precious and attractive. They illustrate the importance that words hold for us. This verse is one of thirty-six where the wisest man who ever lived spoke of the use of words. Wilfred Funk, a noted dictionary publisher of the 20th century, suggests the ten most impressive words in the English language. Like Proverbs 25:11 these words are as apples of gold in a silver frame.

> "Alone"—the most bitter word
> "Mother"—the most revered word
> "Death"—the most tragic word
> "Faith"—the most comforting word
> "Forgotten"—the saddest word
> "Love"—the most beautiful word
> "Revenge"—the cruelest word
> "Friendship"—the warmest word
> "No"—the coldest word
> "Tranquility"—the most peaceful word

May all of your words be apples of gold spoken in due season!

Lord, help me to speak words worth framing.

July 23

God at Work

Have you ever heard someone called a piece of work? Most of the time it is used negatively, but Shakespeare used the phrase to describe how much men were likened unto angels or deity. "What piece of work is a man, how noble in reason, how infinite in faculties, in form and moving, how express and admirable in action, how like an angel in apprehension, how like a god!"

From the Garden of Eden, we hear God saying that he would make man in the image of God. Certainly not the physical image since scripture plainly teaches that God is Spirit. Instead, God made us like unto Himself in several ways. He created us as a triune being. As God is Father, Son, and Holy Spirit, God made man as body, soul, and spirit. God gave man free will and in doing so gave man the ability to choose. Before sin entered the world, God made man eternal as He is eternal and willed that man would have eternal life. Man still is eternal, but that eternity can be spent either in heaven or hell. These are but a few of our likenesses to the Creator.

Like Adam, I know how far I fall from being the piece of work God intends of me, but I will hold to His promise in Psalms 138:8, "The LORD will perfect that which concerns me; Your mercy, O LORD, endures forever; do not forsake the works of Your hands." I am a piece of work that is still being molded and shaped into perfection. There will be times that God will need to break me and taking the pieces in His hands reshape me again into His image.

God performs this under the parameters of His own mercy which endures as He does forever. We are the work of His hands...a piece of work being formed into His image.

Lord, help me to yield my life to Your molding.

211

July 24

He Keeps His Word

 There was a time that a man's handshake was all that was needed. It was symbolic of a signed promissory note. My father told me a story once about borrowing some money from a man that he knew. The gentleman told my dad that the money would be left on the porch swing the next day in front of his house in a brown paper bag. Repayment was to be made the same way.

Each month my father would go to the man's home, put that month's payment in a bag and leave it on the swing. No stack of paper. No one claiming that they did not understand the fine print. Just two men making agreement with a handshake.

It would be nice if things were that way still, but I'm not holding my breath. We can have a word of promise from God, however, that is as valid as a handshake between gentlemen. Hear this description of the God we serve. "God is not a man, that He should lie, nor a son of man, that He should repent. Has He said, and will He not do? Or has He spoken, and will He not make it good?"~Numbers 23:19

For my dad and his friend, a bag and a swing was the place where the promise was kept. For us, it is the word of God in a book called the Bible. Our God has never failed to keep His word. Paul declared God faithful to keep His word because He is our God "...who cannot lie..."~Titus 1:2 I will fail you. Others may fail you. But God is faithful to keep His word. What a joy to have a word from Him who never changes and always follows through on His promise. Rest not until you have a word from God!

Lord, help me to always take You at your word.

July 25

Profit Motive

Profit holds a special allure to many people. The commercial may be advertising a myriad of schemes, but the catch is always the same: high profit. It may be selling some mass-merchandise item or buying a new franchise. The motive is profit. It may be a weight loss plan, but the motive is still how much weight you will loss, thereby, profiting from the sacrifice of food and exertion of exercise.

There is nothing inherently wrong with profit. No one says I'm going into business to lose a lot of money! Even during the days of Jesus' ministry here on earth, profit was a powerful motive. Jesus asked an important question based on profit motive. "For what profit is it to a man if he gains the whole world, and loses his own soul?"~Matthew 16:26 Profit has its place in our motives, but pales when measured against eternity.

As Jesus was teaching his disciples about offending others and their response to offenses, the disciples concluded that they needed Jesus to increase their faith (Luke 17:5) Jesus responded with a parable. "And which of you, having a servant plowing or tending sheep, will say to him when he has come in from the field, 'Come at once and sit down to eat'? But will he not rather say to him, 'Prepare something for my supper, and gird yourself and serve me till I have eaten and drunk, and afterward you will eat and drink'? Does he thank that servant because he did the things that were commanded him? I think not. So likewise you, when you have done all those things which you are commanded, say, 'We are unprofitable servants. We have done what was our duty to do.'"~Luke 17:7-10

All the servant did was the minimum required! Are you trying to figure out how little it takes to please God? Decide today to turn a profit for the King!

Lord, help me to be profitable to You and Your kingdom.

July 26

You Can't Google It

 William Randolph Hearst, was a collector of rare art and spent a great deal of money for his collection. One day he found a description of an artwork that he felt he must own, so he sent his agent abroad to find it. After months of searching, the agent reported that he had found the treasured object and surprisingly it was close to home. It was already in Hearst's warehouse, with many other treasures he owned!

Sometimes the hardest place to find what we are searching for is the spot right in front of us. It is what happens when we search for our glasses and they are on our face. We simply look right through them. Jeremiah tells us in Lamentations 3:40-41, "Let us search out and examine our ways, and turn back to the Lord; let us lift our hearts and hands to God in heaven."

Our way can turn wrong. The amazing thing is that we can be on the wrong path and not know it. To correct this we must turn back to the Lord. Jeremiah's word to us is that we must begin this process of turning back by searching our present way. This search could be overwhelming were it not for heaven's help. Without God's answer to our predicament, it would be like searching the Internet without Google, Yahoo, or another search engine. The way of our return is available to us if we search for it diligently and then turn back to the Lord.

Have you lost your way? Are you searching to find your way back into fellowship with the Lord? You won't be able to google the answer to this question. Simply lift your heart and hands toward heaven and you will be on the right path again.

Lord, help me to someone the way to find You today.

July 27

I'm Telling!

How much easier would it be to seek God's answer if we had the understanding of Job? Job said, "But as for me, I would seek God, and to God I would commit my cause—Who does great things, and unsearchable, marvelous things without number."~Job 5:8-9

You can learn several things about telling God your concerns as you hear Job's response to the tragedies he had faced. His first action was to seek God and commit his cause to Him. In essence, Job was saying, "I'm gonna tell God about this!" If you have ever had something bad happen to you, you know how we take comfort sometimes in repeating the story to others. The word *commit* in these verses means to rehearse or say over again. Quit spending time rehearsing your story to people who can't help you. Job said, "But as for me, I would seek God."

What assurance did Job have as he ran to God with his problems? He had the record of God's accomplishments. He recounted not only his troubles, but rehearsed God's triumphs. He saw God as One who had done great things that were beyond comprehension. Not only had God acted in the past, He had acted with such regularity that the occasions were without number. This was no once in a lifetime, limited opportunity for God to help. This was God's pattern! Never limit your asking because you have a poor understanding of God's ability to answer!

Like the old hymn says, Tell it to Jesus, tell it to Jesus, He is a friend that's well-known; you've no other such a friend or brother, tell it to Jesus alone. The next time the devil picks on you inform him, "I'm telling God on you!"

Lord, help me to tell You first.

July 28

Learning Contentment

 I heard a story once about two teardrops that were floating down the river of life. One teardrop asked the other, "Who are you?" "I am a teardrop from a girl who loved a man and lost him. But who are you?" The first teardrop replied, "I am a teardrop from the girl who got him."

Life can be so much like this story. We cry over the things we can't have, but we might really weep if we had received them.

Paul suffered many trials after he came to know Christ as his Savior. He listed some of those things in Second Corinthians 11 and in other places throughout his writings. Now in prison, he writes to the Philippians, "Not that I speak in regard to need, for I have learned in whatever state I am, to be content."~Philippians 4:11 BE CONTENT! Here was a man stuck in prison under trumped up charges and he was content! How is this possible?

The idea here is to be self-conscious of sufficiency. To know that when you are lacking it is enough and when you are in abundance you need no more. Most of us will probably never suffer all that Paul suffered for the gospel. Amazingly, however, it is the abundance part that carries the most danger. It seems that we are always wanting the next blessing so badly that we miss the joy of the present one.

This ability to be content in *every* circumstance does not come by infusion, It comes by daily instruction. Paul had to learn to be content. The word *learn* means to be instructed through experience and apply the knowledge gained by reflection. So which teardrop are you?

Lord, help me to be content in all things.

July 29

Looking Like Jesus

As Stephen felt each blow upon his body he slowly succumbed to the effect of being stoned to death. He was marking a place in history as the church's first martyr. Just a few hours before the council had saw his face as that of an angel. As he gazed toward heaven he told his executioners, "Look! I see the heavens opened and the Son of Man standing at the right hand of God!"~Acts 7:56

I wonder if it was his words that caused the next scene to transpire or the fact that he had the glow of Jesus on his face. "And they stoned Stephen as he was calling on God and saying, 'Lord Jesus, receive my spirit.' Then he knelt down and cried out with a loud voice, 'Lord, do not charge them with this sin.' And when he had said this, he fell asleep."~Acts 7:59-60

The story is told of a pagan tribe who worshiped a stone god that had been carved into the face of a cliff. A young boy became enamored with this stone god and committed his life to sit daily before it for hours. Decades passed as he spent his days before a false god. One day as he came down the mountain the villagers cried out that their god had come to visit them in the flesh. The boy had spent so long in the presence of the carving that he had taken on the characteristics of the cliff face.

Surely this is how it was with Stephen. Acts 6 says that he was a man full of faith and the Holy Spirit. He had spent so much time with Jesus that his face glowed with His likeness. Our faces will always reflect that upon which we gaze. This brought great conviction on this crowd and even as they had killed the Savior, they killed this man who reminded them of Jesus. Keep looking at Jesus and you will look like Jesus!

Lord, help me forgive like Jesus.

July 30

Behold The Lamb!

 A man was climbing a mountain on his way to worship at the mountaintop chapel. Steep was the climb and with great effort he made each step. Looking over his shoulder, he noticed another man coming along the same path just behind him. The man carried a large burden on his shoulder. Turning around he thought to assist the man would be the "Christian" thing to do. As he looked into the face of the man carrying the burden, he was surprised to see that it was Jesus!

"Are you carrying the sins of the world in this great bundle?" he asked with sympathy and concern.
"No," said Jesus, "Only yours!"

When John the Baptist saw Jesus coming to the river for baptism, he told those gathered, "Behold! The Lamb of God, that takes away the sin of the world!"~John 1:29 What a bold statement for John to make! Up until this time, Israel had offered sacrifices to *cover* their sin, but now John claimed that a Lamb had come to *take them away!*

The same John who wrote the gospel also penned the words of the three epistles named for him. In the first of those three letters, he said, "And He Himself is the propitiation for our sins, and not for ours only but also for the whole world."~1 John 2:2 The word *propitiation* is not one that we use regularly. It means atonement. Christ was the atonement for our sins. Someone broke the word *atonement* into three parts to describe what atonement creates between God and us—at one ment. Do you see it? We are made at one with God because Jesus took our burden of sin on Himself! When we truly see Jesus carrying the burden of sin we only see ours upon His back, though He carries the sins of the whole world in truth.

Lord, help me rest in Your atonement.

July 31

Measuring Up

One of the problems of walking on the moon (I am told this; haven't
been there lately myself!) is that perspective is lost. There is nothing to
make comparison to in arriving at correct height, depth, or distance.
On earth we have obstacles: trees, buildings, etc. These give us
perspective. I can see how small I really am when I stand next to a
towering oak or a skyscraper, for example.

When you lose perspective I would recommend standing next to Jesus. He is the
measure of the fullness of the Godhead. "...till we all come to the unity of the
faith and of the knowledge of the Son of God, to a perfect man, to the measure
of the stature of the fullness of Christ..."~Ephesians 4:13
All will be brought into focus as we draw nigh to Him!

Near to my home is the statue that is called "Christ of the Ozarks." This statue
of cast concrete stands over 65 feet high and is the sixth tallest statue in the
United States. As you approach the statue your perceived height shrinks away
quickly. Standing next to it puts everything into perspective for me.

Without such a structure to make comparison to the Apostle Paul speaks of the
stature of the fullness of Christ being the hallmark of our perfection or maturity.
We know we have arrived when we attain such a measure. This is important to
Paul's discussion of our Christian maturity. The fact that he used the word *measure*
helps us to understand that our growth and maturity is not something abstract,
but tangible. It can be measured, but always against the standard of the
completeness of Christ. "For in Him dwells all the fullness of the Godhead
bodily; and you are complete in Him, who is the head of all principality and
power."~Colossians 2:9–10

Let's quit measuring up to one another and let Christ be the standard!

Lord, help me to measure myself rightly.

August 1

Press On!

 One of my favorite Civil War movies is, *Gods and Generals*. As much as Robert E. Lee is revered by many, I am always touched by the life of Thomas J. "Stonewall" Jackson. The scene of his death in this movie is one that demonstrates a faith that carried him through life and death alike.

The chief surgeon of Jackson's Corps, Dr. Hunter Holmes McGuire, recorded Jackson's final words. A few moments before death, Jackson cried out in delirium: "Order A. P. Hill to prepare for action! Pass the infantry to the front rapidly! Tell Major Hawks..." In the midst of these "battlefield" orders, Jackson suddenly grew silent. Holmes reported that "a smile of ineffable sweetness" came over Jackson's pale face, and then a look of relief. These last words were then quietly spoken: "Let us cross over the river, and rest under the shade of the trees."

Oh, to press on even through death. This same determination of faith was seen in the Apostle Paul. He recorded his commitment to press on in Philippians 3:14, "I press toward the goal for the prize of the upward call of God in Christ Jesus." Never be satisfied with your present position of faith. Paul said, "I press on toward the goal." He was pursuing the goal; moving energetically toward it. Paul like Stonewall Jackson did not shrink back from the upward call. Johnson Oatman, Jr. wrote these words as the chorus of the old familiar hymn *Higher Ground*:

Lord, lift me up and let me stand,
By faith, on Heaven's tableland,
A higher plane than I have found;
Lord, plant my feet on higher ground.

PRESS ON!

Lord, help me to press on to higher ground.

August 2

Follow Me!

A man sitting on his front porch noticed a boy dragging a logging chain along the road. Calling out to the boy, he asked, "Why are you dragging that chain son?" The boy never broke stride and responded, "Have you ever tried pushing a chain?" So it is with leadership. Those following are like the links of a chain. Each is integrally connected, but each link must lead the one following it. No link has the ability to push another.

True leaders seem to be few and far between, but the truth is we are all leaders. No one has the privilege of just following. Twenty times in the gospels Jesus said, "Follow Me!" He used this simple command in calling James and John, "Then He said to them, 'Follow Me, and I will make you fishers of men.'"~Matthew 4:19 He called Matthew with the same two words, "As Jesus passed on from there, He saw a man named Matthew sitting at the tax office. And He said to him, 'Follow Me.' So he arose and followed Him."~Matthew 9:9

If you will be a great leader then follow the greatest Leader: JESUS! He led by the example of servanthood. In John 13 Jesus washed the feet of the disciples and set the precedent of service (John 13:15). His leadership was never by coercion, but always through cooperation. As a leader, He was always preparing the followers for His departure and in doing so prepared them to do greater things than He had done (John 14:12).

You are a leader. Someone is following you, be it a child, a spouse, a co-worker, a friend, or neighbor. There is no way to avoid leadership, however, there is a way to avoid poor leadership. Dwight D. Eisenhower said, "You do not lead by hitting people over the head—that's assault, not leadership." Can you say to someone in your circle of influence, "Follow me!" Take a moment in your quiet time today and ask God to reveal to you your followers. Then lead like Jesus!

Lord, help me follow You.

August 3

True Love

 Two hundred years ago the encyclopedia contained a four line discussion of the word atom and a five page discussion of the word love. Today you will find five pages on the atom and the word love has been omitted entirely. The world simply does not understand the power of love when it is unleashed. Love has fallen on the wayside because its definition has been compromised. Today a person will use the word love and direct it towards anything and everything. The problem is just that. *Things* are the focus of our love because these things benefit us. There is little to no requirement on our part. Paul said, "Let love be without hypocrisy. Abhor what is evil. Cling to what is good."~Romans 12:9 Paul admonished that love needed to be sincere. A hypocritical love is one that tries to cover its deficiencies and look like the real thing when it is not.

In Middle Eastern countries porcelain figurines would sometimes crack during the firing. Dishonest merchants would disguise the cracks with wax. Merchants who sold quality merchandise would mark their wares with two Latin words which translate into English as sincere, literally "without wax." This is what Paul meant when he said that love needed to be without hypocrisy. He meant that it should be sincere.

As followers of Christ, we are known to the world by our love for one another. Paul described this sincere love in the verses 10-13 in this same chapter. Love is to be of brotherly quality, serving quality, and a proven quality. Paul concludes his thoughts on love by saying that we should be "given to hospitality" (Romans 12:13). The word *hospitality* means stranger loving.

As believers let's put the word *love* back in the book. Do a love inventory in your life and make sure that there are no cracks being covered with wax. Be sincere in your love–the world knows when you are.

Lord, help me to be sincere in my love for others.

August 4

Have You Been with Jesus?

A committee of ministers in a certain city was discussing the possibility of having Evangelist D. L. Moody preach during a city-wide evangelistic campaign. One young minister who did not want to invite Moody stood up and asked, "Why Moody? Does he have a monopoly of the Holy Spirit?" There was silence. Then an old, godly minister spoke up: "No, he does not have a monopoly of the Holy Spirit; but the Holy Spirit has a monopoly of D. L. Moody."

The early disciples were noted as men, "that had been with Jesus." (Acts 4:13) These men had no formal education. They were fishermen who had followed Jesus and were now boldly giving testimony concerning Him. They were also the same men who a few days earlier had fled at the sign of trouble. Peter had even cursed the name of Jesus in denial. But on this day 5000 men had come to know Christ and the whole city wanted to know how this was possible.

How will people know that you have been with Jesus? Acts 4 gives us several indicators. First, there will be the evidence of boldness. This boldness is only possible when, like D.L. Moody, the Holy Spirit has a monopoly on you. A professor gave a physics class a project of removing all of the air from a drinking glass. The class came up with all sorts of procedures for removing the air, but the professor demonstrated the simplest way to do so. He took the glass and filled it with water. Voila! All of the air was removed. When we are filled with the Holy Spirit all of us is removed and great boldness is always the evidence of this.

Second, the people saw the transformed lives of these men. A changed life is the best advertisement. Standing with the disciples was a man who days before had been a lame beggar. His changed life could not be denied. We are all lame in some way, but the power of Jesus can change our walk. If you've been with Jesus it will show up in your talk and your walk. Now, have you been with Jesus?

Lord, help me to advertise a life that has been changed.

August 5

Priming the Pump

 A man's vehicle broke down on a country road. He walked to a farm house and discovered no one lived there. Inside he saw an old pump mounted on a sink. The door was open, so he went in to cool his thirst. He could not get any water from the pump, but noticed a jar of water on the window sill. A note attached said, "Pour this down the pump and you will receive cool fresh water in return." His thirst almost made him drink the jar of water, but he obeyed the note. After a few more pumps of the handle, cool refreshing water flowed. He refilled the jar and wrote a postscript to the note: "Praise God! Do It! It works!"

There are just some days that our lives need a little priming. Like an old pump that will only bring up rusty, stale air, our lives need to be primed afresh with a reminder of what God has done for us so we can bless His Name. "Bless the LORD, O my soul; and all that is within me, bless His holy name! Bless the LORD, O my soul, and forget not all His benefits: Who forgives all your iniquities, Who heals all your diseases, Who redeems your life from destruction, Who crowns you with loving kindness and tender mercies, Who satisfies your mouth with good things, so that your youth is renewed like the eagle's."~Psalm 103:1–5

Here's a list of things that God has already primed your life with so you can bless His name like the man who rejoiced over a jar of water in a window sill. We can bless the Lord for His benefits–how He has treated us in the past. We can bless the Lord for His forgiveness–how He has forgotten our past. We can bless the Lord for His healing–how He has remedied our past. We can bless the Lord for His redemption–how He paid for our past. We can bless the Lord for His mercy– how He made Jesus suffer for our past. We can bless the Lord for His goodness– how He satisfies our past. We can bless the Lord for His renewal–how He takes us out of our past. Yes, once our pumps are primed we can see our blessings and be a blessing! And out of us shall flow cool, refreshment for others!

Lord, help me be a refreshment to someone I meet today.

August 6

Drink Deeply

The more arid area of the western United States has trees, but the lack of water causes them to be small and gnarly compared to ones planted near good water and soil. Where there is a ready source of water the trees grow large like the oaks of the Deep South. So the Psalmist speaks of the man of God in Psalms 1:3, "He shall be like a tree planted by the rivers of water that brings forth its fruit in its season, whose leaf also shall not wither; and whatever he does shall prosper."

A mature oak tree with deep roots and a plentiful source of water can drink over fifty gallons a day. Its leaves, twigs, and branches will prosper under these conditions. Like a tree filling itself with water, the believer is filled with God's word. And like a tree producing fruit in its season because of perfect conditions, the believer will bring forth fruit by the perfect word of God.

A prospering believer will be filled with several characteristics. He will be filled with a delight for God's word. He will be filled with a desire to meditate in God's word. He will be filled with the hope of God's word. He will be filled with the abundant fruitfulness of God's word. He will be filled with the beauty of God's word. He will be filled with success by God's word.

It may be a time of drought in your life today, but do not despair. God has planted you where you are. Wait for the refreshing rains to come and then drink deeply. Soon your withered branches will lift and new leaves will burst forth. "Repent therefore and be converted, that your sins may be blotted out, so that times of refreshing may come from the presence of the Lord."~Acts 3:19

Lord, help me to wait for the rain so I can grow where I'm planted.

August 7

Without Complaining

 I read the fictitious account of Matthew Arnold's death. Someone said that he died from a weakness caused by complaining. At his funeral a neighbor quipped, "Poor Matthew, he always complained about everything. I'm sure that he won't like God!" Nothing ruins a witness like complaining.

Gary Preston, in his book, *Character Forged from Conflict*, tells this story:
[O]ne lady never seemed fully satisfied with anything I did. Seldom would she tell me directly of her displeasure; I usually heard it through an intermediary source. I met with her and told her, "I'm unable to live up to your standards of performance and expectations for my ministry. I feel as though I can't please you." I told her that since I couldn't, I was going to stop trying..."So you won't mind if I no longer concern myself with pleasing you with every action and decision?" She said she wouldn't. That took the pressure off and diffused some of her constant complaining.

There really is no place for complaining in the Christian life, though I must confess that I am one of the best complainers at times. It just seems easier to complain than to do something about the situation. Hear Paul's words to the Philippians: "Do all things without complaining and disputing, that you may become blameless and harmless, children of God without fault in the midst of a crooked and perverse generation..."~Philippians 2:14–15

God leaves no room for complaining. He said through the Apostle that we are to do *all* things without complaining. This means without grumbling and murmuring. The result...that you may be without blame and harm in the midst of this generation." Complaining never impresses the lost world in which we live. Don't be like poor Matthew!

Lord, help me stop all of my complaining.

August 8

Barely Saved

Many times I have barely escaped tragedy: the near miss, the slipping knife, the foul ball sailing past my head, and a myriad of other examples. I read a story once of a little girl who had been barely rescued from a fire. A passerby saw her stranded on the ledge of an upper floor window sill. He climbed an iron drain pipe and brought her down to safety. The man disappeared into the watching crowd. Her parents were both killed in the flames of that burning house.

Months later the court had convened to determine who would care for this child since there was no relative to take her into their care. Many came forward, but none were found to be acceptable to the judge. On the last day of the court's deliberation, the door of the courtroom opened quietly. An unassuming gentleman stepped forward claiming that he would care for this orphaned child. When the judge asked him of his qualifications, the man lifted two burned hands toward the judge and child. Case closed!

My salvation is the result of a near miss like Joshua of Zechariah 3 when God said, "Is this not a brand plucked from the fire?" As Joshua stood with the Lord, Satan came to accuse as he always does the believer. But God the righteous Judge rebuked Satan and declared Joshua saved from the fire as a twig plucked from the flames. And there was the Angel of the Lord, Jesus Himself, lifting high two nailed scarred hands.

Oh, how God can deliver! Even from the flames, He can pluck us out of danger and eternal doom! Every believer is the picture of a near miss. The hands of Jesus are wounded to show that He is our Deliverer and Savior!

Lord, help me never forget how close I was to being lost forever.

August 9

Stop Squirming

Many years ago when my children were still very young, we took a vacation which included a stop at Ruby Falls outside of Chattanooga, Tennessee. My second daughter was still in a stroller at that time. We purchased our tickets and joined a group that was headed into the cavern. The guide then informed everyone with children that strollers were not allowed along the trail leading down to Ruby Falls. I was still young, so I saw no problem. My toddler daughter, however, was not interested in stalactites, stalagmites, or rocks shaped like curtains or dinosaurs. She fell asleep in the first few minutes and I spent the next one and one-half hours carrying her in my arms.

As tiring as this was, any parent will tell you that there is something far worse than carrying a sleeping child. How many of you as a parent have said to a child, "STOP SQUIRMING!" My hand's up...how about yours? A squirmer can wear a parent down in no time. First Peter 5:6 says, "Therefore humble yourselves under the mighty hand of God, that He may exalt you in due time..." The word *hand* can best be described as the hollow of the hand. STOP SQUIRMING! God's intent is to protect until the perfect time. Then He will lift you up and out! STOP SQUIRMING!

As long as we are squirming we are not humbled in His hand. Which is really trusting you to hold them: a squirming or a sleeping child? As tired as I was carrying my sleeping daughter, I was in total control and she was in total trust. First Peter 5:7 gives us the evidence of fully resting in His hand. "Cast all your care upon Him, for He cares for you." Squirming keeps us from laying our burden totally on Him. Trust lets us rest in Him.

Do it now! Fling your frailty upon His frame! He'll carry you!

Lord, help me not to squirm so much.

August 10

Lacking One Thing

A few years ago I was diagnosed with pernicious anemia. This malady is caused not by contracting some infection or virus, but by your body lacking a vital property called the intrinsic factor. This factor allows the absorption of B_{12} into the body. The lack of the intrinsic factor causes the anemia to develop. I had no idea that I had this lack in my chemistry. It showed up in a routine checkup where the doctor ordered a total blood analysis. I thought I was just fine.

My diagnosis gave me something in common with the rich young ruler of Mark's gospel. He thought everything was in place for him to obtain everlasting life, but he lacked one thing. "Now as He was going out on the road, one came running, knelt before Him, and asked Him, 'Good Teacher, what shall I do that I may inherit eternal life?' Then Jesus, looking at him, loved him, and said to him, 'One thing you lack: Go your way, sell whatever you have and give to the poor, and you will have treasure in heaven; and come, take up the cross, and follow Me.'"~Mark 10:17,21 This young man came with his best foot forward. He called Jesus a good man. He had the list of commandments he had kept since a child to flash in the face of the Teacher. All he needed was validation of his religious health and he would be set for eternity, but then the report came back with the bad news: One thing you lack!

But Jesus loved him and gave him the answer to his condition: Go and sell all you have, give it to the poor, take up your cross, and follow me. The rich young ruler decided not to follow the orders of the Great Physician, however, and "...he was sad at this word, and went away sorrowful, for he had great possessions."~Mark 10:22 What's keeping you from following Jesus? Don't go away sad...

Lord, help me to be always willing to do what You ask of me.

August 11

Down to Size

 On a windswept hill in an English country churchyard stands an obscure slate tombstone. The faint wording reads:

BENEATH THIS STONE, A LUMP OF CLAY
LIES ARABELLA YOUNG,
WHO, ON THE TWENTY-FOURTH OF MAY,
BEGAN TO HOLD HER TONGUE.

I certainly hope this would not be my epitaph. It is only natural to try to get even sometimes, but as believers we are not natural! We are empowered by God's presence to do that which is supernatural. We probably use our tongues as a weapon more that our fists. When we are harmed by someone who speaks harshly against us, we can quickly put our mouths into gear and seek retribution.

The snail is a very interesting creature. It has teeth on its tongue! If you were to examine the snail's tongue under a microscope you would count as many as 30,000 teeth. The snail keeps his toothy tongue rolled up like a ribbon, until it is needed; then he thrusts it out and uses the tongue like a saw blade. With its tongue a snail can cut through leaves and stems with ease. We use language that seems to be based on a snail's tongue when we talk about cutting someone down to size.

Perhaps this is what Peter was thinking when he wrote these words, "Never give back evil for evil, or reviling for reviling, but on the contrary, giving blessing, knowing that you are called to this so that you might inherit blessing."~1 Peter 3:9 Give blessing (commendation) and inherit blessing (a good word). That will be in a word: Well done!

Lord, help me to hold my tongue.

August 12

God's Reflection

As a youngster in the early 1960's, playing the part of an astronaut was pure joyful fantasy. I turned the swing that hung from an a-frame in our yard into a Gemini space capsule. From there I could force the swing back into the same reclining position that the astronauts took, go through the countdown, "look" down on Earth from my playtime space, and make a safe re-entry.

As astronauts enter their capsules mounted atop huge rockets, you will always see the technicians dressed in clothing that looks more like surgical attire than anything else. They wear face masks and gloves to make sure that no impurities get into the capsule that would make an astronaut ill during his journey or foul up some part of the equipment.

God also desires a purified people. Purification comes by fire. It's not a process of pitting our wills against ourselves until we morph into purity. PURITY COSTS! Something has to be lost so that all remaining looks like Jesus. Psalms 66:10 tells us, "For You, O God, have tested us; You have refined us as silver is refined."

The silversmith will take solid silver and place it in a vat over a source of extreme heat. His intent is not to sooth the metal or to relax it with warmth. He will apply the heat until the metal's very character changes. The silversmith will then begin a process of dredging the surface of the liquified metal. As it boils and writhes under the intense heat, impurities are released. These particles are lighter than the metal and they float to the top where a skimmer is used to remove them. This process continues until the worker sees a reflection of himself in the surface of the silver. May God see His reflection today as He looks into your life!

Lord, help me to lay aside all that doesn't look like You.

August 13

It Can't Hurt

 It never hurts to ask is a common phrase that is used when we have a need and we are not sure that an answer will come. We openly use this concept when seeking help from another person, but do we sometimes use this thought when we pray?

I'm not talking about praying as a last resort. You see, the answer to your prayer begins with the asking. Your prayer asked in His will and couched in the power of Christ's name is answered in heaven at the moment of asking. "And whatever you ask in My name, that I will do, that the Father may be glorified in the Son. If you ask anything in My name, I will do it."~John 14:13-14

Remember, however, that the appearance of the answer on earth does not always coincide with the asking. "Ask, and it will be given to you; seek, and you will find; knock, and it will be opened to you. For everyone who asks receives, and he who seeks finds, and to him who knocks it will be opened."~Matthew 7:7-8 The words, *ask, seek,* and *knock* all are in the present active. This means that we are to keep on asking, seeking, and knocking. We are to be actively waiting for the announcement of the answer to our asking, seeking, and knocking.

Jesus has full intention on answering our prayers. "Ask, and you will receive, that your joy may be full."~John 16:24 He is waiting for us to ask not with the questioning attitude of it can't hurt, but with the full assurance that He desires to answer us and full up our joy.

Lord, help me ask.

August 14

At Home with Jesus

In the South we say things like, "Get down!" We don't mean *get down* like you are a sniper target. Nor do we mean that you are able to do some fancy dance moves. What we mean is to open your car door and exit your vehicle! I guess it's a left over from the days when folks rode a horse and buggy to the neighbor's house.

We also say, "Come in! Make yourself at home!" This phrase isn't all that it sounds like it is saying either. What we mean is that you are welcome to come into my house and make yourself at home as long as you can do so from the proximity of the couch while keeping one hand on the coffee table. We have no intent of you taking liberties with the "make yourself at home" part of that greeting.

Jesus visited the Simon's house and received a poor welcome. Luke writes, "Then He turned to the woman and said to Simon, 'Do you see this woman? I entered your house; you gave Me no water for My feet, but she has washed My feet with her tears and wiped them with the hair of her head. You gave Me no kiss, but this woman has not ceased to kiss My feet since the time I came in. You did not anoint My head with oil, but this woman has anointed My feet with fragrant oil. Therefore I say to you, her sins, which are many, are forgiven, for she loved much. But to whom little is forgiven, the same loves little.'"~Luke 7:44–47

Simon offered Jesus none of the customary courtesies given to guests. It was a woman who most likely was a prostitute that offered to Jesus what Simon should have gladly given. We should never need to say to Jesus, "Make Yourself at home."Not only should He be welcomed into our homes, but He should have full range in every part of our lives. We have been forgiven much and like this woman in Luke's account we should gladly be washing the feet of Jesus. May Christ always be at home in your life.

Lord, help me to make You at home in my life.

August 15

No Obituary Needed

 Remember this old chorus: "I'm gonna live forever; I'm gonna die no never..." Mark Twain probably wished he would have known these words as he read his own obituary in the *New York Journal*. Someone had mistakenly received word of Twain's death and ran the obituary. His response was classic Mark Twain, "The reports of my death have been greatly exaggerated." I'm not sure I would enjoy reading my own obituary, but truthfully we are all writing our own day by day. I hope mine will include at least the true facts that I haven't really died. For as a believer, "I'm gonna live forever!"

The words of Peter give us a theological base for the truth of living forever. He quotes the words of Isaiah the prophet as he connects the eternal quality of God's word to the life of the believer. "...having been born again, not of corruptible seed but incorruptible, through the word of God which lives and abides forever, because

> *'All flesh is as grass,*
> *And all the glory of man as the flower of the grass.*
> *The grass withers,*
> *And its flower falls away,*
> *But the word of the* LORD *endures forever...'* "~1 Peter 1:23-25

As lives the word, so live I. I have been born again through the word of God. Peter's quote of the Isaiah passage makes it clear that physical death will happen, and may I say, quicker than we are planning. But he has surrounded the words about dying with two phrases. The first, *the word of God which lives and abides forever.* The second, *but the word of the* LORD *endures forever.* Those two phrases made very good pall bearers! By the way, the reports of my death have been greatly exaggerated!

Lord, help me live like I'm going to live forever.

August 16

The Baby Sitter

Our five senses give us the ability to receive, respond, and react to the world in which we live. A newborn has all of these senses, but we all have seen that a baby cannot use those senses well.

In John 16 Jesus spoke to the "baby" disciples and said He was leaving soon. Their response was very childlike. They were filled with sorrow and concern. "'But now I go away to Him who sent Me, and none of you asks Me, 'Where are You going?' But because I have said these things to you, sorrow has filled your heart.'"~John 16:5–6

Because of their fear, He promised to send the Holy Spirit who would teach them all things. (John 16:13) The Holy Spirit acts as our spiritual sense so we might receive, respond, and react to the spiritual world that is more real than that which our five senses can detect. The ministry of the Holy Spirit is much like that of a baby sitter. (Do not take this analogy too far. God does not intend for us to remain as children, but to mature into Christians who can sit, walk, and stand on our own.) The sitter must not only take care of the child, but follow explicitly the wishes of the parent.

Jesus told His disciples they should follow the instructions of the Helper He was sending in His place, because "...when He, the Spirit of truth, has come, He will guide you into all truth; for He will not speak on His own authority, but whatever He hears He will speak; and He will tell you things to come. He will glorify Me, for He will take of what is Mine and declare it to you. All things that the Father has are Mine. Therefore I said that He will take of Mine and declare it to you."~John 16:13–15 Wait today for the Promised One! He will guide you into all truth!

Lord, help me to wait for the Spirit's leading.

235

August 17

Bigger Plans

 Many of you know the story of the Macedonian Call. Be refreshed as you read this account. "Now when they had gone through Phrygia and the region of Galatia, they were forbidden by the Holy Spirit to preach the word in Asia. After they had come to Mysia, they tried to go into Bithynia, but the Spirit did not permit them. So passing by Mysia, they came down to Troas. And a vision appeared to Paul in the night. A man of Macedonia stood and pleaded with him, saying, 'Come over to Macedonia and help us.' Now after he had seen the vision, immediately we sought to go to Macedonia, concluding that the Lord had called us to preach the gospel to them."~Acts 16:6–10

We often focus on the call itself, but what of God placing Paul so he could hear the call? Paul was attempting to go in another direction. The Holy Spirit directed him to Troas instead and there the vision came. This action of God placing His servants in just the right place to hear Him speak is repeated over and again throughout scripture. Why is this so important? Couldn't Paul have preached Jesus in one of these other places just as well?

Of course, the answer is yes, but God had a purpose that was bigger than Paul's plan. By going to help the man of Macedonia, the gospel was introduced to the continent of Europe. Without his hearing God through this vision and obeying God in going to Macedonia, the gospel would not have come to America and finally found most of us.

Is God waiting to speak to you? Get to the place He appoints and stay until you hear from Him! Then, watch the doors swing open for ministry. You may never see the full results of your obedience, but God has a plan bigger than yours or mine.

Lord, help me to listen for Your plan to be revealed.

August 18

Shelter in the Time of the Storm

Growing up in south Louisiana, I have been through a few hurricanes. Even though I did not live directly on the coast, we were close enough that we felt the full fury of the storm. I can still remember hurricanes like Hilda, Betsy, and Andrew. Everyone who has the slightest access to news will remember Hurricane Katrina and the devastation it caused in New Orleans and across the Gulf Coast.

These storms show us the absolute power of our sovereign Lord. The aftermath always makes us shake our heads in disbelief that what takes man years to build, a few minutes of a storm can erase. Even more amazing are the stories of survival that come from the rubble of destruction. Even those who choose not to flee in the face of the storm survive sometimes. But often they and others lose their lives in the sheer magnitude of the wind and waves.

I have spent a few nights and days in a shelter. It is important that we do our best to protect life and limb, but there is a safe place for the believer that the world knows not. "How precious is Your loving kindness, O God! Therefore the children of men put their trust under the shadow of Your wings."~Psalm 36:7

We may not be facing a physical hurricane in our life, but we have all faced the wind of pain, sorrow, and death. Like in a Katrina our world can be blown apart and we need a shelter. There is no safer place than under the shadow of His wings. As a hen gathers her chicks and tucks them under her wings, so God desires to keep you safe. No safer place can be found!

Lord, help me to hide under the shadow of Your wings.

August 19

Who Has You Protected?

 You can sometimes see signs in some yards that declare that the property is protected by some alarm service. The idea is to warn burglars that even in the absence of the homeowner someone somewhere is watching or at least listening.

What I have never seen is a sign welcoming burglars into the home. You know something like, "Welcome all thieves! The door is unlocked! Go on in and help yourself! Cookies on the counter are for you! Thank you for visiting us!"

My mission travels as well as my interaction in the communities where I have been a pastor have revealed many who have been visited by a thief. This thief may have not been some man breaking down a door or prying open a window, but the evidence is that someone has come to destroy a household. Perhaps Jesus had such folks in mind when He spoke the words recorded for us in John 10:10, "The thief does not come except to steal, and to kill, and to destroy. I have come that they may have life, and that they may have it more abundantly."

The thief is none other than Satan himself. His intent is to cause great harm. He robs people of their joy and their hope. He kills the dream and sometimes kills the person. He destroys loving relationships. Jesus, to the contrary, has come to give life and the living of that life unto abundance.

If you know Christ as your Savior, then get a sign for your life. "Warning! This life is protected by Jesus–24/7."

Lord, help me live life abundantly under Your protection.

August 20

A Single Piece of Paper

Debt is an interesting thing. You can only get into debt by spending more than you earn and the inevitable consequence is that the day will come that you cannot earn enough to repay what you owe. Debt destroys relationships and breeds deceit and mistrust. The only remedy is either repayment in full or complete forgiveness.

Before I was called to serve in ministry, I owned a grocery business. When I first began this business, I offered credit to those who shopped with me. Most repaid their debt on time. Others had a strange habit of reaching their credit limit and then spending cash at one of my competitors. Some never repaid. I can still remember carrying a charged receipt in my wallet long after I no longer allowed credit accounts at my store. Each time I saw the person who owed me the money, I would cringe with anger. I really believe that I was at the very edge of hatred over this matter.

My thoughts of this debt changed when I came to know Christ as my Savior. I contacted the person who owed the debt, took the receipt from my wallet and handed it to her. The debt was cancelled not out of repayment, but out of forgiveness. That little piece of paper was ruling and wrecking my life.

Only after I met Christ did I understand, I had a debt I could not repay; Jesus paid a debt He did not owe. "Then Jesus said, 'Father, forgive them, for they do not know what they do.' And when Jesus had cried out with a loud voice, He said, 'Father, into Your hands I commit My spirit.' Having said this, He breathed His last."~Luke 23:34,46

Lord, help me to never hold a debt over someone's head.

August 21

Do Not Touch!

 Oswald Chambers noted that God has no museums. We go to a museum to look at objects on display. Most museums are filled with the past and it is perfectly fine to think about how the past has influenced our life today. There is one sign, however, that is prevalent at a museum: DO NOT TOUCH!

Some folks will attend a church this week only to discover unfortunately that it has become a museum. That's a sad commentary on what many houses of worship have become. Hurting, lonely people will enter a church and see a lot of artifacts in the pews and many DO NOT TOUCH signs.

It was not so with Jesus and it should not be so with us. Jesus was always in touch with those around Him. It was Jesus drawing the children close to Him while the disciples were doing their best to keep them away. It was Jesus touching the blind and the leper. It was Jesus who reached down and touched Peter, plucking him out of the waves after his faith had failed.

One of my favorite scenes is when a sick woman touched the hem of Jesus' garment and was healed. "And suddenly, a woman who had a flow of blood for twelve years came from behind and touched the hem of His garment. For she said to herself, "If only I may touch His garment, I shall be made well." But Jesus turned around, and when He saw her He said, 'Be of good cheer, daughter; your faith has made you well.' And the woman was made well from that hour."~Matthew 9:20–22 In Mark's account, Jesus asked, "Who touched Me?" This question seemed foolish to the disciples since the entire crowd was touching Jesus. But Jesus never ignores the touch of faith.

Go ahead! Touch Him!

Lord, help me be the hem of Your garment today.

August 22

The Gentleman

I still open doors for ladies even though some of them don't seem to like it. I'm not claiming any superiority in doing so. I am only living out my upbringing. My parents taught me very early in my life to be a gentleman. Evidently, this has become somewhat strange in our world today.

One of my church members became ill once while working in the Northeast part of the country. I called the hospital to check on his condition. The operator answered and forwarded me to the correct room. My friend said, "I knew it was you, pastor." I asked him how he had guessed that it was me on the phone. He told me that the operator had called his room to see if he was up to the phone call. She told him that a southern gentleman was calling. Her analysis came from just a few words on the phone.

The Holy Spirit is also a gentleman. Jon Courson said in his *Application Commentary* "the Holy Spirit will never force anyone to come to Christ, for He is a perfect Gentleman." When Abram sent his servant to find a wife for Isaac he told him, "And if the woman is not willing to follow you, then you will be released from this oath..."~Genesis 24:8 In this verse Abram was a type of God the Father and the servant a type of the Holy Spirit. The decision to follow the servant would not be forced by Abram's servant.

The Holy Spirit never kicks you into obedience. HE NUDGES.... Ever so gently, He is at work to align your life with God's perfect will. "But the Helper, the Holy Spirit, whom the Father will send in My name, He will teach you all things, and bring to your remembrance all things that I said to you."~John 14:26 Be sensitive today and you will feel the breathe-like touch of His hand. Then yield to His gentle persuasion!

Lord, help me respond to the nudges of Your Spirit.

August 23

Ready for a Deal

 Remember Monty Hall? He was the host of the original *Let's Make a Deal!* All through the show Monty was tempting the contestant to trade what was in a box with what was behind a door on the stage. Sometimes it was a blind choice; other times the contestant literally traded a bird in the hand for two in the bush. If you chose wrong you got *zonked.* A *zonk* was weird stuff like donkeys, wash tubs, or hobos, etc. The big winners entered a final round with the choice of trading their winnings for Door #1; Door #2; Door #W? I know. You're thinking its supposed to be Door #3, but the best choice is Door # "W".

"At Gibeon the LORD appeared to Solomon in a dream by night; and God said, 'Ask! What shall I give you?'"~1 Kings 3:5 Solomon could have chosen anything and had God's permission to do so, but he chose "W"isdom. Solomon understood the immensity of the challenge in being the king of Israel. Though he was young he choose the better "deal." And what was behind Door # "W"?

Only a God who does not deal in zonks would be able to say to him: "Because you have asked this thing, and have not asked long life for yourself, nor have asked riches for yourself, nor have asked the life of your enemies, but have asked for yourself understanding to discern justice, behold, I have done according to your words; see, I have given you a wise and understanding heart, so that there has not been anyone like you before you, nor shall any like you arise after you. And I have also given you what you have not asked: both riches and honor, so that there shall not be anyone like you among the kings all your days. So if you walk in My ways, to keep My statutes and My commandments, as your father David walked, then I will lengthen your days."~1 Kings 3:11–14 So, which door will you choose?

Lord, help me choose wisdom.

August 24

Hog Time

A retired pastor friend and I were scheduled to have a meeting. He forgot, which was no big deal. We rescheduled and took care of our business. He sent me a note and made this statement, "After all what's time to a hog?" I had no idea what he was talking about!

He did explain it to me when I next saw him. The story went like this. One hog farmer was speaking to another and said that he was going to truck his hogs all the way up to Omaha, Nebraska, because he could get a better price there. His friend asked, "Do you know how long it will take to get your hogs all the way to Omaha?"

The farmer who was planning on driving his herd of hogs up north stopped and thought for a moment and then replied, "It don't matter none. After all, what's time to a hog?"

Now there is a man who understands the true essence of time. Time really does not matter if you are a hog. But we are not hogs! God has given us time, placed great value upon it, and given us responsibility in it. He tells us that we are to redeem it (Ephesians 5:16.) We are instructed to arise for it is high time that we get busy for the Kingdom (Romans 13:11.) And we are to glorify God while there is still time. In other words, right now!

"To Him be the glory both *now* and *forever!*"~2 Peter 3:18 We often think about the forever part, but sometimes forget that we are called to glorify Him right now! What are your glory plans for today? As the old hymn says, "Hallelujah, Thine the glory!"

Lord, help me never to be so busy that I forget Your glory.

243

August 25

All Mixed Up

 I still remember when my parents bought me a chemistry set for Christmas one year. Can you still buy chemistry sets? Oh well, I had grand aspirations. With no instructions (if there were any I threw them away) I began mixing chemicals.

I found out very quickly how hot some of that stuff gets when you mix several of these chemicals together! Sometimes nothing happened. Other times I created smoke or smell or just pretty colors. I do know that I stained a lot of things. Maybe a chemistry set wasn't such a good idea! Maybe that's why they don't sell them as "toys" anymore either.

Solomon advised us on what to mix with our stuff. "Better is a little [mixed] with the fear of the Lord than great treasure [all by itself] with trouble."~Proverbs 15:16 This was great wisdom coming from the richest man who ever lived. Solomon's great treasure got him into all sorts of trouble. Things got hot at times for Solomon because he forgot to add the fear of the Lord to his formula for life. At other times things got smoky because he substituted the wrong ingredients in place of the fear of the Lord and he could not see the leading of the Lord in his life.

We can gain great wisdom from Solomon's experience. Doing so will keep us from blowing things up and leaving a lot of stains behind from our trial and error process. We have the formula for success. Take the little you have and always keep it mixed with the fear of the Lord. The outcome will always be better than riches mixed with trouble.

Happy mixing!

Lord, help me keep a healthy fear of You in my life.

August 26

Self-Effort

I find that one of the most amazing characteristics of humans is that we so quickly revert to what we know best and are comfortable with in our lives. For example, I am now the proud owner of a self-propelled lawnmower. It has been years since I owned one of these contraptions. I always pushed and was proud of my pushing. At least I know that now!

Now you might be wondering how I discovered my pride at work in a lawnmower. Here's how it happened: This morning I pulled out my new mower and got all ready to begin the process of giving my lawn a fresh cut. Checked the oil, filled the gas, etc., etc. etc. Up to this point I'm doing fine. I have a mental recognition that this mower is self-propelled. I cranked the mower and promptly began to push the mower back and forth across the lawn!

The thing that made me realize my error was when I came to an understanding that this mower is really heavy and is not designed to be pushed. It has been designed with the purpose of propelling itself. My only input is to guide it and release the drive mechanism at the appropriate times. What a revelation! I bought the mower. I brought it to my home. I read the manual. I understood with my head that this mower would propel itself, but I insisted with my heart that I would push it along. Result: Wasted effort based on self-effort!

Paul speaks of this in Ephesians 2:10, "We are His workmanship, created in Christ Jesus for good works, which God prepared beforehand that we should walk in them." God desires to work through us, not in spite of us! Yes, we serve a part, but we are not the source of our strength...He is! God's purpose for us has been prepared beforehand. Now walk behind that purpose and let Him propel you to accomplish His will for your life.

Lord, help me to work within Your purpose.

August 27

With or Without Preservatives?

 In our modern world we are very used to the idea of preservatives. I love them. I think they are a great idea. Some will not agree with me, I know, and that's okay too. I'll take my food that has an expiration date six years from now and you can spend the extra time scraping away that fuzzy stuff growing on yours. I'm only kidding on my way to make a point about preservation. God wants to preserve us. The natural route doesn't work in spiritual matters!

Satan's complaint about Job was that God had put a hedge around him. The hedge was there for Job's preservation and protection. David sang these words in Psalm 16:1, "Preserve me, O God; for in You do I put my trust." The word *preserve* in this verse also means to hedge or protect. God is attentive to the protection of His own.

When we are out from under God's protective hand we soon feel the full effects of our sinful natures. We were conceived in corruption. We have been dying from the start and no amount of pampering of the flesh will make us last one day longer than has been appointed by God. The life of King Saul is a demonstration of stepping away from the preserving hand of God. In 2 Samuel 1:21 we are told that the shield of Saul was not anointed with oil. Olive oil was used a preservative. The idea here is that Saul's protection was gone because of his disobedience. Like spoiled food, he would be cast away from his throne.

Jesus prayed to His Father in John 17 that He had kept safe all those given unto Him. We can trust in His preservation! We are hedged about by the hand of the Lord. We have the oil of the Spirit upon us to keep the effects of sin's corruption from destroying us. O BLESSED THOUGHT!

Lord, help me to stay inside Your hedge of protection.

246

August 28

Paid in Full

I'm sure you have noticed, but we are in a serious situation with the debt owed by our country. Congress, states, and even cities simply cannot balance the books. The problem is *not* the debt. The problem *is* their system of accounting. Until there is an honest appraisal of the debt, it can never be reckoned.

Mankind has a similar problem when it comes to resolving our sin debt. We want to blame our sin debt on something other than the debt itself. Our tendency is to blame the previous generation for our debt. We sometimes take it all the way back to Adam and Eve and blame them for our sin debt. We will be just like our civic leaders if we do not get honest. *It is our debt.*

So, what can we do now that we've owned up to it? Listen to Paul in Romans 6:11, "Likewise reckon yourselves also to be truly dead to sin, but alive to God through Jesus Christ our Lord." Until we account for sin's debt as God does, we will never have our books balanced! It is our debt, but Christ who had no sin debt took all that we owed and placed it into His account. Then God in His grace took all of the righteousness of Christ and placed it in our account.

Finally, He took his stamp of holiness, dipped it in the shed blood of Jesus, and pressed it on the page of accounts. The words are written in red:

PAID IN FULL!

Lord, help me to rejoice in the full payment for my sins.

August 29

Something New

 When was the last time you bought the newest model only to get home and find out a few days later that a new and improved one was on the shelf? The Bible tells us that there really is nothing new, but somehow we believe we have finally discovered the new gadget that will change our world.

Solomon, the wisest man in the world said, "That which has been is what will be, that which is done is what will be done, and there is nothing new under the sun. Is there anything of which it may be said, 'See, this is new?' It has already been in ancient times before us. There is no remembrance of former things, nor will there be any remembrance of things that are to come by those who will come after." ~Ecclesiastes 1:9–11

Now that may be a sad commentary, but it is nonetheless true. Someone else said, "If it's new it probably isn't true and if it's true it definitely isn't new." This piece of sage advice most likely has some serious holes in it, but I must admit that I agree with Solomon, "there is nothing new under the sun." It may be a different color or shape, but it is usually just something old in a new box.

Before you get too discouraged I have good news. There is one thing that can be made new and it is you. God can take you just as you are and make an entirely new creation out of you. "Therefore, if anyone is in Christ, he is a new creation; old things have passed away; behold, all things have become new." ~2 Corinthians 5:17 If you're looking for something new, don't go to the mall; go to the Master Creator!

Lord, help me live like I've been made new in You.

August 30

An Eye on the Sea

Ever since I watched the movie, *Jaws*, I have been afraid of the
ocean. I just don't trust what I can't see. Like big fish with teeth! I
will walk along the beach and let the waves wash up on my feet, but
not much more. Several years ago I visited Hawaii and learned a
common saying of beach-goers. "Never turn your back on the
ocean." Not long after my visit, I read that a man had been swept out to sea by
a rogue wave. He lost his life by not heeding the danger of the sea.

James warns us about turning our back on faith. "If any of you lacks wisdom, let
him ask of God, who gives to all liberally and without reproach, and it will be
given to him. But let him ask in faith, with no doubting, for he who doubts is like
a wave of the sea driven and tossed by the wind. For let not that man suppose
that he will receive anything from the Lord; he is a double-minded man, unstable
in all his ways."~James 1:5-8

God will move when faith acts. In this case, he tells us that we can ask God in
faith for wisdom. Not only does he freely give us wisdom, He gives it to us again
and again. Thus, the phrase *without reproach*. God never responds to our request
offered in faith by wondering why we keep asking over and over. He knows we
are slow learners sometimes!

But hear the warning. Never turn your back on faith. Like the sea, a faithless
request acts as a rogue wave that can knock us off our feet and sweep us out to
sea. The doubt of faithlessness blows across our life and quickly drives the waves
upon the beach of our minds. Soon the erosion of doubt cuts a channel of
confusion and we become double-minded. This word literally means two-spirited
or divided in opinion. Like a home built on the sand doubtful and faithless living
takes its toll on our foundation and collapse soon follows. Never turn your back
on the ocean or on God! Both can bring sure disaster!

Lord, help me to never turn my back on You.

249

August 31

In This Corner

Jacob entered the night as a deceiver and schemer. His entire life had been one of trickery. From his birth, where he grabbed the heel of his firstborn twin brother, to the deception he played out upon his aged father, on to his dealing with Laban, and his marriages to Leah and Rachel, Jacob lived up to his name.

He entered the night assuming that it could be his last. The morning held confrontation with his estranged brother whom he assumed would surely kill him for stealing away the birthright. But Jacob did not know that he would wrestle with the Lord that night. "Then Jacob was left alone; and a Man wrestled with him until the breaking of day."~Genesis 32:24 Jacob lay himself down for a restless night of sleep, but found himself in hand to hand combat with Jesus! He expected to meet his brother, but he met instead his Big Brother. All night he wrestled to no avail until morning broke upon the scene. Here he demanded, as Jacob would, a blessing. The Man, Jesus, touched his hip. As Jacob collapsed in a heap, Jesus asked his name. Of course, Jesus knew his name, but this was for Jacob's benefit not the Lord's. Then came the blessing. "And He said, 'Your name shall no longer be called Jacob, but Israel; for you have struggled with God and with men, and have prevailed.'"~Genesis 32:28

He limped away the next morning as one who had wrestled with God. No longer Jacob, but now Israel! This truth leaps out of this Biblical account: Contact with God always changes us! Interesting that the one thing we need most is the one thing that we avoid with a passion. We do our best to not deal with our own character. Like Jacob we spend our days conniving our way through life and wondering why there is so much frustration. Maybe it's time for a wrestling match. It will never happen until we are alone. God can arrange for that just like He did with Jacob. The encounter can begin today. Yield to God's plan today and be changed forever!

Lord, help me to stop wrestling with You.

September 1

Watch Your Step

Have you ever stepped wrong? Minding your own business you step off a curb or stumble at little or nothing. Ever turned an ankle? Sometimes little harm occurs in our misstep, but one wrong step can lead to tragedy.

Psalms 37:23 says, "The steps of a good man are ordered by the LORD, and He delights in his way. Though he fall, he shall not be utterly cast down; for the LORD upholds him with His hand." God orders our steps. He renders them sure so we will suffer no misstep. Literally, God frames our steps, sets the boundaries, and keeps us from straying. Because of this, God delights in the way or course of life we are traveling. When we are sure of God's direction, we can walk with confidence.

Don't you wish the text had just stopped there? Why did God have to bring up the falling down part? You would think that if we were walking in the path that God has ordered there would be no missteps. But we know better than that! We do fall down, but the good news is we don't stay down for long. Like a child learning to walk, the only real way to get the hang of it is to fall a few times. And like a child learning to walk, a parent is usually close to take them by the hand and encourage them to get up and try it again.

God upholds us with His hand. He sustains us when we trip and find ourselves flat on our faces. The key here is to walk in the path that delights the Lord. On this path you will always know that God is right there to pick you up, dust you off, and encourage you to keep walking.

May each step you make today be a "God-step!"

Lord, help me to watch my step today.

September 2

One Piece at a Time

 Incredible what an artist can do in creating a mosaic. Tiny pieces of glass, shell, or other fragments are polished and pieced together into a work of beauty. All of these pieces, once a part of something else, now with the touch of the master's hand are remade into something bigger than any individual piece.

I have learned that life is not a photographic snapshot, but a mosaic. If someone was to hand you a single photo of a particular scene from their life, you could not possible deduce from that one picture the totality of their existence. You may surmise a lot about one day and you could probably well define that particular moment frozen in time as captured by the lens of a camera and imprinted on the film. That picture could, however, be added to thousands of others and soon a true representation of your life would unfold.

This is how our Christian life is being shaped. One tiny piece at a time is being cut and polished and laid in place. No particular piece telling the whole story, but each piece vital to conveying the whole. As the Apostle Paul described it in 2 Corinthians 3:18, "But we all, with unveiled face, beholding as in a mirror the glory of the Lord, are being transformed into the same image from glory to glory, just as by the Spirit of the Lord." We are not finished works. We are in process. A transformation is taking place piece by piece.

Anything shattered in your life? Give God the pieces. Watch the Master do His work!

Lord, help me to yield every piece of my life to Your masterful hands.

September 3

God's Refinery

My dad worked at a refinery where crude oil was transformed into many products from fuel to plastic. As a matter of fact a forty-two gallon barrel of crude oil only produces about nineteen gallons of fuel. The remainder is used to produce thousands of items of everyday use. Most of which we would never connect to a barrel of crude oil.

Isaiah 48:10 says God also has a refinery, "Behold, I have refined you, but not as silver; I have tested you in the furnace of affliction." God wants to take the "raw" material of your life and transform you into the image of His Son. Only one "product" comes from God's refinery:

PEOPLE IN THE IMAGE OF THEIR SAVIOR!

We see here the refining work of God, but also the restraining work of God. He said through the prophet that his intent was to refine Israel by trying them in times of affliction. But note that He also said that he would not refine them as silver. The process of refining silver takes silver to a liquid form. Extreme conditions bring silver to a pure state. "The words of the LORD are pure words, like silver tried in a furnace of earth, purified seven times."~Psalm 12:6

The product that comes from God's refinery will be His people who are shaped into the image of His Son, but He restrains the process lest we be melted down in the heat of purification. This verse demonstrates the mercy of God in His dealings with us. In petroleum refineries the crude must pass through a unit called a cracker. Here complex molecules are reduced to simpler compounds. It is not God's intent to bring so much pressure that we crack. He is not making us simpler, but more complex...into His image.

Lord, help me daily to be refined into Your image.

September 4

Stand Still and Go Forward

 When I was a much younger man, I managed a trailer park for my parents. In those days, rent was collected weekly. Many renters were very transient. Some would move in with all they owned in the trunk of a car. It made for some interesting times!

A man came once to rent a trailer home. After discussing the cost of rent, etc. I asked if he had any other questions. He said, "Just one. Can I park my car in a place where I don't have to back up to leave?" His concern was valid. His car had no reverse gear! I arranged such a spot for him and he stayed for some time before moving on to another place with the right parking spot.

This story reminds me of the children of Israel as they were exiting Egypt. They came to the Red Sea and found themselves trapped between the waves and the Egyptian chariots. The people began to cry out to Moses. "And Moses said to the people, 'Do not be afraid. Stand still, and see the salvation of the LORD, which He will accomplish for you today. For the Egyptians whom you see today, you shall see again no more forever. The LORD will fight for you, and you shall hold your peace.' And the LORD said to Moses, 'Why do you cry to Me? Tell the children of Israel to go forward.'"~Exodus 14:13–15

Faith only moves us in one direction: FORWARD! Reverse or neutral are not options. Standing before the Red Sea with all of Israel waiting, Moses said, "Stand still!" God said, "Go forward!" Both of these statements are true. Faith gives the ability to remain at peace while stepping out in obedience to faith's call. Are you stuck today? Go forward in faith! Vance Havner said, "I thank God for the Unseen Hand, sometimes urging me onward, sometimes holding me back; sometimes with a caress of approval, sometimes with a stroke of reproof; sometimes correcting, sometimes comforting. My times are in His hand." Stand still and go forward!

Lord, help me to never backup.

September 5

It's Off To Work I Go

Labor Day is celebrated during the first week of September each year, specifically on the first Monday so to give a three day weekend. Its purpose is to set aside a day to celebrate the economic and social accomplishments of the American worker. Similar holidays are observed in several other countries around the world. The day itself is actually a full-fledged work day for many. The same entrepreneurial drive that lifted the American worker to have the status of a holiday named for them has opened the day to be exploited for financial gain. Ah, the joys of a capitalistic mind set!

The Bible speaks of the importance of honoring honest, hard labor. In particular, Paul commended the Thessalonians for their work of faith and labor of love. There is no harder labor than that of faith and love. "We give thanks to God always for you all, making mention of you in our prayers, remembering without ceasing your work of faith, labor of love, and patience of hope in our Lord Jesus Christ in the sight of our God and Father"~1 Thessalonians 1:2–3

The word *work* in the original Greek language gives us the idea of occupation, effort, and toiling. This is not a casual working at something, but a primary function of a person's life. Hence, one might say my life's work.

The labor of love that was exhibited by the Thessalonians again takes on the meaning of toiling, but to the point of exhaustion. The world exhibits a casual love that focuses on self. A laborious love is one that is so deep that it is likened to a hard day's work. Don't get tired of working on a life of faith and loving so much that you end the day physically tired. You'll sleep well at night when you do so!

Lord, help me to work at loving others every day.

255

September 6

GIGO

 Somewhere somebody has got a very bad job. I certainly don't want the job, but I guess somebody had to do it. The job...figuring out how much garbage the average person produces each day in America. The answer is 4.6 pounds per person per day. The question is how do you calculate something like that? I guess that's why that other guy has the job and not me!

I grew up in the country where a man came by our house once a week with a truck and collected our garbage. I still remember his satisfaction guarantee on the side of the truck. It read, "Satisfaction Guaranteed or Double Your Garbage Back!" He could keep this guarantee, because he had plenty of garbage in reserve to answer any customer's complaint. I don't think he got many phone calls!

What about our personal lives? How much garbage is coming out of us on any given day? There is a word for this: GIGO. It's an acronym for garbage in, garbage out. You can't get garbage out if none has ever been input. Consider what Jesus declared in John 7:38. "The one who believes in Me, as the Scripture has said, will have streams of living water flow from deep within him." That doesn't sound like a GIGO scenario.

Recently while traveling in Haiti we crossed rivers choked with garbage, sewage, and who knows what else. None of the pollutants came from the source. Somewhere upstream a pure flow began. Along the way it was clogged with garbage. If you believe in Christ then He is the headwater of life flowing from you. What gets dumped in the river during the day is controlled by you! Remember, GIGO.

Lord, help me to never be a spiritual polluter.

September 7

Unhidden Grace

Grace is probably one of the most common and well known terms in Christianity. The term is chosen by some churches as an identifier of their ministry and is even given as a name to some females. My favorite acrostic for the word grace is *getting redeemed at Christ's expense.*

Grace has many descriptions. Amazing and abounding are two that come to mind. Peter described grace as *true* in 1 Peter 5:12. "By Silvanus, our faithful brother as I consider him, I have written to you briefly, exhorting and testifying that this is the *true* grace of God in which you stand."

What did he mean? Is there a false grace? A deeper look will reveal the truth. *True* in this case means not hidden. He could have just said that grace is in the open, but he used a word that describes grace like this. *I testify that this is the <u>NOT HIDDEN</u> grace of God.* You simply cannot ignore God's amazing, abounding, unhidden grace!

So many people use what they perceive as difficulty in experiencing God as an excuse for not knowing who God really is. Peter here in this verse says that he is writing about a grace that is openly revealed. We do not have to be theologians or preachers to understand the grace of God. It is easily recognizable in every person who has experienced its liberating and life-changing qualities.

Not only is it easily seen, but the person who has been affected by the work of grace will stand upon it as a platform to tell others about it. It truly is an amazing, abounding, unhidden grace. It heals the broken hearted, restores relationships, and enables one to abide in the truth.

Lord, help me to stand in Your unhidden grace.

September 8

How Much Do You Weigh?

 Before God's call to ministry I owned a country grocery business. Country grocery men are a bit of everything to their customers: doctor, counselor, veterinarian, nutritionist, etc. I had an old-time scale in my store. Besides weighing what I sold, I weighed lots of things for customers including BIG fish and LITTLE babies!

I could rejoice with the fisherman who had just caught the biggest fish of his life and wanted the weight validated and I could ooh and ah with the mama who wanted to see how much weight her little one had gained. Being a country grocery store operator prepared me for a lot of my ministry as a pastor and then as an associational missionary.

God is in the weighing business too. "For the Lord is the God of knowledge; and by Him actions are weighed."~1 Samuel 2:3 The set of scales in my store had to be calibrated regularly to make sure they were weighing items correctly. The weights division of the state would stop by periodically to test the scale and place a sticker on it verifying its accuracy.

God's scale is always right and it never has to be calibrated because it is based on His standard of holiness. God does not place items like fish or babies on His scale. God weighs things like the thoughts and intent of the heart. The word *actions* has hidden away in its meaning the idea of gleaning. It is a searching out of the little things that might be otherwise overlooked. God's scale system gives Him the knowledge of more than what we have done. By His scale He knows *why* we did what we did. Having this understanding that God knows our thoughts and intents will certainly cause us to be more careful with our actions.

Lord, help me to submit all of my life to Your set of scales.

September 9

Little is Much

There is one miracle of Jesus that is recorded in all four gospels: the feeding of the 5000. At the center of this miracle is the unselfishness of a lad with five barley loaves and two small fish. (John 6)

Let me write this story with a 21st century background.

A boy wakes up in a three bedroom, two car garaged home, with his mother preparing to head out to work. She is a single mom who has limited resources and daycare for her son during the summer months is out of the question. She has good neighbors who have promised to keep a close eye on her son, so her fears are somewhat soothed.

As she cranks her car, she hands her son some money and tells him to get some lunch at McDonald's. She tells him that she loves him and off she goes. The boy can't wait for lunch time since he just loves those fish sandwiches at McDonald's! When noon finally comes, he hurries to buy his sandwich. He has heard that a teacher is speaking in the park. His name is Jesus. So with his food in hand, he walks to the park to hear the teacher. To his surprise thousands are gathered and he overhears one of the men say that someone needs to feed them all. The lad looks at his sandwich and offers it to Jesus. You know the rest of the story.

The question: What is so little among so many?
The answer: With God little is much!

Let's not measure with our limited sight, but in and through a heart of faith. Yield your little to the majesty of the Maker! Then step back and be amazed!!!

Lord, help me give you my little so You can make much of it.

September 10

Follow Me

 We live in a world that operates under the axiom of lead, follow, or get out of the way. Some have even added the little phrase, "or get run over!" I know that we must have good leaders and that being a good leader means that someone is following, but this leadership style does not line up with biblical teaching. The greatest leader of all time of course is Jesus and His leadership style was to lead as a servant.

We see this time and again in the gospels as the writers give their perspectives on the ministry of Jesus. Each saw things from their own eyes and heard with their own ears, but they never varied on Jesus being revealed as a servant leader.

His instructions to His disciples in the first days of their calling was very simple. *Follow Me!* These common men were called upon to make radical changes in their lives. They are, for the most part, described in the book of Acts by others as ignorant and unlearned. Yet, they followed Jesus and turned the world upside down for Him.

This lesson on leadership did not come easily to the disciples. They struggled with it as you and I will from time to time. Two of the disciples sought a place of exaltation at the left and right of Jesus in His Kingdom, but Jesus reminded them that self-serving leadership was not the model for believers. He told them in Matthew 20:28, "The Son of man came not to be served, but to serve." Do you want this to be a great day? Here's a thought–follow Jesus. How about a really fantastic day? Find someone to minister to in the name of Christ! You'll lie down tonight with a smile upon your face and your heart!

Lord, help me to serve someone in Your name today.

September 11

Guided By His Eye

Amazing! A doctor can use a camera guided by his own hand to peer inside the human body. Since the doctor guides the camera, he always sees exactly what he wants to see. He doesn't ask the body into which the camera is inserted to guide the lens. Once the patient has submitted to his care, the doctor becomes the one to decide what will be seen.

God says in Psalm 32:8-9 "I will instruct you and teach you in the way you should go; I will guide you with My eye. Do not be like the horse or like the mule, which have no understanding, which must be harnessed with bit and bridle, else they will not come near you." Like the physician, God has our best interest at heart. He is not looking inside us with a camera to determine what is diseased or to make corrections. He is looking with His own eye to guide us.

Imagine this—everything you experience today God has already seen with His own eyes. The doctor may find a surprise as he looks through his lens, but God will never be caught unaware. He desires to instruct and teach us in the way we should go. He does not want us to respond to His leadership like a horse or mule. These will not turn without the bit and bridle. God desires our submission to Him.

We can trust God and draw near to Him because of His all-seeing eye. He sees the entire landscape. He sees around the next bend. He sees through the darkness. Trust and follow Him as He leads!

Lord, help me to follow You willingly.

September 12

A Day to Worship

 What a wonderful day to worship! It doesn't matter if this happens to be a Sunday or not. If it is Sunday then I hope that you have spent or will spend the day worshiping with fellow believers. If not, shouldn't this be a day of worship just like a Sunday?

Sometimes I think we might have relegated worship to a checkbox. GOT THAT DONE...What's next? Psalms 29:2 says, "Give unto the Lord the glory due to His name; worship the Lord in the beauty of holiness." Our modern word *worship* comes from the Old English word *worthship*. It means to attribute worth to something or someone. The Hebrew person would understand the worship of God as the act of falling prostrate as before royalty.

This verse not only instructs us to worship the Lord in general, but expands our understanding of what is required of us as we worship. The first word noted in this verse tells us that we are to give. So much of what we call worship seems to be very man-focused. We have even labeled our service times as "worship." Worship is not about a time frame.

When we truly worship, it should be a giving time. We are instructed in this as well. Our giving is of glory due to Him. The word *glory* means splendor or weightiness. Our worship should never be done in a flippant or casual manner. One of the indications that we have been worshiping the Lord is a sense of heaviness. That is, there is no such thing as worship lite.

Finally, worship God wherever and whenever God is holy. So be it Mon...Tues... or on to next Sunday...WORSHIP HIM EVERY DAY!

Lord, help me to worship You today.

Working for the King

There have been and always will be the unnamed host of people who do the bidding of King Jesus with little or no recognition. These men and women work not for fame or glory, but for His pleasure alone. Their reward is the security of God's hedge around them.

Many of us never take the time to read the lists of names that are included in the Bible. Many are hard to pronounce and we just don't see the value in reciting such lists. I have learned that the Holy Spirit did not move on the hearts of the Bible writers to include these lists as filler. They are there for a reason. They are there for our edification and instruction.

Tucked away at the end of a list of names in the book of First Chronicles is this verse which includes some obscure workers. "These were the potters and those who dwell at Netaim and Gederah; there they dwelt with the king for his work."~1 Chronicles 4:23

These folks lived with the king to do his work. This was no nine to five job. It was a ministry to the king. They were planted, the meaning of the word *Netaim*, and secure within the hedges, the meaning of the word *Gederah*. They may have been unnamed and maybe even unappreciated, but they are included in the scriptures. Be faithful where you are planted and you will be protected by the King who employs you.

There is no safer place than within God's wall. Those thorny hedges are for your protection! Settle down! You're in the King's employ!

Lord, help me work for You within the hedges.

September 14

That Hurts

 There's a real market for stupidity. Entire television programs are designed around people doing dumb things. Somebody shoots a video and suddenly an imbecile becomes an overnight sensation. Most of it is funny, but if your response is like mine, you usually find yourself saying, "I bet you that hurt!"

Anger is like that. We do something that catches us off guard and there goes our mouth or a hand or a foot while our brain is still in neutral. And like being stupid, there is usually someone there with a camera. Ecclesiastes 7:9 tells us, "Do not hasten in your spirit to be angry, for anger rests in the bosom of fools." The word *fools* here means those who are stupid. Let me restate this verse to help you understand it better. "Don't let agitation be at home in your deepest self for doing so is stupid!" I know! You've told your kids not to say stupid, but the Bible clearly tells us to be angry is stupid!

Anger is a very natural response and therein lies the problem: IT'S NATURAL! Since it is natural and of the flesh we must guard against it. A lady once told her pastor that she couldn't control her anger. She went on to say that she felt that it wasn't a big deal though, because her anger never lasted a long time. The pastor told her that a shotgun blast doesn't last long either, but look at all the damage it does. Scripture plainly teaches that we should be angry and sin not (Ephesians 4:26.) Being angry is not the sin; pulling the trigger is! Afterwards you will be saying, "I bet you that hurt!"

Lord, help me not to be stupid today!

September 15

Walking the Valley

Dwight L. Moody put the valley of the shadow of death in its place as he lay dying. With his family gathered around he exclaimed, "This is my triumph! This is my coronation day! I have been looking forward to it for years." Mr. Moody closed his eyes and drifted into unconsciousness. Rousing, he spoke again. "No pain! No valley! If this is death, it's not bad at all! It's sweet!"

The evangelist was giving his opinion on valleys as he passed from this life into eternity. He had connected the valley with pain, suffering, and death, but at the end of his life he concluded it wasn't bad at all. Valleys are depicted as dark and wearisome. Mountains get all the glory and praise. Shadows in the valley; sunshine on the mount.

Psalms 104:10 tells us that "He (God) sends the springs into the valleys; they flow among the hills." The valley is the gathering point of the springs. Rivulets become brooks, rivers, and ultimately oceans. The word *valley* comes from the same Hebrew word as that which means inheritance.

All of us will have to traverse the valley at some time in our lives. If we enter these times with our only concept of valleys as being filled with dread, then this will be a perilous journey. If on the other hand, we see the valley as part of our inheritance our step will be easier and our burden lightened. Here in the valley is where the still water resides. Here in the valley is where the green grass grows. All of God's promises gather in the valley. We find the comfort of His rod and staff here and we fear no evil.

Valleys are meant to bless us! Remember this during your next valley visit. No valley extends forever, but sooner or later opens upon the plains where the sun shines again. Until then, He goes with you all the days of your life.

Lord, help me walk with assurance through the valleys.

September 16

Take Your Vitamins

 Three biblical concepts that we often think of in a segmented way are: faith, obedience, and joy. They are connected intricately, however. Each is dependent in some way on the other. Faith is impossible without obedience. Obedience strengthens our faith. Joy is directly proportional to obedience. Faith flourishes in the joy-filled life. Like a multi-vitamin for the body you need a balanced diet of all three to grow spiritually.

Now as you consider faith, obedience, and joy as essential resources to spiritual health, look at these three verses that contain these "vitamins." First, you can see the element of faith in Ephesians 3:16-17, "...that He would grant you, according to the riches of His glory, to be strengthened with might through His Spirit in the inner man that Christ may dwell in your hearts through *faith*..." Faith is integral to the indwelling of Christ.

Second, the element of obedience is seen in Romans 6:17. "But God be thanked that though you were slaves of sin, yet you *obeyed* from the heart that form of doctrine to which you were delivered." Obedience gives to us the evidence that sound doctrine is at work in our spiritual systems.

Third, the vital ingredient of joy is added to our multi-vitamin for spiritual health. "Behold, My servants shall sing for *joy* of heart..."~Isaiah 65:14 We are servants, but in our service our hearts are filled with joy. And there you have the perfect multi-vitamin for good spiritual health covering everything from your heart to your mind, and muscles.

Lord, help me by faith to obey You in joy.

September 17

Come on, Ump!

Christy Mathewson was a pitcher for the New York Giants in the early 1900's. He won thirty-seven games during the 1908 season and was admired as an athlete and as a Christian man. Mathewson's Christian virtue was demonstrated in one particular game when he found himself on third base. The coach has called for a squeeze play. In baseball the squeeze play is a maneuver consisting of a sacrifice bunt with a runner on third base. The batter bunts the ball, expecting to be thrown out at first base, but providing the runner on third base an opportunity to score.

As the play unfolded, there was a huge collision of bodies around home plate. Dust was flying and the umpire had no idea how to call the play. It simply could not be determined whether Mathewson was safe or out. A conference of all the umpires was called and finally they determined that the only thing they could do was ask for the runner to call the play.

Mathewson walked around home plate adjusting his trousers, dusting off his uniform; finally, removing his cap, he announced: "He got me". The runner had declared himself out and a run did not score. Later, in the dressing room, his teammates asked him why he had thus judged the play; whereupon Mathewson said, "I am an elder in the Presbyterian Church."

I don't know many people who enjoy being corrected; fewer who will correct ourselves. Sometimes this comes from thinking we are right; sometimes from not wanting to admit that we are wrong! "Behold, happy is the man whom God corrects; therefore do not despise the chastening of the Almighty."~Job 5:17 *Corrects* holds the idea of God being an umpire. His correction is based on the rules of His holiness! Our happiness doesn't come from God overlooking our error or allowing us to make the call. The chastening penalty teaches us to play the game of life better.

Lord, help me to stand corrected.

September 18

Lose the Box

 How many of us have given a child a wonderful gift and then watched them have the time of their lives playing with the box! The little girls make a house and the little boys build a fort. I think I'll just start wrapping a nice big refrigerator box, sit back, and watch imagination at work.

We adults have our boxes too. Unfortunately, we don't build houses and invite our friends over for tea. Nor do we build forts and invite our buddies to come play with us. No, we all like to build our boxes and then require everyone to fit inside of it. We measure folks by our own set of rules. There is no standard, but our own. We make the ruler according to our own definition of an inch and everybody has to measure up or they don't get in!

Now you are "welcome" in these adult size boxes, but whatever doesn't fit just gets cut off with disastrous consequences. I am thankful that God doesn't relate to us like that! The *infinite* God *chose* to dwell in us and have us dwell in Him as well. "Now, therefore, you are no longer strangers and foreigners, but fellow citizens with the saints and members of the household of God, having been built on the foundation of the apostles and prophets, Jesus Christ Himself being the chief cornerstone, in whom the whole building, being fitted together, grows into a holy temple in the Lord, in whom you also are being built together for a dwelling place of God in the Spirit."~Ephesians 2:19-22

You see, we were all strangers when God invited us into His box. He makes a place for us and brings us into unity with other believers. The amazing thing is that His box is always big enough. It's us that must be enlarged by God to accommodate MORE of Him! Lose the box!

Lord, help me to never place You in a box.

September 19

Bugs

Amazing what happens when you shine a little light on the subject. An Oriental fellow was shocked when he looked at some grains of rice under a microscope. The rice was crawling with bugs unseen by the naked eye. His response? He destroyed the microscope! Some folks would rather eat bugs in ignorance than know the truth.

We live in a dark world. However, it really is no darker than it was in the days of Jesus' ministry here. At the Feast of Tabernacles the large seven stemmed lampstand of the temple would be lit as part of the festival. This was a reminder to the Jewish community of the pillar of fire that had led Israel at night through the wilderness. In the brilliance of this golden lampstand burning, "Jesus spoke to them again, saying, 'I am the light of the world. He who follows Me shall not walk in darkness, but have the light of life.'"~John 8:12 He had proclaimed that He was not just another light burning, He was *the* light. No longer could the world "eat bugs" in ignorance.

But what about today? Is there a light for our world? Jesus said that *we* were to shed light in our dark world. "You are the light of the world. A city that is set on a hill cannot be hidden. Nor do they light a lamp and put it under a basket, but on a lampstand, and it gives light to all who are in the house."~Matthew 5:14-15

Yes, it is amazing what happens when you shine a little light on the subject. All of a sudden the "bugs" are exposed. Don't be surprised though by the world's reaction to the light. They may decide to destroy the microscope!

Lord, help me be a light so others can see You.

September 20

Treasure Hunting

 The movie, *National Treasure,* is one of those movies that keeps you on the edge of your seat. The script is filled with unexpected twists and turns, as the actor Nicolas Cage and others enter into a massive treasure hunt. Just in case you have never seen it, I'll not spoil it for you. It is, however, one big treasure that is found in a very remarkable place.

Sometimes our life can be like a treasure hunt. We have a map, but like the treasure hunters in the movie, we keep running into dead ends and plot changes. We are ever seeking the next clue and asking, "What in the world am I going to do?" Here's the answer. The world doesn't hold the answer you are looking for...Jesus does!

I know you may be thinking that's too spiritual or just too simple. Somehow we have come to the conclusion that it has to be hard or hidden for it to truly be the answer to life's most difficult questions. But the simple truth is Jesus holds the key to all wisdom and knowledge because He *is* the answer. We just live in Him and the answer is ours! "In whom are hidden all the treasures of wisdom and knowledge. As you therefore have received Christ Jesus the Lord, so walk in Him." ~Colossians 2:3,6

God has made our treasure hunting so easy. So easy, in fact, that many will overlook it. Just like in *National Treasure,* many of the clues were hidden in plain sight. We discover all of the treasures of heaven when we simply walk in Christ. Ok, ready? Take ten paces east of the big tree, turn right, go twenty-five paces, look for...Never mind! Just walk in Christ as you have received Him as Lord and all wisdom and knowledge is yours. No need for a map!

Lord, help me discover the treasures of heaven.

September 21

Incoming!

It seems that no matter how much we prepare for trials they have a way of slipping up on us. James put it this way: "My brethren, count it all joy when you fall into various trials knowing that the testing of your faith produces patience."~James 1:2 The word *fall* here could be translated fly upon. Trials fly upon us as if from thin air!

That never changes. I don't know of anybody who schedules troubles. In battles where artillery is used the whistling sound of incoming shells can be heard and the cry of soldiers will warn all that the blast is not far behind. We cannot prevent the trials from flying upon us, but we can control our reaction. We need to add a new column in our ledger and label it *JOY*, before we hear the shout of, "Incoming!"

In the *Letters of Samuel Rutherford*, the 15th century theological said,

"If God had told me some time ago that he was about to make me happy as I could be in this world, and then had told me that he should begin by crippling me in arm or limb, and removing me from all my usual sources of enjoyment, I should have thought it a very strange mode of accomplishing his purpose. And yet, how is his wisdom manifest even in this! For if you should see a man shut up in a closed room, idolizing a set of lamps and rejoicing in their light, and you wished to make him truly happy, you would begin by blowing out all his lamps, and then throwing open the shutter to let in the light of heaven."

Do you need a new accounting system? It's time to add joy to your trials!

Lord, help me to never leave joy out of the equation.

September 22

I Can See!

 Many folks my age now find it necessary to wear glasses. I have been doing so since I was 16 years old. I still remember being able to shoot the basketball better after I could see the rim! Now I just remember when I could play basketball!

If you wear glasses you know the routine. New glasses, new feel, new look, and new focal points! I'm at the age (and have been for a long time) that I need lots of focal points. So, I wear transitions. They are wonderful because they let me see at all distances. But each new pair has just a slight change in focal point. If I am to wear these glasses comfortably and get the full benefit from them I must adjust. The glasses cannot reset the focus to accommodate me. Most important in all of this is the fact that I can see much better when I am willing to use the glasses according to their design.

Jesus told his disciples that they were blessed because they could see what others could not. "Then He turned to His disciples and said privately, 'Blessed are the eyes which see the things you see; for I tell you that many prophets and kings have desired to see what you see, and have not seen it, and to hear what you hear, and have not heard it.'"~Luke 10:23-24

The followers of Christ can sometimes be like a person wearing a new prescription pair of eyeglasses. What is there to be seen, will be seen, when they allow the prescription to work for them. Jesus told the disciples that what they were seeing was always available to be seen and many had tried with due diligence to see it, but they could not. Now they were blessed to have received the ability to see it for themselves. Jesus is like that. He rejoices in giving sight to the blind whether it be physical or spiritual blindness. If you are a believer today rejoice! YOU CAN SEE!

Lord, help me to be thankful that You have given me sight.

Overloaded

In my missionary travels I have experienced some unusual sights. Some of the most unusual have been methods of transportation used in other countries. Not only the methods, but how many people and goods are often placed on one of these vehicles?

I have seen motorcycles with five people and a goat riding all at the same time. At other times, I have seen motorcycles moving mattresses, lumber, propane tanks, and the list goes on and on. Two other pastors and I were crammed into the back of a *very* small car once. We could not close the doors, so someone on the outside of the vehicle had to do so for us. Seatbelts...uh, no!

Buses and trucks can be seen with such massive loads that the axles collapse. In Haiti taxis are called tap-taps. Dozens of people are mashed and compacted into the bed of small pickup trucks. The driver is notified that a stop is needed by a person tapping on the cover of the truck bed, hence the name tap-tap.

Have you ever thought about God getting overloaded? Now we know better, but so that we might understand what He experiences when we will not hear His word, He gives us this illustration. "Behold, I am weighed down by you, as a cart full of sheaves is weighed down."~Amos 2:13 Israel refused to hear the word and it was like an overloaded cart whose wheels were wobbling under the weight.

Listen to God! When we hear and obey it will lighten both your load and His!

Lord, help me to obey and thereby lighten my load.

September 24

Camp Hope

 In 2010 the world's attention was riveted on the scene of a mine collapse in Chile. Thirty-three men were trapped over one-half mile deep for nearly ten weeks. With experts from around the world devising methods on-the-fly, these men were all returned to their families with little permanent health issues. The camp that surrounded the site of the collapse was dubbed *Camp Esperanza*, Camp Hope.

How would you respond if you found yourself in need of rescue? Would you cry out, fret and worry, or maybe even concoct your own escape? Hear what God's had to say about rescue. "It is good that one should hope and wait quietly for the salvation of the Lord."~Lamentations 3:26

As each one of the men who had been trapped were rescued, there was a shout of excitement and a great release of anxiety. Many broke out in singing the Chilean national anthem; all rushed to hug and kiss their family members. Mario Sepúlveda said, "I was with God, and with the devil–and God took me." It seems that God's name comes up when rescue is needed. This is why Jeremiah could say in the book of Lamentations that it is good for us to wait for His rescue.

The hard part sometimes is waiting quietly. Settle down! God knows EXACTLY where you are! Make your own *Camp Esperanza*. Wait with expectant hope and silently expect the rescue of the Lord.

Lord, help me hope in You and wait patiently.

September 25

Truth Telling

One of the earliest things I remember learning from my parents was to tell the truth. I never had to learn lying. It came completely naturally! No one has to instruct us in the self-protecting process of telling a lie. Truth telling on the other hand came by clear precise instruction.

The lesson went something like this: When you do something wrong you need to tell the truth and own up to it. And yes, I did do lots of things wrong. And no, I didn't always follow the teaching of my parents, but little by little I learned that honesty is the best policy.

I know that sounds awfully old fashioned in our world today. We have created all shades of deception and many cannot tell the difference between a lie and the truth. God cannot use us effectively in His service unless we are trusted as truth tellers. When Jethro instructed Moses to share the burden of leading the children of Israel through the wilderness, he gave him specific details about the men he should choose for this work. These details included seeking out men of truth. "Moreover you shall select from all the people able men, such as fear God, men of truth, hating covetousness; and place such over them to be rulers of thousands, rulers of hundreds, rulers of fifties, and rulers of tens."~Exodus 18:21

One of the characteristics of those chosen was that they were to be men of truth. This was in addition to ability, reverence for God, and unselfishness. How many people have not been chosen because of this one serious flaw in character? Being truthful means that you are stable, assuredly certain, and trustworthy. It does not mean that you are perfect or that you will never make a bad decision or choice. It does mean that you will own up to it when you do fail to meet the standard.

Be a truth teller and God will entrust you with more of His Kingdom business. There's probably a Moses out there that can use your help!

Lord, help me to be a person of truth.

September 26

Not Ashamed

 Disgraced! When I think of this word, I envision someone with a huge scarlet "A" stitched on their garments as in Nathaniel Hawthorne's novel, *The Scarlet Letter*. It means to be out of favor, without respect, loss of confidence.

In Romans 1:16 Paul says, "For I am not ashamed of the gospel of Christ for it is the power of God to salvation for everyone who believes, for the Jew first and also for the Greek." The word *ashamed* carries the idea of disgrace. Paul was saying in this verse that he would not be disgraced as one who was avoiding the sharing of the good news of the gospel.

It seems incredible that anyone who knows the grace of the gospel could be disgraced by the gospel! Yet there is almost an embarrassment when we begin to tell someone of this good news. The power of the gospel is wrapped up in the very fact that it is *good news*! We do not have a message of despair or doom to deliver. Sharing the gospel should not be like a scarlet letter that we must work around.

The gospel puts us in favor with God and man. The gospel is a powerful force that can break down every barrier to itself. It stands alone. It does not need to be defended. Its power is available to all who believe. To be ashamed is to lose the respect and confidence of those who need to hear. Dispatch the grace of the gospel at every opportunity; never be disgraced by it.

Lord, help me to never be ashamed of You.

September 27

Go Clean Up

Cleanliness can sometimes be very deceptive. That is, we can attempt to clean something, but fail because we do not have the right cleaning agents or enough light or perhaps nothing to which we can compare our efforts.

This happened to an evangelist friend of mine several years ago. He and his family traveled in a bus from church to church for meetings. As happened from time to time their bus broke down on the road. He tried to make repairs, but could not. Friends came to get the family off the highway while he stayed and slept on the bus. Before retiring, he looked in the mirror in the pale generator light and attempted to remove some of the grease on his hands and face. After washing thoroughly and a quick look in the mirror he was off to bed. The next morning's bright sunshine revealed the deception of his cleaning attempt. He had not removed the grease on his face and hands. He had just thinned it and spread it evenly, so that it only appeared that he was clean.

Solomon asked a question in Proverbs 20:9, "Who can say; 'I have made my heart clean, I am pure from my sin?'" It seems the answer is NO ONE! Yet Jesus said, "Blessed are the pure in heart for they shall see God."~Matthew 5:8 Who's correct? BOTH!

We can't cleanse and purify ourselves, but we can be cleaned by the purging of the Holy Spirit. Jesus said the pure in heart shall see God. The word pure carries the idea of catharsis—an emptying out of vile impurities either physically or emotionally, but most importantly spiritually. Purity comes by an emptying and a refilling! Like the group Third Day puts it, "I FEEL LIKE I'VE BEEN BORN AGAIN!"

Lord, help me to keep my heart pure today.

September 28

Living the Gospel Out Loud

 History tells us of a pagan soldier in Constantine's army named Pachomius who was deeply moved when he saw Christians bringing food to fellow soldiers who were suffering from famine and disease. Curious to understand a doctrine that would inspire such generosity, Pachomius studied Christianity and was converted.

Someone is always looking with interest upon the everyday living of the Christian. Before ascending to heaven Jesus left these words with his disciples and ultimately with us through Luke's writings in the book of Acts. "But you shall receive power when the Holy Spirit has come upon you; and you shall be witnesses to Me in Jerusalem, and in all Judea and Samaria, and to the end of the earth."~Acts 1:8

So often we only read this verse with a mindset of missions that moves out in concentric circles until all of the world is touched and this is a true interpretation of this verse. Jesus was telling his disciples that with the power of the Holy Spirit their ministries would be much bigger than just the city of Jerusalem. But we can and should be witnesses right where we live. Some of us will never go much further than right where we live. The greatest witness we have is in our everyday interaction with those who cross our paths right where we live.

Those Christians who were ministering in their Jerusalem to the sick and hungry touched the life of Pachomius. Here he was a soldier in Constantine's army. An army whose mission it was to "convert" the world to Christianity, yet in its midst was a soldier who needed Christ as Savior. It was not the might of an army that pointed him to Jesus, but the caring and compassionate witness of the Christians who were living out the life of Jesus openly in his sight.

There is a Pachomius somewhere watching you today! Will he see Jesus?

Lord, help me be a faithful witness.

September 29

Redeemed to be a Slave

One of the great dangers of the Christian life is that we forget what God did in saving us. Time can eat away at that first excitement we had at the moment of our salvation. We, like the church at Ephesus, leave our first love (Revelation 2:4.) Our salvation has set us free from our bondage to sin and its consequences.

He was always reminding Israel of this: "And remember that you were a slave in the land of Egypt, and the LORD your God brought you out from there by a mighty hand and by an outstretched arm..."~Deuteronomy 5:15 You *SHALL* remember! It's a command not an option.

We were really slaves under the control of flesh and the world's influence. The phrase, *brought you out from*, has the connotation of being redeemed. We were on the shelf in the devil's shop. Our days were spent building pyramids in sorrow for the devil and God literally bought us out by paying the price. That price was laid upon the back of Jesus and nailed to a cross on Calvary. We should never forget that!

Get up! Get out of Egypt! And never forget from where you came. It will help you live free today as slaves. Yes, even though we are free in Christ we are indeed still slaves. We serve Him who saved us! "But now having been set free from sin, and having become slaves of God, you have your fruit to holiness, and the end, everlasting life."~Romans 6:22

What a privilege to yield our lives to His control knowing that He holds our future securely in His hands because He redeemed us unto Himself!

Lord, help me to live like one who has been redeemed.

September 30

Faith to Die By

 Today's devotion has a very personal connection for me. It was on this day in 2008 that my wife finally beat the effects of ALS or as it is better known Lou Gehrig's disease. On this date, Kay was welcomed into the presence of the Lord and left a horrible disease behind. This disease had completely paralyzed her except for the movement of her eyes. She could no longer eat without the benefit of a feeding tube. Each breathe she took was a challenge as the effects of the disease compromised her diaphragm and her ability to inhale sufficient oxygen. "Precious in the sight of the LORD is the death of His saints."~Psalm 116:15

I know that my wife's death is not the only time that a spouse has been widowed, so my inclusion of Kay's death is not intended to be unique. Death is certainly not unique, but how we die certainly can be.

She was diagnosed with ALS on her birthday in 2008. We had just left the doctor's office and returned to our vehicle. It was just when we were about to depart that I heard from Kay the first evidence of how she intended to deal with the reality of a death sentence.

Kay had 10 brothers and sisters. She was one of 11 children who had all come into this world as single births. At the time of her illness very few of her siblings showed any evidence of having trusted Christ as their Savior. I can still hear her response as we backed away from the parking space, "Thank God, it's me and not one of my brothers or sisters." It was so matter of fact. No complaining. No weeping. Just thanks to God that her siblings who might not know Christ had been spared.

The next hard part of the diagnosis was telling our four children the news. We asked all of them to come home so she and I could inform them and their spouses. I began talking, but I cannot honestly even remember what I said, for whatever I had said was overshadowed by her remarks. She calmly said to these four children whom she had carried and delivered into this world, "I only have two things to say to you all. First, I am not mad at God and I don't want you to be. Second, if God never does another thing for me, He has done enough." And with that she was finished. No complaining. No weeping. Just two simple statements of faith.

I do not know if I will ever have faith of this dimension. I do know that if the occasion calls for it, God will provide. "For I say, through the grace given to me, to everyone who is among you, not to think *of himself* more highly than he ought to think, but to think soberly, as God has dealt to each one a measure of faith."~Romans 12:3

I was privileged to be married to a saint. Not a saint because of her own goodness, but a saint because she gave her life to the only One who could give her life beyond ALS.

Lord, help me to always remember the faithful witness of those who have gone before me into Your eternal presence.

October 1

Thanks for the Memories

Remember when it was courteous to write thank you notes?

One of the things that I have tried to do during my ministry years is to send thank you notes. I have been the recipient of many blessings through the kindness of folks I have pastored. This month is set aside each year as Pastor Appreciation Month. I hope you remember your pastor and his family during October and say thank you in some tangible way. One of my fondest memories was when the congregation at First Baptist Church in Livingston, Louisiana declared the entire month, Sheep to Shepherd Month. I can still recount so many of the blessings my family and I received from God through the hands of those church members.

I also hope that you as a pastor remember to say, "Thanks!" Take the time to hand write a note even in this day of texting and emails. There is nothing more personal than taking a moment to reflect on the gift received, offer thanks, and an explanation of intent as to the use of the gift. Now before you conclude that this is a daily devotion on etiquette, let me tie all of this into the word of God.

Believers have received gifts from our Father. 1 Peter 4:10 tells us, "As each one has received a gift, minister it to one another, as good stewards of the manifold grace of God." When was the last time you sat down and wrote a thank you note to the Father? The scripture is plain: Each one has received a gift! There are no exceptions. Tell God your intentions as to the use of this gift, then use it to minister to others. Never forget you are only a steward of the gift. It is a gift of grace. Undeserved, yet yours. Don't you think it's time to say thanks?

Lord, help me to be thankful today.

October 2

Comfortability

Obedience is not easy! If it were everyone would be doing it. We have a tendency to attempt levels of obedience. We falsely assume that something less than full obedience will be accepted. Our obedience seems to follow the logic of comfortability. The conclusion that we derive from this logic is that I only need to obey up to the point that my conscience no longer bothers me, that is, we become comfortable.

The trouble with this line of logic is that we are using the wrong standard. Like the man who wrote a letter to the IRS and included a fifty dollar bill for back taxes. His letter stated that if he could not sleep at night he would send another fifty. Therein is the logic of comfortability.

The standard God sets is total obedience and the results of this level of obedience is not comfort, but happiness. "But He said, 'More than that, blessed are those who hear the word of God and keep it!'"~Luke 11:28 Notice that there are two steps to this standard of obedience. We are to hear and then to keep or observe. The result is to be blessed or as it could have been translated, *be happy.*

To keep or observe means more than blindly obey. It also means to protect and hide. As we hide God's Word in our hearts obedience gets easier. As we obey, we protect the Word from being taken from us. The difficult part of obedience is not the doing part; it is the holding on part.

There is one who is doing his best to steal away God's word and thereby bring us to disobedience. It is that old deceiver himself, Satan. He has been doing this since the Garden when he convinced Eve to disobey. Disobedience began when she listened to Satan's line of questioning. "Yea, has God said? (Genesis 3:1) The moment God's word was replaced then the logic of comfortability came into being and thereby disobedience. Hear and keep! Simple obedience!

Lord, help me to never get too comfortable.

283

October 3

The Unseen Line

 Life is a race with an unseen finish line. We have many finish lines that we cross, but none looms larger than the final one called death. I have friends and family that are closer (or so it seems) to the finish line than I. No one knows where the finish line is...only that it is.

The Apostle Paul used the analogy of life being a race. "Do you not know that those who run in a race all run, but one receives the prize? Run in such a way that you may obtain it."~1 Corinthians 9:24 Paul was thinking of the Isthmian games which were a forerunner of our present day Olympics.

In these games there was only one winner crowned and the crown was not gold, but a simple laurel wreath placed upon the brow. But, oh, the preparation and diligence that went into these races! Only one born a Greek could run. You could be disqualified even during the days leading up to the race itself. So, Paul spoke of keeping his body under control and running with great certainty not for a perishable crown of leaves and twigs, but for a crown that would be placed on his brow by Jesus.

During the Civil War, Lee sent word to Stonewall Jackson to see him on a matter of no great importance the next time he rode in the direction of headquarters. General Jackson received the message and immediately prepared to leave. Rising very early, he rode the eight miles to Lee's headquarters against a storm of wind and snow. Much surprised, Lee inquired why Jackson had come through such a storm. Jackson replied: "But you said that you wished to see me. General Lee's slightest wish is a supreme command to me."

So let us run as though our commander has summoned us to meet Him in the morning. So let us run as though our next step will break the ribbon. So let us win this race and expect the victor's crown from our Father.

Lord, help me to run well...all the way to the end.

October 4

Faith Bank

Imagine going to a bank to make a withdrawal where you had no account. I think that's called robbery! Believers have been given an account of faith in the Bank of Heaven. The account can never be reduced in value or ever depleted. We make deposits of praise in the dark times and withdraw the accumulated interest on the principal deposit of faith. The more we praise the higher the interest.

Now even though we have this sure account of faith in heaven, we still must be careful how we conduct our spiritual business while we journey here on earth. Jude wrote his brief letter to warn believers. "Beloved, while I was very diligent to write to you concerning our common salvation, I found it necessary to write to you exhorting you to contend earnestly for the faith which was once for all delivered to the saints."~Jude 3

Notice that Jude calls on us to contend for the faith that has been delivered to us. Delivered has the idea of entrusting to another as in a deposit at the bank. There is an intensity in the holder of this trust that portends the fact that someone is trying to take from us that which was delivered.

Beware whoever or whatever tries to make a withdrawal when they have not made a deposit. That is robbery! And we know who is the master thief and robber. It is Satan himself. He would love to destroy our faith. Guard it with all diligence!

Lord, help me to contend daily for the faith.

October 5

Happy Under His Hand

 Happiness is a subject often chased but seldom caught. When caught it is so very fleeting. We spend vast sums of money trying to be happy. Vacations, amusement parks, and new cars are just a partial list of things that we utilize as we seek happiness. Of course, all of it is fleeting and has little lasting effect on us.

Have you ever considered the happiness that can be found under the chastening hand of God? We don't normally think of chastisement as enjoyable much less as something that could remotely bring happiness. Job's response to God's chastising hand was one of happiness. "Behold, happy is the man whom God corrects; therefore do not despise the chastening of the Almighty."~Job 5:17 Incredible! There is a sense of excitement in this verse. It could have been written, "HOW HAPPY!"

The writer of Hebrews saw great value in the chastising work of God. "If you endure chastening, God deals with you as with sons; for what son is there whom a father does not chasten? But if you are without chastening, of which all have become partakers, then you are illegitimate and not sons. Furthermore, we have had human fathers who corrected us, and we paid them respect. Shall we not much more readily be in subjection to the Father of spirits and live? For they indeed for a few days chastened us as seemed best to them, but He for our profit, that we may be partakers of His holiness. Now no chastening seems to be joyful for the present, but painful; nevertheless, afterward it yields the peaceable fruit of righteousness to those who have been trained by it."~Hebrews 12:7–11

Now a question, "How happy are you under God's hand of correction?" Your response will determine how this day unfolds. BE HAPPY!

Lord, help me to be happy under Your chastisement.

October 6

Tank of Condemnation

We once had a fairly large aquarium. As a matter of fact we had two aquariums at the same time. In one we kept a variety of tropical fish. In the other we kept only one fish, a gourami. Gouramis are interesting. They tend to grow as large as the aquarium in which you house them. They also eat live food. We fed them goldfish which is one of their favorites.

In our smaller tank where the different varieties of fish existed, we would have a fish every now and then that just could not co-exist with the other fish. They would attack and agitate the other smaller fish. I remedied this problem. I let them visit the gourami. None ever returned. The gourami tank became our tank of condemnation.

Some people cannot fathom the concept of being in a state of condemnation and may even have issues with my fish story. I understand that. But condemnation is a reality if you do not have a relationship with Jesus. By the way, I no longer have any aquariums!

John 3 gives us the account of Nicodemus coming in the dark to see Jesus. The setting is indicative of man's heart condition: "And this is the condemnation, that the light has come into the world, and men loved darkness rather than light, because their deeds were evil."~John 3:19

Compare what men love and what God loves. God loves the world and openly gave Jesus on the cross for our redemption. Men love the dark. They hide in it and blame God for condemning them. We have every indication that Nicodemus believed that Jesus was indeed the Savior and was brought out of the dark into the light. Come to the light, believe and be saved today!

Lord, help me shed some light so others might come to You.

October 7

Electronic Withdrawal

 Suppose God told you to put down everything that had to be charged. You would possibly start shaking as you entered the full blown effects of electronic withdrawal. Now before you stop reading and return to your *iPhone, iPad, iPod,* or "iExistence", understand that I am not anti-gadget. After all I have even included the gateway to electronic Bible study with the embedded QR-codes for each day's devotion in this book. I hope that you have used them to further your devotional life. But...

We live in such a connected world today that we have a hard time being alone—particularly alone with God. Someone said that being alone is the anteroom before one steps into the presence of God.

Before Daniel received one of the greatest visions ever, he was alone. "Therefore I was left alone when I saw this great vision and no strength remained in me; for my vigor was turned to frailty in me, and I retained no strength."~Daniel 10:8

Before God spoke, terror fell on Daniel's companions and they fled leaving him alone. Then came the vision. For many of us we have a host of electronic friends, all of which can only help us until the battery fails or we drop them too hard on the concrete. Daniel's friends sensed the presence of God and fled out of fear. Our electronic gadgets are dumb tools that will not flee. You are their conscience. WE MUST PUT THEM AWAY AND BE ALONE WITH GOD! Try it. Be alone and be amazed at what God has to say in the stillness...then pick this book up again and read the daily devotional. You may be amazed at what God really has been trying to say.

Lord, help me use my times of being alone to see You.

October 8

Out of Your Mind

You must be out of your mind! Well, at least beyond your mind...but that's a good thing. When we give our cares and concerns to the Lord in prayer we are the recipients of peace that goes beyond our comprehension.

"Be anxious for nothing, but in everything by prayer and supplication, with thanksgiving, let your requests be made known to God; and the peace of God, which surpasses all understanding, will guard your hearts and minds through Christ Jesus."~Philippians 4:6–7 While we may not comprehend how God's peace comes to us in our times of anxiety, we are not left clueless as it calms our spirits. Instead, we are more fully prepared by His protection and guarding against the next assault which would work to steal away our peace.

It never ceases to amaze me how easily you can determine who has their confidence firmly anchored in Christ. Over the years I have visited church members and family in many hospitals and funeral homes. The response of people to sickness and death is always connected closely to their walk with Christ. There is a calmness and assurance in the face of trying times for those who have cast their care on the Lord. There is a peace that surpasses understanding.

This surpassing quality that comes by the peace of God at work cannot be mimicked or faked. It comes out of a living relationship of trust. It is a tranquility that presents itself in the midst of and aftermath of the storm.

So, it's okay to be out of your mind or at least beyond it! May the peace of God be yours today!

Lord, help me to prayer for understanding today.

October 9

Greater Grace

 I have heard people say things like, "God can't forgive me. I've sinned too much." Here's the answer for you or them. "In Him we have redemption through His blood, the forgiveness of sins, according to the riches of His grace..."~Ephesians 1:7

God's forgiveness is not measured by the badness of our sin, but by the extent of His grace! In essence, God's grace is proportional to our sin. So we can understand why Paul tells us where sin abounds grace does more abound! Whatever the immensity of your sin the riches of grace stands ready to pay the cost! This is not license to sin, but a limiting factor to sin. Understanding the penalty of sin that was placed on Christ and the pain He suffered for our sin, should cause us to hesitate at the very thought of sin.

Julia Johnston wrote these words that became the old familiar hymn, *Grace Greater than Our Sin*:

Marvelous grace of our loving Lord, grace that exceeds our sin and our guilt! Yonder on Calvary's mount outpoured—there where the blood of the Lamb was spilt. Sin and despair, like the sea waves cold, threaten the soul with infinite loss; grace that is greater—yes, grace untold—points to the Refuge, the mighty Cross. Dark is the stain that we cannot hide; what can avail to wash it away? Look! There is flowing a crimson tide—whiter than snow you may be today. Marvelous, infinite, matchless grace, freely bestowed on all who believe! You that are longing to see His face, will you this moment His grace receive? Grace, grace, God's grace, grace that will pardon and cleanse within; grace, grace, God's grace, grace that is greater than all our sin!

Lord, help me to take time to delight in your rich grace.

October 10

Living Up to Your Name

I wonder what the world is thinking about Jesus today. Where do they get their opinion? You don't need to think long or hard about this. Just go look in the mirror!

Paul's wrote in his second letter to the Thessalonians, "Therefore we also pray always for you that our God would count you worthy of this calling, and fulfill all the good pleasure of His goodness and the work of faith with power, that the name of our Lord Jesus Christ may be glorified in you..."~2 Thessalonians 1:11-12 Paul clearly describes for us where Jesus is displayed: *IN YOU!* The idea is that Jesus is made known and exalted in our everyday lives.

It is very evident what or who is being honored in our lives. It is Christ in us and demonstrated by us that the world sees. Paul prayed that the believers at Thessalonica would understand the magnitude of the calling upon their lives and the powerful work of faith that had taken place among them. This work of God was that which produced a proclamation of Jesus to the world.

The name of Jesus is either adored or abused, but very seldom ignored. For those who were watching the early church they only knew the character of Jesus by the lives of the believers. I can still remember my dad telling me as a boy that when I was away from home I should never forget that I was a Clark. The name represented my father and because of that I had a responsibility to live up to it.

Napoleon once came upon a soldier in his ranks who bore the same name as the emperor. Calling the young man to his tent he told him, "I have been told that your name is Napoleon. Either honor that name as a soldier or change your name!"

Now one last time. What does the world think about Jesus today?

Lord, help me to clearly be a picture of You to the world.

291

October 11

Fly Away

 A boy with a cage of sparrows was met by a man along the way. The birds flapped and fought to find their release, but to no avail.

"How much for the lot?" asked the man.

"Oh, these are worthless sparrows," replied the boy. "I'm taking them home to play with and then I'll feed them to my cat."

The man quickly responded, "They are valuable to me, son. Name your price."

A price was set and paid in full by the man. Taking possession of the cage of sparrows he surprised the lad as he opened the cage and set the captives winging and singing away. Remind you of someone you know? You are the bird; the man is JESUS!

It was Jesus who read in the temple the words from the prophet Isaiah, "The Spirit of the Lord is upon Me, because He has anointed Me to preach the gospel to the poor; He has sent Me to heal the brokenhearted, to proclaim liberty to the captives and recovery of sight to the blind, to set at liberty those who are oppressed;"~Luke 4:18

The price set for you and I was not established by the one who held us captive. The price was declared by God Himself. A price so high that no one but God Himself could pay it. And pay it He did on an old rugged cross. There He set the captives free proclaiming all of the benefits of which Isaiah spoke. More than an open door, we have had our broken hearts healed, our sight restored, and our repression remedied.

So fly away and sing of His love for you! The days of your captivity have ended!

Lord, help me fly today with a song of redemption.

292

October 12

A Working Heart

It is easier to fill a mind than to mend a heart. Most people are not impressed with what you have stuffed between your ears. Rather they are convinced by how deeply your heart beats with the compassion of Christ. Your friends don't really care how much you know; they know how much you really care. The shortest verse in the Bible is "Jesus wept."~John 11:35 It is in this short verse that we see the real heart of Jesus at work.

Jesus wept. Just two words, but they reveal the compassionate heart of Christ. He had been summoned because his friend Lazarus had become ill and the sisters of his friend knew He could heal their brother. But Jesus delayed His arrival and in the time that elapsed Lazarus died.

When He arrived at the home of Mary and Martha the crowd was in full grieving mode. Mary and Martha both greeted Jesus with a shallow accusation that questioned His delay. Both of the sisters and the others knew that He was too late. Their brother was dead and their hopes now rested in the future resurrection. Jesus asked where they had laid his friend. Upon seeing the despair of Mary and Martha and the hopelessness of the mourners, Jesus wept.

Jesus wept and the crowds thought His weeping was for Himself and His grief at the death of His friend. They could not imagine that He wept for them, but as the song says, "O, how He loves you and me!" Then at His word the stone over the tomb was removed, the command for Lazarus to come forth was issued, and His friend walked out of the grave. No! The weeping was not for Himself for He knew that Lazarus would live again. It was for you and for me and that's a *heart* not a *head* at work!

Lord, help me to remember that You have wept over me.

October 13

Parable of the Root Canal

 Have you ever started to watch a television program and there was a disclaimer that what you are about to see may be disturbing to some viewers. Well, for those of you are squeamish about dentist, you might want to read the next few lines with your eyes closed or at the minimum with your mouth closed!

Here's the account as it happened. Several months ago my dentist ground down what I thought was a perfectly good tooth and crowned it. Now covered in beautiful porcelain I thought all was fine. However, that tooth began to throb. The dentist had to drill through that porcelain exterior to fix the ROOT problem. No amount of veneer could fix the deep down problem.

Jesus' words to the scribes and Pharisees matched the condition of my tooth perfectly. "Woe to you, scribes and Pharisees, hypocrites! For you are like whitewashed tombs which indeed appear beautiful outwardly, but inside are full of dead men's bones and all uncleanness."~Matthew 23:27

The scribes and Pharisees had become religious experts. They attended all of the holy days and kept the Sabbath. These men knew the Scriptures like the back of their hand. Correct in their dress, culinary habits, and avid tithers these would have been models of moral correctness, but Jesus applied the x-ray of holiness to their religiosity and found a deep rooted problem.

They had covered themselves with outward beauty like my dentist did with the porcelain exterior of my crown. However, the poison of their pride and deceit was eating away night and day on their souls. It took Jesus coming along and touching the nerve to expose the real root problem they were facing. Like my porcelain crown would have kept the problem concealed, it could never correct the root problem. And that's the parable of the root canal.

Lord, help me get to the root problem today.

October 14

Grace Power

What mountain stands before you today? Be it mere obstacle or overarching concern, the answer is not your strength or ability. The power which levels the mountain is GRACE!

This from Zechariah's vision will help you. "This is the word of the Lord to Zerubbabel: 'Not by might nor by power, but by My Spirit,' says the Lord of hosts. 'Who are you, O great mountain? Before Zerubbabel you shall become a plain!' And he shall bring forth the capstone with shouts of 'Grace, grace to it!'" ~Zechariah 4:6-7

Now there are times that we would like to shout a lot of words at a problem. Some of these words may even rush up from our past. Words that we do not use any longer as believers, but the most powerful answer is GRACE! It is in grace that the Spirit of God both levels the mountain and sets the capstone of rebuilding.

We do not usually think of grace in terms of power. Grace is thought of at the moment of salvation or in times when we are simply out of strength and endurance. But in Zechariah's vision, we see the power of grace at work. Grace reveals our lack of power and might for it can never exist as long as we are struggling to accomplish the task on our own. Grace not only exposes our inability, it gives us the ability to do what God has ordained.

Whatever obstacle is keeping you from obeying God today, shout grace to it and watch it flatten before you. And once that mountain is removed then build upon the foundation of grace realizing that nothing is done in the believer's life apart from it. Let your victory cry be, "Grace, grace, God's grace!"

Lord, help me to realize today that it is not my strength, but Yours.

October 15

Easy or Hard

 Water always seeks the easiest route to the lowest level which is eventually the sea. Thus when you look at the course a river chooses it is always curving and twisting. The water is always looking for the *easy* route. Not so with the Christian...God chooses our path which sometimes is *hard*. Hard enough to bring us to the place of trusting Him and eventually ending up at His side.

We, as believers, are called to walk the path that has been laid out before us. "Therefore we also, since we are surrounded by so great a cloud of witnesses, let us lay aside every weight, and the sin which so easily ensnares us, and let us run with endurance the race that is set before us, looking unto Jesus, the author and finisher of our faith, who for the joy that was set before Him endured the cross, despising the shame, and has sat down at the right hand of the throne of God."~Hebrews 12:1–2

This path will be no less difficult than that which Christ Himself walked. Since He endured and finished His race, we too, have the encouragement to complete our race as well. Easy is simply not in the layout of the Christian course. Some of the difficulty in our race comes not from design, but from external forces who are bound and determined to make it hard for believers. These difficulties were foretold in Paul's last letter before he was martyred. "...men will be lovers of themselves, lovers of money, boasters, proud, blasphemers, disobedient to parents, unthankful, unholy, unloving, unforgiving, slanderers, without self-control, brutal, despisers of good, traitors, headstrong, haughty, lovers of pleasure rather than lovers of God, having a form of godliness but denying its power."~2 Timothy 3:1–5 Seek His course for your life! Mind not the hardness! Look not for the easy!

Lord, help me face the hard times and not look for the easy way out.

October 16

Craft Fair Time

This is a beautiful time of the year here in the Ozarks of Northwest
Arkansas. Along with the fall colors come the caravans of shoppers.
Not only is it fall in the Ozarks, it is Craft Fair time. Some of the largest
craft fairs in America occur in my back door. It's a busy, congested
time!

I enjoy looking at some of the creations that have come from minds and hands
that are much more nimble than mine, but I can take it or leave it. In essence
crafters might be defined as people who create stuff out of stuff and stuff it into
a display hoping someone will take all of their stuff home and add it to their stuff!
Does that make me stuffy about crafts? I hope not!

Craftiness on display...unlike our crafty adversary, the devil, who never puts his
stuff out to be seen easily. He has been crafty since he first tempted Eve in the
garden with his partial truths. "But I fear, lest somehow, as the serpent deceived
Eve by his craftiness, so your minds may be corrupted from the simplicity that is
in Christ."~2 Corinthians 11:3 Sometimes when I look at a display of crafts I
must ask, "How did they do that?" So it is with the craftiness of Satan. We must
not marvel at his cunning.

The Apostle Paul warned the Ephesians, "that we should no longer be children,
tossed to and fro and carried about with every wind of doctrine, by the trickery
of men, in the cunning craftiness of deceitful plotting,"~Ephesians 4:14 He is
the master of trickery. He likes to slip his stuff into our lives. Somehow when I
attend a craft fair, I always come home with some article; another piece of stuff.
Beware the devil's stuff; it always cost more than it's worth!

Lord, help me to never fall for the devil's craftiness.

October 17

Goose, Goose

 We have near our home a pond on which a large flock of geese reside. Each morning they take flight with much fanfare. God spoke through these geese this morning, as I began to write this devotional. Now you may not think that God can speak through geese, but I do.

If He can speak through Balaam's donkey (Numbers 22), I certainly think that He can speak through a flock of geese. If you are still not convinced, then what of Psalm 19, where David proclaimed that the very heavens declare the glory of God and the earth shows his workmanship? So, with that point settled...*God does speak through geese*...here is what I learned and what I believe God wanted you to hear today as well.

As these geese began to lift off from their pond you could hear them before you could see them. Each goose honked as if to herald the fact that they were about to occupy the sky and the intention of each honker was that all the flock should join in the process. Geese are like that you know. They seem to understand the importance of cooperation, challenge, and camaraderie. Taking flight they formed their usual "V" formation and began to honk encouragement to the goose out front. Every goose in this formation was making it easier for the goose that followed.

These same qualities were seen in Jonathan's relationship to David. "Then Jonathan, Saul's son, arose and went to David in the woods and strengthened his hand in God."~1 Samuel 23:16 What a great friend of encouragement was Jonathan! Oh, to be a Jonathan and to have a Jonathan in formation with us.

Will you be a Jonathan today? Let me hear you now, "HONK!, HONK!"

Lord, help me be like a Jonathan to someone today.

October 18

Are You Ready?

Ready! Set! Go! Are you prepared to meet God? No, I'm not talking about dying although that's a possibility for all of us. I'm just talking about making things ready BEFORE you approach God.

Whether it be in prayer or in communion we should make sure that things are in order before we come into His presence. Hear God's word to Moses before he ascended the mountain to receive the 10 commandments: "So be ready in the morning, and come up in the morning to Mount Sinai, and present yourself to Me there on the top of the mountain."~Exodus 34:2

Be ready. Put everything in order. Prepare through faithfulness to meet with God. This was the commandment given to Moses. He did not have the privilege of simply marching up the mountain and coming into God's presence. God instructed him to come and present himself. The idea here is to show oneself in the best state possible.

I have been in worship services in many countries around the world. I have noticed that those who come to worship in those places come wearing their very best even though they may live daily in poverty stricken villages. This is in sharp contrast to what I see here in the states many times. It seems that casual is in and the idea of *presenting* oneself is not considered for the most part.

I'm not saying that we must wear a suit and tie to go to church, but I do think that the admonition given to Moses cannot be overlooked. Make everything ready and present yourself before the Lord with the very best you have. Ready? Set...

Lord, help me to be ready...always!

October 19

Keeping It on the Level

 Okay, here's the scoop. I was never able to make foul shots when I played basketball. Whew! I'm glad that's off my chest! I've discovered in my later years that the problem was not with my hands, but with my eyes. I have a malady called vertical displacement. My eyes perceive that things are tilted when they are not. The result: my brain tells my muscles to compensate for a tilt that doesn't exist... and voila a missed shot! That's my excuse and I'm sticking to it!

The same thing happens in our Christian walk also. We need God's help to make sure that the path we walk is level. "Teach me Your way, O Lord, and lead me in a level path, because of my enemies."~Psalms 27:11

Notice we need this because of our enemies. The word translated as enemies carries the meaning of those who have hostile intentions toward us. Thinking back on my basketball days, I can only imagine what folks in the stands must have said when I went to the free throw line. The opposing team's fans rejoiced knowing I would probably miss and our fans would think, "Oh no! Clark's on the line!"

Either way, there was some hostility toward my ability to shoot a foul shot. Things would have been different if I had known that my vision was not on the level. Just as this verse calls on God to make our path level, I could have quieted my "enemies" with eyes that saw in a level fashion. Our enemies are always watching our walk. They are ready to call attention to an unleveled gait. May God correct our vision and level our paths for everyone's sake!

Lord, help me to walk level in a tilted world.

October 20

Fearing God

Fear is not always a bad thing. Fear is one of the responses that we have been given to help us, especially in times of danger. Fear can also keep us from engaging in too much risk. However, fear can quickly degenerate into paralysis that prevents us from acting. And then there is the healthy form of fear...the fear of God.

There are a lot of people who struggle with the idea of fearing God. The person who has never trusted Christ fears Him who holds their soul's destination in His hands. The backslidden Christian fears God's hand of correction. And even the one walking in fellowship finds times that leave the heart wondering about a HOLY God.

David gives us a totally different perspective on fear in Psalm 19:9, "The fear of the Lord is clean, enduring forever; the judgments of the Lord are true and righteous altogether." Let me paraphrase his statement: The reverential awe of God has a cleansing effect that lasts forever allowing us to stand before the Lord without fear of his true and righteous judgments.

It is important for us to properly understand that the fear of the Lord is to be filled with reverential awe. This proper respect for the majesty of the Lord has as a side effect the ability to keep us clean. For those old enough it's better than *Bon Ami*; a little younger it is more powerful than *Mr. Clean*; and for the 20-somethings it'll make you whiter than *OxiClean*! Furthermore, we can approach God without fear because His judgment has already fallen upon Christ on Calvary. Fear the Lord and watch your life sparkle!

Lord, help me stand before You in awe today.

October 21

Tickets, please!

I am not a black tie—got to have a reservation type of person. I fit in a lot better in a setting that allows me to just be me. The welcome mat is always out for me at McDonald's and that's just fine with me!

There is a place, however, that a reservation is required and I'm planning on going there one day. How about you? No tickets are sold at the door. You must make all of your plans TODAY, because you never know when you will show up. So, would you like to go with me one day? Where is this place you are wondering? Wonder no more! The place is HEAVEN and you can go!

Are you ready? Is your reservation made? "Blessed be the God and Father of our Lord Jesus Christ, who according to His abundant mercy has begotten us again to a living hope through the resurrection of Jesus Christ from the dead, to an inheritance incorruptible and undefiled and that does not fade away, RESERVED in heaven for you."~1 Peter 1:3-4

The wonderful promise of this verse is for all who will place their trust in the death, burial, and resurrection of Jesus. The moment you answer His call upon your life a reservation is made for you. Remember, no tickets at the door. The cost of your admittance has already been paid. No black ties needed...only a yielded life.

Lord, help me to rejoice in the fact that I have a reservation.

October 22

Rescue

So...what's the bad news today? You do not have to look far to find it. Somewhere evil is moving. Doesn't that just bless you? DON'T DESPAIR! Our rescue is on the horizon!

Our rescue begins the moment we trust Christ as our Savior. At that moment we are delivered from the penalty of sin. "[Jesus] gave Himself for our sins, that He might deliver us from this present evil age, according to the will of our God and Father."~Galatians 1:4

You may have noticed, however, that we still suffer the effects of sin after we have trusted Christ. This verse goes on to tell us that He is in the process of delivering us from this present evil age. It is in this age that we sense the power of sin.

Paul spoke of this in Romans 7 as he wrote of his struggle with doing the right thing and ending up doing the wrong thing. He concluded that only Jesus could deliver him from the power of daily sin. But the news gets better!

We will ultimately be delivered from the presence of sin at His glorious return. Sin will have no place in His presence. Tell the good news! It is God's will to rescue us by plucking us out of this world! LOOK UP! Your redemption draws near!

Lord, help me to always look up!

October 23

Riddle Time

 Here's a riddle for you. What is the one thing God has never seen? Remember now He is omnipresent. He is everywhere at once. He is omnipotent. He is all powerful. He is omniscient. He knows all things. So, what's your answer? What is the one thing God had never seen?

Answer: God has never seen His equal!

"Who has measured the waters in the hollow of His hand, measured heaven with a span and calculated the dust of the earth in a measure? Weighed the mountains in scales and the hills in a balance? Behold, the nations are as a drop in a bucket, and are counted as the small dust on the scales; look, He lifts up the isles as a very little thing. 'To whom then will you liken Me, or to whom shall I be equal?' says the Holy One."~Isaiah 40:12,15,25

God has described Himself in relationship to various parts of His creation and concludes that the answer to my riddle is correct. He has never seen His equal! He can measure all of the oceans and seas in the palm of His hand. That same hand's width measures the whole of the earth. He measures the mountains, hills and islands and weighs them upon His scale. Even the billions of people upon this earth today are like a drop in His bucket. These descriptions of God quickly overwhelm our ability to comprehend.

Now, if this unequaled God whom we serve can hold all that is like so much dust, is He not able to hold you and your concerns with ease? We really are out of our league when we think that we know better or have the ability to meet our own needs. Never try to be God's equal!

Lord, help me to remember that You have no equal.

October 24

The Mystery of the Mystery

Mysteries have a way of fascinating us. As soon as someone gives a hint we want to know more. If we find out that the information is only for a select few, well, that makes it all the better as our curiosity is piqued.

Since the early days of radio and television, the mystery has been an audience grabber. One of the early programs was *The Shadow* which first aired in August 1930. The tag line for the opening of this radio mystery was, "Who knows what evil lurks in the hearts of men? The Shadow knows!"

The Bible has a few mysteries in it as well. There is a problem, however, in conveying a biblical mystery when it is compared to a modern fictionalized mystery. For example, the Apostle Paul speaks of a mystery in 1 Corinthians 15. "Behold, I tell you a mystery: We shall not all sleep, but we shall all be changed—in a moment, in the twinkling of an eye, at the last trumpet. For the trumpet will sound, and the dead will be raised incorruptible, and we shall be changed. For this corruptible must put on incorruption, and this mortal must put on immortality. So when this corruptible has put on incorruption, and this mortal has put on immortality, then shall be brought to pass the saying that is written: 'Death is swallowed up in victory.'"~1 Corinthians 15:51–54

The English word *mystery* is a word that means something covered, hidden, and undiscoverable. The Greek word used here means something that was previously hidden, but is now revealed at least to a select group. So, the mystery of the word *mystery* is solved. God has no intent in hiding from believers the truth about death, resurrection, and the second coming of Christ. We may die, but we shall be raised first at the moment of His coming. We may live, but we will be changed from corruptible to incorruptible.

It is going to happen quickly like the blinking of an eye. It will happen so fast that not even our vision will be blurred. One moment here; the next moment there. The truth of this transition is evident for the living and those who have already died. All of this transpires at the trumpet sound of God. He alone is in control of this next great experience for the believer in Christ. That which is so mysterious, if you have never trusted Christ, is revealed to all who believe. And like all good mysteries the story must end with the "good guy" winning and the "bad guy" being defeated. Read again the last sentence of our text for today:

Death is swallowed up in victory.

The good guy is Jesus. We are on His side. We win!

Mystery solved!

Lord, help me to not be mystified by Your coming.

October 25

A-Maze-ing

This is the time of the year for fall harvest and the rejoicing that accompanies a bumper crop. You would think that a farmer would anticipate the day he could load his crop onto his wagons and garner it, but there is a new use for corn crops that has begun to catch on across the country side.

Farmers are taking perfectly good corn fields and cutting mazes into them! This is really amazing (no pun intended.) More amazing is that people will then pay him to walk into these mazes and get lost! No wonder *Fritos* cost so much! We are either turning the corn into fuel for our automobiles or seeking a confused state of mind as we trample through it!

Paul found himself in a state of confusion at times: "We are hard-pressed on every side, yet not crushed; we are PERPLEXED... but not in despair;"~2 Corinthians 4:8 To be perplexed is to not know the way through to the exit. But notice—Paul's perplexity never led to despair or hopelessness.

Why? Because he knew the Farmer who carved out the maze as a Friend and Companion for the journey. Jesus may have said something like this, "Lo, I am with you as you traverse the maze called life for I AM THE WAY OUT!"

Lord, help me never be lost in life's maze.

October 26

Bon Appetit

 Why does it seem so difficult to get folks to listen to the good news of the cross, salvation, and God's infinite love displayed in Christ? The message is not wrong and doesn't need to be altered. The problem lies in the delivery.

We must make sure that our words are tasty! Job put it this way. "Can flavorless food be eaten without salt? Or is there any taste in the white of an egg?"~Job 6:6

Work on making your delivery delicious! God has written the recipe for salvation to be appetizing. The word gospel means good news. Let's make sure that our delivery doesn't leave a bad taste in people's mouths!

If you are looking for a good restaurant, then be on the lookout for a full parking lot. This is usually a good indication that the menu lists lots of great tasting food. Folks will travel long distances for a tasty tidbit. And having eaten at a really good restaurant, the customers will be walking billboards for that business.

Always remember, you are just the waiter delivering the food. "[So] let your speech always be with grace, seasoned with salt, that you may know how you ought to answer each one."~Colossians 4:6 We did not write the recipe. We have no right to make substitutions to the menu. God is the "master chef" of this establishment. He has prepared the menu before the foundation of the earth was set. To those who consume the good news of the gospel, they will find themselves full and overflowing with joy, peace, and life. BON APPETIT!

Lord, help me to be flavorful to those I meet today.

No Time for Berry Picking

If you happened upon a burning bush would you take your shoes off and walk on holy ground or spend your time figuring out how to pick berries without getting burned? God certainly knows how to get our attention, be it a burning bush or an interruption that ignites our interest. Turn aside now and see what God is doing and what He has to say. Your day will be better for it.

Moses was minding his own business on the back side of the desert. He had long ago fled from Egypt after a failed attempt to deliver Israel from bondage. His plan evidently was to set them free one Egyptian at a time. The Exodus account tells of Moses coming upon an altercation between an Egyptian taskmaster and an Israelite slave. Moses interceded and the result was a dead Egyptian. Isn't it amazing how we can mess things up so badly trying to perform God's will our way?

The story picks up some 40 years later. "Now Moses was tending the flock of Jethro his father-in-law, the priest of Midian. And he led the flock to the back of the desert, and came to Horeb, the mountain of God. And the Angel of the LORD appeared to him in a flame of fire from the midst of a bush. So he looked, and behold, the bush was burning with fire, but the bush was not consumed. Then Moses said, 'I will now turn aside and see this great sight, why the bush does not burn.'"~Exodus 3:1–3 God knows exactly where you are and what it takes to get your attention. Moses must have assumed he was well hidden from both the Egyptians and God, but God came calling to him from the burning bush. Moses' response was exactly as ours might have been. "I will now turn aside and see this great sight, why the bush does not burn." God can use curiosity to move us back into the center of His will and service. What is God using as a burning bush in your life today? It's time to turn aside and take off your shoes; it's not time to pick berries!

Lord, help me to turn aside and hear You today.

October 28

No Place Like Home

Home. Just a place. Always good to find oneself there. But Paul said in 2 Corinthians 5:1, "...we have a building of God, an house not made with hands, eternal in the heavens."

Home? Not quite yet since I am still writing daily devotions for my friends. One day I'll write my last one and then I will really be home and it won't just be a place!

I find myself more desirous to be at home these days. Especially, since I have had the privilege of traveling nearly all the way around the globe as part of my ministry as an associational missionary. Most folks, no matter how much they enjoy traveling, eventually want to go home. We all get a little Dorothy in us. We would like to click our heels, so we could instantly be home.

Paul would later write to the Philippians these words which describe his desire to go home. "For to me, to live is Christ, and to die is gain. But if I live on in the flesh, this will mean fruit from my labor; yet what I shall choose I cannot tell. For I am hard-pressed between the two, having a desire to depart and be with Christ, which is far better. Nevertheless to remain in the flesh is more needful for you. And being confident of this, I know that I shall remain and continue with you all for your progress and joy of faith, that your rejoicing for me may be more abundant in Jesus Christ by my coming to you again."~Philippians 1:21–26

So, as I arrive home again from another mission trip I must admit that this is not really home. It's just a place to rest until we really rest. May I ever see this place as temporary!

Lord, help me to remember that I'm not home yet.

310

October 29

I Will

What will you do today? One of the amazing aspects of God's sovereignty is that He allows the human will to function. He is not threatened by our ability to decide. He is not afraid of us making a wrong decision. He is willing to allow us the freedom to choose.

After the Psalmist conveyed the might of God in Psalm 104, he announced, "I will sing to the Lord as long as I live; I will sing praise to my God while I have my being. May my meditation be sweet to Him; I will be glad in the Lord."~Psalms 104:33-34

There are times our wills need to be realigned to bring glory to Him who allowed us to have free wills in the first place. God could have easily made us like robots. He could have put the thoughts in our heads and the words in our mouths to the extent that we would simply parrot our response to Him. But He did not!

He graciously allows us to think and speak on our own. But because of our tendency to drift away and forget His grace, it does us well, like it did the Psalmist, to recount the majesty of His work. Take the time to read this entire Psalm and you will join the writer as he adjusted his will to "sing to the Lord as long as I live."

So what WILL you do with your God-given ability to choose? As for me, I join the Psalmist: I will sing; I will praise; I will meditate; I will be glad!

Lord, help me make a choice to sing praises to You today.

October 30

Spot On

Ever felt like you were on the spot? Especially if you feel like you've been put there! Well, you are and you have been! God has a very specific purpose for placing you in the exact spot where you reside.

Paul tells us in 2 Corinthians 2:14, "Now thanks be to God who always leads us in triumph in Christ, and through us diffuses the fragrance of His knowledge in every place."

The word *place* in this verse means the very spot where we are. God's reason for placing you here is simple really. We are the diffusing stick through which God fills our spot with the scent of Jesus! This means that your family is your spot. Your job is on the spot. The school you attend has a spot that fits you. Where you shop is a spot that needs filling and you are the one to fill it. I could go on, but I think you get it. You're on the spot!

If you were not in the very spot you occupy there would be no fragrance of heaven flowing from your life to fill an otherwise pungent predicament. It may seem some days that life stinks. I agree. But we can be the sweet fragrance of Jesus to fill our space and turn an otherwise disagreeable scent into one that causes us and others to take in a deep, deep breath.

Will you be a *Glade* Christian today? If you will stay in your place, God can use you like the aerosol of heaven. Now, breathe deeply and stay put until the spot you're in smells like Jesus.

Lord, help me to fill my spot with a fragrance of You.

October 31

Under Construction

I visited the grave site of Ruth Bell Graham, wife of evangelist Billy Graham, a couple of years ago. Her epitaph reads: "End of Construction; Thank You for Your Patience." She had read these words at the site of some road construction that had been completed. She had remarked that she would like these words as her epitaph. Her family had them inscribed on her tombstone.

Paul spoke similar words about our journey as Christians, "being confident of this very thing, that He who has begun a good work in you will complete it until the day of Jesus Christ;"~Philippians 1:6

Like Ruth Graham our lives are undergoing massive construction. God did not begin a repair job in our lives when we came to know Christ. He released the power of His Holy Spirit to tear out the old, put a new foundation in place, and begin a new good work in us. As in all construction projects I have ever experienced, they take longer than I would have expected. God, however, is never behind schedule and the work will be completed on time.

Until that day comes keep your sign posted:

"UNDER CONSTRUCTION!"

Be ready for a lot of complaints from passers-by who have no idea what God is up to in your life nor what it takes to make something new out of something old. You can endure the process knowing this: One day the work will be completed. In the meantime:

THANK YOU FOR YOUR PATIENCE!

Lord, help me be patient until You finish working on me.

November 1

Now That's Beautiful!

 Beauty...What do they say? Fleeting, skin-deep...You know very temporary! We apply the term to everything from sunsets, to brides, to great catches in the end zone. But where can we find true lasting beauty?

It is only found in God's presence. The Psalmist tells us in Psalm 96, "Honor and majesty are before Him; strength and beauty are in His sanctuary. Oh, worship the Lord in the beauty of holiness!"~Psalms 96:6;9

Twice in these two verses the word *beauty* is used. The first speaks of His gleaming glory while the second holds the idea of decoration and ornamentation. His beauty is one of His attributes even as His glory is part of his character. Added to this is the fact of His holiness which is a beautiful characteristic as well. It is this holiness of God that adds the honor and majesty that we see in His presence.

We have never really seen beauty yet. You and I have been wowed by a lot of stuff in our lives, but in that day we will just be speechless in His sanctuary. All of the wows of our meager experience will be left in the dust and ashes of earth's beauty. Until then we can experience a little foretaste of real beauty as we worship Him by living in His holiness.

WOW! THAT'S BEAUTIFUL!

Lord, help me worship You today in all your beauty.

November 2

Grace, Grace

Limitless grace! Paul only came to the knowledge of God's supply of grace after he had walked the road of suffering. He spoke of this revelation of grace in this way, "And He said to me, 'My grace is sufficient for you, for My strength is made perfect in weakness.' Therefore most gladly I will rather boast in my infirmities, that the power of Christ may rest upon me."~2 Corinthians 12:9

Charles Spurgeon related it this way to a class of ministerial students. I couldn't think of a better description. "Gentlemen," he said one Friday to his students, "there are many passages of Scripture which you will never understand until some trying or singular experience shall interpret them to you. The other evening I was riding home after a heavy day's work; I was very wearied and sore depressed; and swiftly and suddenly as a lightning flash, that text laid hold on me: 'My grace is sufficient for thee!' On reaching home, I looked it up in the original, and at last it came to me this way: MY grace is sufficient for THEE. 'Why,' I said to myself, 'I should think it is!' and I burst out laughing. It seemed to make unbelief so absurd.

It was as though some little fish, being very thirsty, was troubled about drinking the river dry; and Father Thames said: 'Drink away, little fish, my stream is sufficient for thee!' Or as if a little mouse in the granaries of Egypt, after seven years of plenty, feared lest it should die of famine, and Joseph said, 'Cheer up, little mouse, my granaries are sufficient for thee!'

Again, I imagined a man away up yonder on the mountain saying to himself, 'I fear I shall exhaust all the oxygen in the atmosphere.' But the earth cries: 'Breathe away, O man, and fill thy lungs; My atmosphere is sufficient for thee!'" Sufficient is so much better than limitless because it is always exactly matched to my situation. Amazing, SUFFICIENT grace!

Lord, help me to breathe in Your grace today.

November 3

Vote for Jesus

On one of the first few days of November elections are usually held here in the United States. Every four years we vote for a president. Indeed, we are blessed to have such a wonderful privilege.

In a country where we elect leaders it is difficult to understand the concept of a Potentate ruling over us. However, Paul uses this term to describe Jesus in 1 Timothy without apology.

"I urge you in the sight of God who gives life to all things, and before Christ Jesus who witnessed the good confession before Pontius Pilate, that you keep this commandment without spot, blameless until our Lord Jesus Christ's appearing, which He will manifest in His own time, He who is the blessed and only *Potentate*, the King of kings and Lord of lords, who alone has immortality, dwelling in unapproachable light, whom no man has seen or can see, to whom be honor and everlasting power. Amen."~1 Timothy 6:13–16

As Jesus stood before Pilate He informed Him that Pilate had no authority except that which had been given him. When Pilate asked Jesus if He was a king, little did he know that before him stood the King of Kings, the Potentate of the universe!

The designation of Jesus as Potentate gives us insight into His potential. He can do all things because the dynasty is His! He is not running for election to office. His term never expires and He will never surrender His throne! Therefore, as the Apostle Paul stated it, "AMEN!!!"

Lord, help me to pray for our leaders today.

November 4

Testimony in Chalk

On one of my morning walks I saw a place along the sidewalk that some children had been scribbling with chalk. Since it had not rained in a while their art had lasted for days, but I knew the rain would come and their chalk Picasso's would be washed away. This made me think about what testimony of my passing would be left the morning after life's rain washes me away.

The book of Revelation speaks about those who literally overcame the old Deceiver, Satan, himself by the word of their testimony. "And they overcame him by the blood of the Lamb and by the word of their testimony, and they did not love their lives to the death."~Revelation 12:11

Many of you have experienced a testimony service where individuals stand to proclaim what God has been doing in their lives. Sometimes these accountings can be very moving and filled with detail. Other times you have to wonder how long it has been since the person has been with Jesus. The phrase *word of their testimony* is much more than a simple recounting of what's been going on in one's life. The testimony spoken of here places great weight on the content of the one giving the testimony. The *word of their testimony* was an outflow of what was filling them on the inside. It was the evidence of a personal experience with the One who shed His blood for them. "...even as the testimony of Christ was confirmed in you..."~1 Corinthians 1:6 Here the Apostle Paul declared that the believers in the Corinthian church had a testimony that could be confirmed as true and was evidenced as being part of their very lives.

Chalky testimonies are easily drawn from shallow experience, but they are washed away when the trial comes by the hand of the Deceiver. So, is your testimony written in chalk or in blood? The only testimony that will stand the test of time is one that confirms you as a child of God through the shed blood of His Jesus.

Lord, help me to always have a fresh testimony.

317

November 5

The King's Highway

 It is amazing how easy God makes it to find peace, yet how much trouble man goes to avoid it. In Isaiah 59:8 we read, "The way of peace they have not known, and there is no justice in their ways; they have made themselves crooked paths; whoever takes that way shall not know peace."

A few years back the interstate system was still in its infancy. As people traveled along the miles of concrete, signs would be placed for businesses just off the main highway. Some exits were just that—an exit with no return or at least not an easy one. These signs carried a message somewhere in their design that read like this: EASY OFF—EASY ON. The message of these few words was that the driver could be assured of quick access to their services, but also an easy return to the interstate highway. You do not see this statement on signs anymore. Off ramps are always accompanied by on ramps and no one even thinks about getting off the highway and not being able to get back on easily. The verse from Isaiah tells us that some depart from the way of peace and find themselves traversing a crooked path. They do not know how to return to the highway of peace.

The *way of peace* speaks of a well-marked highway whereas their *ways* and *paths* can best be described as trampling about in a circle. To miss the peace of God a person must purposefully leave the highway and cut his own path of lostness. Like the old days on the interstate, leaving the highway of peace is easy, but finding your way back can be challenging. This is especially true in this case for a willful choice is made to make one's own way.

The admonition is clear: WHOEVER TAKES THIS PATH SHALL NOT KNOW PEACE! Are you seeking peace in your life today? Come to the King's Highway and find peace and safety for your life!

Lord, help me show someone the on-ramp to the King's Highway.

November 6

Game of the Century

Sports fills a lot of our lives today. I'm not so sure that it was any different in the Apostle Paul's day, however. He made many references to sports as he wrote to the New Testament churches. I remember reading the manuscript of a message written in the first century. In it the pastor bemoans the fact that so many had gone to the chariot races!

Every now and again a game takes on epic proportions. Commentators will label it the game of the century! You have to wonder at descriptions sometimes. I enjoyed watching just such a game recently. I was glad that my team beat the other team. I was glad that it was a close and exciting process which was won in overtime fashion. But just minutes after the winning field goal I felt the whole house shake!

We had felt the rumble of a 5.7 magnitude trembler that occurred about 120 miles to the southwest of my home. I know that's not much shaking for folks that live where earthquakes happen regularly, but for Arkansas we felt every shake, rattle, and roll!

That earthquake made me realize that God has an amazing ability to put everything into context. The day is coming when games won't matter and there will be no overtime to determine the winner. God's not looking for a contest to prove Himself; He is already the undefeated Champion!

"May the glory of the Lord endure forever; may the Lord rejoice in His works. He looks on the earth, and it trembles; He touches the hills, and they smoke."~Psalms 104:31-32 GAME OVER! GOD WINS! And yes, it is the game of all eternity!

Lord, help me always know that You win.

November 7

Great Expectations

 Great expectations! Had any lately? Great expectations can lead to great disappointments. If you have ever read Dickens' *Great Expectations* you will remember the struggles of Pip as he traversed the ups and downs of life and found that his life was filled with both great expectations and great disappointments.

Am I telling you not to engage in expectancy of grand proportions? *ABSOLUTELY NOT!* The answer lies in the *where* of our expectations and in the *who* of our expectations. Our expectations excel exponentially as our trust in God increases.

"Keep my soul, and deliver me; let me not be ashamed, for I put my trust in You."~Psalms 25:20 This verse provides the right perspective on this subject. It begins with the *where* of expectancy: "KEEP MY SOUL." The idea here is that of being hedged in by God and protected in our minds, wills, and emotions. The *who* of my expectations is God Himself.

The word *trust* in this verse has a root meaning of fleeing. When we flee to God and hide behind His hedge of protection we will never be ashamed of having great or even greater expectations for He will deliver us from ourselves and unto Himself.

We serve a *great* God. EXPECT GREAT THINGS TODAY!

Lord, help me to have great expectations today.

Opinionated

I really appreciate my opinion!

Now wait just a minute you might be saying. That's mighty arrogant of you! And you are right, but I think I join a lot of others who are always ready to give opinions away really quickly whether they happen to be valid or not. As they say, "My opinion and a quarter used to buy a cup of coffee. Now, neither is worth much!"

The real danger is when we bring our opinion to the prayer closet. Too often we pray to give orders to God instead of simply reporting for duty. "He who answers a matter before he hears it, it is folly and shame to him."~Proverbs 18:13 It is not that God has no interest in hearing from us because He really does. What God does not have any desire to hear is our opinion. So often we are like the man that Solomon wrote of in the verse above. We are too busy giving our opinion instead of listening to what God has to say on the matter.

How can we know that we are becoming opinionated in our response to the Lord? There is one easy way to know this. Our response to a given command from the Lord will begin with the little word *but*. God speaks and we say, "But, Lord..." In that brief statement we are preparing to lay before the Lord our opinion. How can our finite minds contrive any opinion that will stand up against the omniscience of God? He already knows all from the end to the beginning. Our opinion on the matter has no weight in the eternity of decisions.

Let your opinion on the matter be, "Yes, Lord! You are right in all of your judgments!"

Lord, help me make my opinion be that You are always right.

November 9

Risky Faith

 Hebrews 11 is noted as the faith chapter in the Bible. This entire chapter list one biblical personality after another who exhibited faith in his or her life. Moses is one of those mentioned and his faith life is often overlooked in the shadow of him being the law-giver.

"By faith Moses, when he was born, was hidden three months by his parents, because they saw he was a beautiful child; and they were not afraid of the king's command. By faith Moses, when he became of age, refused to be called the son of Pharaoh's daughter, choosing rather to suffer affliction with the people of God than to enjoy the passing pleasures of sin, esteeming the reproach of Christ greater riches than the treasures in Egypt; for he looked to the reward. By faith he forsook Egypt, not fearing the wrath of the king; for he endured as seeing Him who is invisible."~Hebrews 11:23–27

Moses demonstrated in his life that faith can be risky. Vance Havner said of Moses, "He chose the imperishable. He saw the invisible. He did the impossible." His parents took the risk of placing him in a basket and setting him afloat in the crocodile infested Nile River. He took the risk of siding with the Hebrew people and turning his back on the easy life of the palace. He did all of this by keeping his eye fixed on that which is invisible so he could partake of the imperishable and accomplish the impossible. A faith that risks nothing quickly degenerates into a religion of mediocrity. We will always seek the path of least resistance and thereby miss the blessings of God's hand at work.

Isn't it time to take a risk? How would you need to live so that your name could be recorded in a list like that of Hebrews 11? Risk is easy when the outcome is based on trusting Him who cannot fail.

Lord, help me to have risky faith.

November 10

The Giving Scale

Where do you fall on the giving scale? Are you trying to keep some minimum quota or have you decided to be as the churches of Macedonia? "For I bear witness that according to their ability, yes, and beyond their ability, they were freely willing, imploring us with much urgency that we would receive the gift and the fellowship of the ministering to the saints. And not only as we had hoped, but they...first gave themselves to the Lord, and then to us by the will of God."~2 Corinthians 8:3-5

Many people do not like it very much when the subject of giving is discussed whether it be in the context of personal discourse or from the pulpit of a church. Somehow we have forgotten how much we have received and how much of a blessing it is to give.

Jim Elliot who was martyred by the Auca Indians in 1956 said, "He is no fool who gives what he cannot keep to gain what he cannot lose." Jim was right in step with the church at Macedonia. Their giving and his was marked by several characteristics that would serve us well to emulate.

The believers at Macedonia gave beyond themselves and their ability. Because of this their gifts were made of their own free wills. No one begged them to give, but on the other hand they implored Paul to please take their gifts. These believers saw the need of others and it prompted them to give abundantly and sacrificially. The reason all of this transpired with such ease is that they first gave themselves to the Lord and then to others. Maybe it's time to rethink our giving based on the Macedonian and the Elliot scale!

Lord, help me give myself to You afresh today.

November 11

No Promised Return

 Life seems overwhelming at times. It can be that the path we are on is all uphill and we are just too tired to take another step. As you think about your particular journey take a moment today to reflect on the sacrifice of many who have served our country and given us the freedom we enjoy.

I read an interesting account once of a team of soldiers who were to engage the enemy under very hostile conditions. The orders were very clear. Take a boat out to the island in the dark of night. Find and destroy the enemy encampment.

One of the soldiers remarked to the officer who had handed down the orders, "Sir, the wind is strong, the waves are high, and the boat is small." He added, "We may not return from this mission."

The officer calmly responded, "Son, the orders are to go; there's nothing in here about returning!"

On this Veteran's Day I am grateful for all who obeyed the call to serve their country with no promised return! They have served well as have unnumbered martyrs before them who served their Commander with no guarantee of return. "As it is written: 'For Your sake we are killed all day long; we are accounted as sheep for the slaughter.'"~Romans 8:36

Remember today all who have served in every branch of our armed services and also remember the multitudes, many unnamed, who have laid down their lives for the cause of Christ.

Lord, help me go unconditionally.

November 12

What's Your Password?

Usernames. Passwords. Security questions. Oh, for the days when the worst nightmare was your mail being placed in a neighbor's mailbox. Even then the neighbor would most likely deliver it to your door before you had been to your own mailbox or discovered that it was missing.

Recently someone hacked into one of my online retailer accounts and tried to make a purchase in Ogden, Utah. Thankfully, I was able to get everything corrected and the fraudulent order was cancelled, but I did feel just a little disconcerted that my identity had been fiddled with so easily.

Thank God that the devil cannot hack into my salvation account! "In Him you also trusted, after you heard the word of truth, the gospel of your salvation; in whom also, having believed, you were SEALED with the Holy Spirit of promise, who is the guarantee of our inheritance until the redemption of the purchased possession, to the praise of His glory."~Ephesians 1:13-14 This is great news for the believer!

Once our "account" is established with the Father we have nothing to worry about when it comes to our salvation. Our identity is protected by the sealing of the Holy Spirit. No matter how many combinations Satan tries on us, he simply will be foiled in his attempts to access our connection to our heavenly Father.

I am so sure of this that I will give you the password to my salvation account. It is: J-E-S-U-S. All caps if you please...

Lord, help me rest assured that my identity in You is secure.

November 13

Two Words

 I understand. Two simple words, but so often used without real meaning. They are more courtesy than fact. Unless you have experienced a certain matter you cannot really understand. That doesn't mean you don't care; you just don't really understand.

There was a time that I could not say I understand truthfully when someone lost a parent, a brother, or a spouse. Now I can say those two words and really mean them, because I have experienced the death of all of the above. Now I do not even need to say those two words at all. I can simply put an arm around a friend, look them in the eye, and convey a deeper meaning to those two words than ever before.

You may not have ever suffered great loss and feel that you cannot properly comfort another person with those two words, but you can direct the hurting heart of your friend to God. God does understand.

Hear the Psalmist declare this of God: "Great is our Lord, and mighty in power; His understanding is infinite..."~Psalms 147:5 Unlike us, God knows all with infinite accuracy. The word *infinite* carries the idea of actually counting until you run out of numbers. You cannot enter any experience that God does not understand, because He has already experienced it and that makes our God both GREAT and POWERFUL!

Do you understand? We might not...God ALWAYS does!

Lord, help me to understand that You understand all things.

Testimony for a Rough Day

Expecting a rough day? Just coming out of a storm and wondering why everything is still spinning? Maybe your world is upside down and you're having a hard time figuring out which way is up? In times like this a testimony always helps…

Robert Baillie was a Presbyterian preacher who after many years of faithful preaching ran crossways of the Scottish crown. The State, unwilling for Baillie to suffer a natural death, condemned him on Christmas Eve, 1684, to be hanged at the Market Cross of Edinburgh between two and four that afternoon. His head was to be cut off and nailed in a public place. His body was to be stretched taut, carved into four pieces, and affixed to other sites.

Here are some of his final words upon hearing his sentence. Baillie replied, "My lords, the time is short, the sentence is sharp, but I thank my God who hath made me as fit to die as you are to live." While waiting in his cell for the appointed hour, he thought of the promise in Philippians 3:21. At the resurrection God will transform our decayed, discarded bodies to be like that of the risen Christ.

When someone asked him how he felt, Baillie answered, "Never better. And in a few hours I shall be well beyond all conception. They may hack and hew my body as they please, but I know assuredly nothing shall be lost; but that all these my members shall be wonderfully gathered, and made like Christ's glorious body."

"I have had sharp sufferings for a considerable time", he said in a final message to his friends, "and yet I must say to the commendation of the grace of God, my suffering time hath been my best time, and when my sufferings have been sharpest, my spiritual joys and consolations have been greatest. Let none be afraid of the cross of Christ, His cross is our greatest glory." O, to live and die as such will smooth out the roughest days!

Lord, help me live to die well.

November 15

The Fourth Man

 HOT! No one has to tell you to pull your hand away when you grab something too hot. Imagine the three Hebrew boys about to be cast into a furnace heated to the point that the executioners were consumed as they threw them into the flames. They would not bow, so the king decided they had to burn.

Willing to enter the fire was an incredible step of faith, but even greater was these three boys remaining there. When the king saw them walking about freely in the fire and a fourth man walking with them, he had to command them to come out of the flames! "'Look!' he answered, 'I see four men loose, walking in the midst of the fire; and they are not hurt, and the form of the fourth is like the Son of God.' Then Nebuchadnezzar went near the mouth of the burning fiery furnace and spoke, saying, 'Shadrach, Meshach, and Abed-Nego, servants of the Most High God, come out, and come here.' Then Shadrach, Meshach, and Abed-Nego came from the midst of the fire."~Daniel 3:25-26

AMAZING! I wonder if I would have stayed in the fire. Their bonds fell away and they stayed in the fire with Jesus! In a hot spot? Stay with Jesus!
Are you standing at the mouth of the oven wondering when you will be thrown into the flames? Take a peek!

The king saw four men in the fire. Only three came out not so much as smelling of smoke. Where was the fourth man? Still in the fire! Jesus is still in the fire today, so never fear the furnace. Go in and don't come out until your testimony is complete and your life tells the story of the fourth man in the fire!

Lord, help me to remember that I'm never alone in the fire.

November 16

Purified Unto Gold

It is amazing that Job wasn't guilty of murder. If I would have been him I probably would have killed a few "friends!" After being accused of sinning against God and forsaking righteous living Job responds to his "friends."

"Look, I go forward, but He is not there, And backward, but I cannot perceive Him; when He works on the left hand, I cannot behold Him; when He turns to the right hand, I cannot see Him.... But He knows the way that I take; when He has tested me, I shall come forth as gold. My foot has held fast to His steps; I have kept His way and not turned aside."~Job 23:8-11

It's one thing to walk the path of God in the sunlight when we sense the fullness of His smile upon our face. But it is quite another to keep His way and not turn aside when we have no sense of His presence. Job had no comfort of God being at work, yet he chose to remain faithful.

He seized the path! Literally, he got a toehold and decided to not bend! A toehold is any means of gaining access or support; a small foothold that facilitates climbing higher. Job said his foot had held fast to *HIS* steps. He was holding on even when he could not see the One who was holding him.

Does it seem as if God has hidden Himself today? Fear not! When He has finished the test you will come forth like purified gold!

Lord, help me to stand fast even when I can't sense Your presence.

November 17

We Wait or the Lord Waits

 Are you a person that enjoys waiting?

It's always a "joy" to go to register a vehicle, pull a number, then hear that the next number called places you 23 spots away from the counter! For the most part few of us enjoy waiting. We are not alone in this waiting process. Israel didn't wait well either. They often sought help apart from the Lord instead of waiting for the Lord to intercede. Isaiah tells us this: "Therefore the Lord will wait, that He may be gracious to you; and therefore He will be exalted, that He may have mercy on you. For the Lord is a God of justice; blessed are all those who wait for Him. Your ears shall hear a word behind you, saying, 'This is the way, walk in it. Whenever you turn to the right hand or whenever you turn to the left.'"~Isaiah 30:18,21

Israel had turned to Egypt (the world) for help instead of the Lord. They refused to wait for the Lord's help. Note the Lord's response: *THEREFORE THE LORD WILL WAIT!* When we refuse to wait for instructions then God just waits. Remember, He has eternity on His side; we don't! Waiting is not a problem for the Lord. He is willing for us to be 23 spots away from His counter if that's what it takes for us to trust Him and walk in His will and way for our lives.

The blessing of waiting is the voice of instruction that will surely come. "This is the way, walk in it." Wait and be blessed!

Lord, help me to wait for Your instruction.

November 18

Powerless Busyness

I don't think that I could name a single friend who would openly declare that their intention is to share in God's glory as they serve here on this earth. However, I, and perhaps you do from time to time bask in the brightness of busyness.

Somehow we have come to believe that God is so impressed with our energy that He will let us shine in each other's presence. As a matter of fact it is almost unacceptable to not give a busy answer when someone ask what we're doing.

Major Ian Thomas, founder of Capenwray Missionary Fellowship and the international Torchbearer Ministry put our busyness into context with these words: "All that God is … is available to the man who is available … to all that God is!"

How paltry our potential. How plentiful His power! It's not ABILITY. It's AVAILABILITY! Thomas was speaking of Christ in this context and we see clearly the power that was available to Christ because He made Himself available to all that the Father is. Jesus functioned in His earthly ministry constantly connected to the Father's power source. Was Christ busy? Yes, but not with busyness!

So...ease up on the throttle. Let God reveal Himself in you and He will get all of the glory. "If then you were raised with Christ, seek those things which are above, where Christ is, sitting at the right hand of God. Set your mind on things above, not on things on the earth. For you died, and your life is hidden with Christ in God. When Christ who is our life appears, then you also will appear with Him in glory."~Colossians 3:1-4

Lord, help me to always be available for Your service.

November 19

Praying for Those Who Serve

 J. Wilbur Chapman became the pastor of Bethany Presbyterian Church in Philadelphia as a young man. After his first sermon an elderly gentleman approached him. "I am afraid you will not make it as pastor here." Allowing some time for that sober assessment to sink in, the man continued, "This is a large church with great responsibility falling upon its pastor. We need a man with equally large experience. But I have made up my mind to help you. I have resolved to pray for you every day…and I have made a covenant with two other men to do the same."

What would have been your response?

Well, here's the rest of the story… Within three years the pastoral prayer group had grown to over 100 and in that three years over 1100 professions of faith had been recorded! Why not begin today to pray for those who serve the Lord in ministry?

This was the Apostle Paul's request to the church at Colosse. "Continue earnestly in prayer, being vigilant in it with thanksgiving; meanwhile praying also for us, that God would open to us a door for the word, to speak the mystery of Christ, for which I am also in chains, that I may make it manifest, as I ought to speak."~Colossians 4:2–4

Pray for your pastors, elders, missionaries, Sunday School teachers, and others who have given their lives to teach and reach those under their watch. Begin this TODAY and watch what God will do TOMORROW!

Lord, help me to pray for my pastor and all those who lead in my church.

November 20

No More Dumping

I am sure that you have noticed this. We live under a massive load of information. And like the land fill that has become stuffed to capacity it appears at any moment a proclamation will need to be made: NO MORE DUMPING!

All of this information is not all bad. We are blessed to live in a time where we can access the resources we need at the touch of a button. These devotionals are written with quick response codes attached for just this reason. One pass of a "smart" device and you can instantly have biblical resources at your disposal—no pun intended!

Somewhere and at some time we need to back off a little, however. The overload of data can let error slip through our defenses. We can begin to assume that just because it came to us electronically or in mass quantities that it must be true. I am sure that John would have been amazed to live in our day and experience the massive flow of information that can cross our desk on any given day.

None of this has caught God off guard. He moved the hand of John to record these words. "Beloved, believe not every spirit, but try the spirits whether they are of God."~1 John 4:1 Substitute the word *information* for the word *spirit* in this verse and suddenly we have a warning for our day. Do not be guilty of believing everything that flashes across your computer screen or even your "smart" device.

The really smart thing to do is to test the information against the truth of God's word. If it's not of God... DUMP IT!

Lord, help me test everything against Your truth.

333

November 21

The *Un*God

 Remember when 7-up advertised as the Uncola. The company focused on what it was not and the advertising campaign lasted for years. They were successful in promoting their "un". What about the "uns" of God?

He is *un*relenting in His pursuit of us. "For the Son of Man has come to seek and to save that which was lost."~Luke 19:10

He is *un*matched in His grace and love for us."Thanks be to God for His indescribable gift!"~2 Corinthians 9:15

He is *un*deniably the only source of peace and hope. "Now may the God of hope fill you with all joy and peace in believing, that you may abound in hope by the power of the Holy Spirit."~Romans 15:13

He is *un*searchable in the fullness of His glory. "For this reason I bow my knees to the Father of our Lord Jesus Christ, from whom the whole family in heaven and earth is named, that He would grant you, according to the riches of His glory, to be strengthened with might through His Spirit in the inner man, that Christ may dwell in your hearts through faith; that you, being rooted and grounded in love, may be able to comprehend with all the saints what is the width and length and depth and height— to know the love of Christ which passes knowledge; that you may be filled with all the fullness of God."~Ephesians 3:14–19

Certainly this is not an exhaustive list of "uns", but I am *un*able in this context to add any more. Why not spend this day thinking of some more "uns" that describe God. In the end you will find that the *un*God is all the God you will ever need! Hallelujah! Amen!

Lord, help me see you in all of Your unsearchable riches.

November 22

Someone Is Always Following

It is vitally important as we walk the path of Christ that we keep the way clear for others who will follow us. A blind man was seen walking in the dark with his guide stick in one hand and a flashlight burning brightly in the other. Someone asked why a blind man should be carrying a flashlight. He responded, "I want to make sure that no one stumbles over me in the dark!"

This blind man understood his responsibility of walking in such a way that other might follow without difficulty. Hear the warning of Jesus: "'But whoever causes one of these little ones who believe in Me to stumble, it would be better for him if a millstone were hung around his neck, and he were thrown into the sea.'"~Mark 9:42

These are strong words from Jesus. The idea being conveyed is not one where a person actually trips another. Instead, causing one to stumble means to provide the circumstances that contribute to the fall. You may have passed by some time ago, but like a passing speed boat you leave a wake in your path. If a person stumbles in your wake you are responsible.

We do not get to walk our path alone. There is always someone following us in our journey. We can smooth out the pathway and clear out the obstacles that might be a hazard to those following.

Walk rightly; someone is always following…

Lord, help me to walk rightly.

November 23

God's Will

 Want to fill a room with thoroughly interested people? Place this sign on the door: *ENTER HERE TO KNOW GOD'S WILL.* The room will be brimming with folks. Let everyone take a seat. Have a moment of getting to know each other and then give them the answer they all came for in the first place. Have them open their Bibles and read in unison the surprising answer found in First Thessalonians 5:18 "In everything give thanks: for this is the *WILL OF GOD* in Christ Jesus concerning you." You won't have to dismiss them; the room will empty by itself!

Discovering God's will is not as hard as it might seem, but *really* discovering God's will may not be as pleasant as expected. When we understand that God's ways are beyond our ways and His thoughts beyond our comprehension it may be easy to just give up on the search. But I do believe we should search the deep things of God which certainly include His will for our lives.

Scripture is plain concerning the knowledge of God's will as seen in the verse listed above. We can begin in God's will by giving thanks in everything. *EVERYTHING?* Yes, everything. Notice that the verse tells us to give thanks *in* everything not particularly *for* everything. We would not be thankful for certain tragedies, but we can be thankful in the midst of them.

This is the doorway to finding God's will in our lives. It makes perfect sense that if we are in God's will by giving thanks for all things that we would be so much more likely to know God's will for the rest of our lives.

Start today by practicing the art of thanks giving. It will seem strange at first, but you will get the hang of it. And when you do, post a sign on your door: *ENTER HERE TO KNOW GOD'S WILL.* When folks show up—show them the verse and let them begin finding God's will too.

Lord, help me to give thanks in everything today.

November 24

Faith Lesson

What does it mean to live by faith? Is it somehow connected to a spiritual pep rally in which we drum up an emotional excitement that energizes a fanciful wish list? NO! It will always be preceded by obedience and proceed in action.

Here's a good example in Luke 5. The disciples had been fishing all night as was customary for fishermen on the Sea of Galilee. They had caught nothing and were busy on the shore mending nets. They probably were quite disappointed with their efforts and the stubbornness of the fish for that matter. Then along comes Jesus who climbs into Peter's boat, asks him to shove the boat out a little ways, and preaches from the floating pulpit.

Up to this point there is no cost to Peter, except for the interruption of Jesus and His need for a pulpit. But Jesus was not just there to preach. He was there to teach. And the lesson of the day was FAITH. Jesus told Peter to launch out into the deep and let down his nets for a great catch. Day time fishing was not the norm. Fishing after an exhausting night on the sea was not convenient. But the catch had to be preceded by obedience: launching out into the deep.

The lesson of the catch and of faith proceeded as they let down the nets. Launching was not faith. Letting down the nets was. There is never any guarantee that you will get your net back again nor that your net will troll a supply of fish. Letting down nets is totally an act of faith.

End of story: obedience led to faithful action that resulted in a miraculous catch! Have you fished all night and caught nothing? Then follow Peter's example, "Nevertheless, at your word I will let down the nets."~Luke 5:5

Lord, help me to always obey Your word in faith.

November 25

Shaking in Your Boots

Have you noticed the return to the 1960's? One symbol has come to the top of the heap...the peace sign. I sure thought we were done with that, but there is a reason for this. People (in particularly, young people) are searching for peace. It is not found in another toy or gadget, but in the words of Jesus as He was preparing the disciples for His death, burial, and resurrection. "Peace I leave with you, My peace I give to you; not as the world gives do I give to you. Let not your heart be troubled, neither let it be afraid."~John 14:27

Jesus is the true source of peace. Jesus used two words to describe the action used in bestowing peace upon His disciples and ultimately upon us. He said he would *leave* peace and *give* peace. There is a real difference in these two words. The word *leave* means to remit or deposit into place. This word alone means that the reality of peace is here, but not necessarily within our grasp. The word *give*, however, means to place in the hand something of value.

It would have been one thing for Jesus just to leave peace on the earth. We could see it like a mountaintop looming before us, but it would remain out of our reach. He went further to explain that this peace he spoke of is now placed in the palm of the hand. It can be touched. It can be experienced practically not just experimentally.

Finally, He delineates between His peace and that of the world. Clearly, the world has a form of peace, but its value is not consistent with the peace of Christ. It cannot alleviate our fears. So he adds the words that our heart should not be troubled nor should we be afraid. Literally, Jesus is telling us that His gift of peace will keep us from shaking in our boots!

Lord, help me have a calm heart as I rest in Your peace.

November 26

How Far Will You Go?

In his book, *The Innocents Abroad*, Mark Twain wrote the following thoughts in which he relates his amazement as to the effects Christianity has had on the world while the ministry of Jesus was limited to such a small geographical area.

"One of the most astonishing things that have yet fallen under our observation is the exceedingly small portion of the earth from which sprang the now flourishing plant of Christianity. The longest journey our Saviour ever performed was from here to Jerusalem - about one hundred to one hundred and twenty miles...Instead of being wide apart - as American appreciation of distances would naturally suggest - the places made most particularly celebrated by the presence of Christ are nearly all right here in full view, and within cannon-shot of Capernaum...He spent his life, preached his gospel, and performed his miracles within a compass no larger than an ordinary county in the United States. It is as much as I can do to comprehend this stupefying fact."

Even with Mr. Twain's observation of Jesus's travels, we can be assured that He visited every location His Father desired. He even traveled through areas of which the Jews of His day would have seriously frowned. "He left Judea and departed again to Galilee. But He needed to go through Samaria."~John 4:3–4 On this journey he met the woman at the well and the rest of the story is as Mr. Twain put it *stupefying*.

Jesus conducted His earthly ministry in a very small geographical area. We on the other hand can be on the other side of the world in less than a day. Let us make good use of ALL that God has blessed us with in His service! If His desire for us is the other side of the world then go, but if His desire is for you to visit the neighbor across the street then by all means go there as well.

Lord, help me go as far as You lead to tell Your story.

November 27

Right Measurements

 Candy making is my specialty. I love getting in the kitchen and turning sugar, cream, nuts, and flavorings into tasty bits of confection. If the candy is going to come out right I have to follow the recipe. I do not have the privilege of using my own ideas of quantities or ingredients. Neither can I use measuring implements of my own design. They must meet a proper standard of measurement to insure the correct results.

Scripture tells us that whatever measure we use in giving will be the measure used in our receiving. "For with what judgment you judge, you will be judged; and with the measure you use, it will be measured back to you."~Matthew 7:2

The widow of Zarephath almost missed a blessing by using the wrong measurements. "So she said, 'As the Lord your God lives, I do not have bread, only a handful of flour in a bin, and a little oil in a jar; and see, I am gathering a couple of sticks that I may go in and prepare it for myself and my son, that we may eat it, and die.'"~1 Kings 17:12

With drought-stricken conditions in the land Elijah asked for a piece of bread and water from this widow. At first she clung to her meager portion and thought only of her son and herself. Eat and die was her conclusion! But when she yielded her little into the hands of God she received a blessing that could not be contained! She gave all she had and she received all she needed!

Throw out the measuring cups...bring in the buckets!

Lord, help me to never limit You by unbelief.

November 28

Something's Going On Here

"Then Mary took a pound of very costly oil of spikenard, anointed the feet of Jesus, and wiped His feet with her hair. *And the house was filled with the fragrance of the oil.*"~John 12:3

The account of the woman pouring the oil from the alabaster box onto the feet of Jesus is recorded in all four gospels. But only John adds the phrase noted above.

Jesus received the gift of oil, but the whole house was blessed by the act! Some closest to Jesus thought the act was a waste. Some in the room thought it was indecent. But ALL in the house knew something had happened!

The container that held the precious ointment was likely not a box at all, but instead a sealed flask. The perfume would have been stored in this alabaster flask with the intent of only being opened for a special occasion such as a wedding. Once the alabaster box was opened it could never be resealed. The arid conditions of the near east would have immediately begun its work of evaporating the perfume.

The woman's gift was an all or nothing act, and once engaged could not be hidden from anyone in the house. The scent of her act was evident to everyone. All of the perfume would need to be spilled out once the neck of the flask was broken. Ask God to break open your life today. Hold nothing back. Pour your all on the feet of Jesus and as a by-product you will be a blessing to ALL in the house!

Lord, help me to give my all today.

November 29

The Last Dime

 My daddy was a master at conveying truths in simple stories. I still remember him telling me if I ever came to the place of only having one dime in my pocket this is what I should do. Go to the store and buy a bar of soap with the dime. (You could still buy a bar of *Ivory* for ten cents then.) Take the soap to the river and bathe. Then go back to the same store and ask the man for something to eat. He concluded his example by telling me that I might be hungry, but I should never be filthy.

This works fine for the physical world, but not for the spiritual. Jesus said, "Those who are well have no need of a physician, but those who are sick. I did not come to call the righteous, but sinners, to repentance."~Mark 2:17

The young man who came to Jesus later in Mark's gospel is an example of one trying to clean himself to the point of righteousness, but only becoming more self-righteous in the end. "Now as He was going out on the road, one came running, knelt before Him, and asked Him, 'Good Teacher, what shall I do that I may inherit eternal life?'"~Mark 10:17 This young man went away sad at the word of Jesus because of his riches.

The rich young ruler could have bought cleanness, but Jesus is not waiting for us to spend our last dime trying to scrub our lives to the point of purity. He has come to seek those who are spiritually filthy and cannot make themselves clean. My daddy's advice still holds a valid place in this physical world, but I thank God for the day that Jesus lifted me up out of the filth of sin and *made* me clean in His presence!

Lord, help me to never forget the day You made me clean.

November 30

What's Your Story?

Paul, who was then known as Saul, had an amazing encounter with Jesus on his way to persecute the people of God and wreak havoc on the Church. He assumed that he was in full control of his life, but soon discovered that an encounter with the living Christ would change his life forever.

"Then Saul, still breathing threats and murder against the disciples of the Lord, went to the high priest and asked letters from him to the synagogues of Damascus, so that if he found any who were of the Way, whether men or women, he might bring them bound to Jerusalem. As he journeyed he came near Damascus, and suddenly a light shone around him from heaven. Then he fell to the ground, and heard a voice saying to him, 'Saul, Saul, why are you persecuting Me?' And he said, 'Who are You, Lord?' Then the Lord said, 'I am Jesus, whom you are persecuting. It is hard for you to kick against the goads.' So he, trembling and astonished, said, "Lord, what do You want me to do?" Then the Lord said to him, 'Arise and go into the city, and you will be told what you must do.' And the men who journeyed with him stood speechless, hearing a voice but seeing no one. Then Saul arose from the ground, and when his eyes were opened he saw no one. But they led him by the hand and brought *him* into Damascus. And he was three days without sight, and neither ate nor drank."~Acts 9:1–9

Now that's an amazing testimony! So, what's your story? I'm not talking fishing story, show your scars story, etc. I'm asking you about your Damascus Road story. The radical life-changing moment when you met Christ. Yours may not be as dramatic as Paul's encounter with Jesus on his way to Damascus, but salvation will always change us and send us in the other direction. The same Jesus who met Paul on the Damascus Road paid the same dear price for your soul. It's a story worth telling!

Lord, help me to tell my story today.

December 1

Only A Few More Days

 As we begin this final month of the year it is evident how fleeting our days really are. How will you complete this year? Decide today to make an everlasting impact on someone in these final days of this year by sharing the good news of the gospel with them. Today is the day to make plans for all the days still on your calendar.

The calendar is a daily reminder of our finite state, but these words in Hebrews 1 describe the eternality of Christ: "You, Lord, in the beginning laid the foundation of the earth and the heavens are the work of Your hands. They will perish, but You remain; and they will all grow old like a garment; like a cloak You will fold them up, And they will be changed. But You are the same and Your years will not fail."~Hebrews 1:10-12

Imagine that! All of this that we cherish will one day be folded and put away like the storing of a coat after winter's cold, but He will remain unchanged! Even His own creation grows old day by day and crumbles away into the pages of history, but His days will never come to an end. The writer of Hebrews stood in awe at the immutability of Christ as he wrote, "Jesus Christ is the same yesterday, today, and forever."~Hebrews 13:8

That puts a year almost gone into perspective! Now, go spend this day well…

Lord, help me remember in changing times that You never change.

December 2

Stumped

I have learned a lot of things throughout my life. I enjoy learning and I am blessed with fairly good recall. I am amazed sometimes at a piece of information that rushes into my mind from childhood days. Usually it is useless to everyone else, but brings nostalgic memories to me.

As Christians we have been taught many things through the working of the Holy Spirit in our lives. If we are growing in the Lord we are still learning. We are the blessed recipients of the work of the Holy Spirit in this matter. "But the Helper, the Holy Spirit, whom the Father will send in My name, He will teach you all things, and bring to your remembrance all things that I said to you."~John 14:26

I have had the privilege of counseling with people throughout my ministry years. I have been amazed as the Holy Spirit reached into the recesses of my life and brought forth truths that were relevant for particular occasions. Jesus said to His disciples, "'Now when they bring you to the synagogues and magistrates and authorities, do not worry about how or what you should answer, or what you should say. For the Holy Spirit will teach you in that very hour what you ought to say.'"~Luke 12:11–12

If you are stumped to find an answer today, wait for the teaching and recalling ministry of the Holy Spirit. He will come to your aid in just the right moment!

Lord, help me trust You for the right word to say.

December 3

What Are You Talking About?

 Do you remember the show *Different Strokes*? Gary Coleman would always say somewhere in the program, "What 'chu talkin' 'bout, Willis?" That's a good question for us as Christians.

The Psalmist put it this way, "I will also meditate on all Your work and talk of Your deeds."~Psalms 77:12 In essence you will talk about what you meditate upon each day. Now that helps me understand why some people talk about the things they do!

Begin today to keep a list of all that God is doing in your life. When those times come that you begin to speak about the wrong things, go back to your list and meditate on all of His works. Then you will be able to speak of His deeds not your misdeeds or those of your neighbor.

Start keeping a prayer journal of requests and answers to your prayers. If you hear yourself talking about that which does not bring glory to His name, then spend some time meditating on those answered prayers. It will not be long until you are singing His praises again.

Stay in the word. This is the treasure chest of His marvelous deeds. Journey across the Red Sea with the Israelites; fight Goliath with David; watch fire come down on Mount Carmel; be there at His birth in Bethlehem, His crucifixion at Calvary and His resurrection on Easter morning. These and many more of His deeds will set you talking about the right stuff. So, "What 'chu talkin' 'bout?"

Lord, help me to talk of Your great works today.

December 4

Laboring in Prayer

The letters of Paul which compose a large part of the New Testament follow a familiar pattern. In those times a letter began with what we would normally place at the end of ours, a salutation. His letters would then conclude with a greeting from several who were ministering with and to him.

Colossians ends this way with a note about Epaphras. "Epaphras, who is one of you, a bondservant of Christ, greets you, always laboring fervently for you in prayers that you may stand perfect and complete in all the will of God."~Colossians 4:12

Epaphras LABORED in prayer!

Can you imagine having your life noted as one who LABORS in prayer? How was this possible?

The key is in the little phrase "who is one of you." I don't think that one can possibly LABOR in prayer until he takes on the character and heart of those for which he prays. The idea is that of empathy instead of sympathy. Sympathy says, "I'm sorry this is happening to you." Empathy says, "I KNOW your struggle, because I have lived its pain." May God help us to LABOR in prayer!

How about you? What would Paul write about your prayer life? Are you noted as one of those for whom you are praying? Only a life of empathy will lead to a labor of prayer.

Lord, help me to be a laborer in prayer.

December 5

God Revealed

 As this day begins be sure you keep in mind that God is always there with you. In each conversation and each transaction of life He is there. And from time to time He makes Himself VERY visible. Take for instance what happened in Daniel chapter 5.

"Belshazzar the king made a great feast for a thousand of his lords...In the same hour the fingers of a man's hand appeared and wrote opposite the lamp stand on the plaster of the wall of the king's palace; and the king saw the part of the hand that wrote."~Daniel 5:1,5

The king thought he was entertaining his friends and that God was on the backside of the universe somewhere, but suddenly God made Himself visible! These verses could certainly cause you to tremble if you were not a believer, but for the follower of Christ they are evidence of a God who is intimately involved in the affairs of man. Whatever this day holds for you God is already there with His finger pressed against the wall ready to write truth into your life.

In this case, judgment was declared, but God can make Himself known in grace just as well. When it appears that your day is about to crumble—take heart! Look for the finger of God writing His message of hope on the wall of your heart!

See it now...

I AM WITH YOU ALL THE WAY TO THE END!

Lord, help me to see Your fingerprint in each day of my life.

December 6

Going All to Pieces

Each year my daddy would mix up a batch of whitewash so we could paint the trees in our yard. You probably have to be from the South or have traveled here to see this. With a big wide brush we would paint from the ground up about four feet high on the bark of each tree. I thought we were just decorating the trees, but it really served a purpose of protecting the trees.

Now whitewash is fine for painting trees, but it does not serve well in wall building. In Ezekiel 13 God warns Israel about following false prophets. He likens their advice to building a wall and using whitewash as mortar. In the end the wall will tumble.

We too are building a wall day by day as we live out our lives. What are we to use as mortar to hold the pieces of our lives together? It is the truth of God's word! It will *not* fail to keep us *from* failing. Jesus put it this way, "Heaven and earth will pass away, but My words will by no means pass away."~Matthew 24:35 The word of God serves as a dependable mortar to keep us from going to pieces.

Whitewash may be pretty on a sunny day, but will prove useless in the storm! Apply the mortar of God's word to your life today and years from now your efforts will still be standing. Happy wall building!

Lord, help me apply Your word to my life today.

December 7

A Birthday Wish

On this day I received a son. I rejoice in the three daughters that I have as well, but I still remember this day in 1984 when God gave us a son. When our children get older it is a little difficult to give birthday presents that really speak of our love. So today I write this devotional for you as a small birthday present. And just so your sisters don't think that I love them less, all of these words are for you three girls as well.

On your birthdate in 1691 a great Puritan pastor, Richard Baxter left this world having suffered many times for his beliefs. His biography speaks of his strong faith and hope. As he died, he quoted these verses: "But you have come to Mount Zion and to the city of the living God, the heavenly Jerusalem, to an innumerable company of angels, to the general assembly and church of the firstborn who are registered in heaven, to God the Judge of all, to the spirits of just men made perfect, to Jesus the Mediator of the new covenant, and to the blood of sprinkling that speaks better things than that of Abel."~Hebrews 12:22-24

My desire today as your daddy is that you live your life with such focus that one day when you also must lay down this temporary house that you will have the same confidence as Richard Baxter. The only difference will be that Richard and I will be there in that general assembly to greet you.

Hallelujah for the calm assurance of knowing Jesus! Happy birthday, son! May God grant you many years to live for His glory! May you be blessed to have sweet harmony with your sisters and with all those whom God brings across your path.

Lord, help me to have an everlasting assurance in You.

Just a Little Drop

Everyone is busy this time of year! I read a story about a man who carried a little can of oil with him as he hurried about his everyday affairs. As he passed through a squeaking door he'd put a drop of oil on the hinge. A sticking gate found relief by the touch of his oilcan. Each day before he set out he would refill his can.

This story reminds me of Elisha's encounter with a certain widow. Her debts had risen to an uncontrollable amount and her sons were about to be indentured to her creditor. Her only resource left was a jar of oil.

Elisha instructed her to gather all of the vessels she could find in her house and from her neighbors. She then was to pour her little jar of oil into all of these containers. And this she did until she ran out of vessels into which to pour. It was at this moment that the oil stopped. "Now it came to pass, when the vessels were full, that she said to her son, 'Bring me another vessel.' And he said to her, 'There is not another vessel.' So the oil ceased."~2 Kings 4:6 It is clear that had the vessels kept coming the oil would have kept pouring. But the oil ceased.

In the story of the man and his oilcan above, it is important to note that he refilled his can every morning. You and I must be like the vessels in this widow's home. We must present ourselves daily to be filled. Note that the filling always came from the original jar of oil. Certainly we can gain valuable support from others, but our filling must come from the original source.

Present yourself for a filling today. Then find someone today who could use a little loosening up and be their touch of oil.

Lord, help me to give my emptiness to You for the filling.

December 9

Looking for Little House

 Most of us are already feeling some of the holiday pressures. It matters not that we would rather Christmas and the holiday surrounding it to be more like *Little House on the Prairie*...It's not gonna happen!

So, instead of totally succumbing to the hustle and bustle let's make a decision to live godly through it! Micah put it this way: "He has shown you, O man, what is good; and what does the Lord require of you, but to do justly, to love mercy, and to walk humbly with your God?"~Micah 6:8

Here's the value of this verse for the upcoming holiday season. As you shop, visit, travel or whatever, decide now to do three things. These three things are not mere suggestions; they are requirements. God has *shown* them to you. The idea is that God has announced them by word of mouth–His mouth!

So here they are as given in Micah's discourse:

DO WHAT IS THE RIGHT THING TO DO AT ALL TIMES.
BE KIND AS YOU ARE DOING IT.
HUMBLE YOURSELF BECAUSE YOU WALK WITH GOD.

These are not incremental steps. They are interactive and interchangeable as you traverse the pathway before you. They are not the natural response to life, so they must be practiced over and over again. As you do so, they will become second nature and I think this will make for a happier holiday!

Lord, help me to practice doing that which is right.

December 10

Live Like You Are Dead

Yikes! Two weeks till Christmas! How will you handle the maddening rush? Here's the simple answer. "For you died, and your life is hidden with Christ in God."~Colossians 3:3

See! Very simple! Live like you're dead!

When the next car cuts you off, when someone takes your parking spot, when the line you moved to STOPS, when the store just sold the last one of what you drove 20 miles to purchase...just respond like a dead person!

Have you noticed that folks quit responding to their senses when they stop living? Our five senses and our emotions are all part of this world. We use them to relate and respond to conditions around us. Dead men have no use of senses or emotions because they are no longer in this world. I know that we must still live here, but we can live here as if we are unseen. The word *hidden* holds the meaning of concealment as in something kept secret. It is not us that is doing the hiding. We *are* hidden in Christ to the degree that all the world sees is Him.

You see it really is quite simple when we live our lives hidden in Christ. Start living like a dead man...it'll make life more enjoyable and the holidays more sensible!

Lord, help me live unseen in You.

December 11

It's That Time Again

 How many of us have not asked this question, "Can it really be Christmas time again?" As we age it seems that time takes on a new urgency to evaporate! The years fly by in a more rapid succession as we mark off the days on the calendar.

The Psalmist pours out his heart unto the Lord in near desperation of the days of his life, but concludes that only the Lord endures forever. "My days are like a shadow that lengthens, and I wither away like grass. But You, O Lord, shall endure forever, and the remembrance of Your name to all generations."~Psalms 102:11-12 The Psalms have a not so subtle way of bringing our temporary states to the forefront.

Our days are described with such fragile substances like shadows and grass. Time marches on and so our shadow lengthens as the day draws to a close. Grass that appears green for a day crumbles under the rigors of drought or succumbs to the biting cold of frost. We appear for a little while and soon our last Christmas will be spent.

Can it really be Christmas time again? More importantly, have you put off again that decision to trust Christ? Perhaps a decision to commit your life to His service has again found a year added to that decision and still you have not engaged the task.

Yes, it really is Christmas time again! Time to give yourself fully and completely to the One whom this entire season is set aside to honor. It's time!

Lord, help me never forget how few days I have to live.

December 12

Someone's Waiting

Most of us run in the same circles. We take the same route to work, to school, or to shop for all those Christmas gifts. Some of this is generated out of convenience. We don't need to think about where to turn or what sights are along the route. If you don't believe this, ask yourself the next time you get to your destination, "Did I stop at that last red light?" See, you are thinking about it now and you don't really know!

Jesus conducted His journeys with intentionality. It certainly would have shocked the disciples the morning He said, "I must go through Samaria." (John 4:4) This was way off the beaten path for Jews. The Samaritans were considered mixed-breeds. They were a despised people that the Jews considered ceremonially unclean; to all except Jesus.

Not only were the disciples amazed at His departure from routine by this side trip into Samaria, the woman He met there was also. This woman was a double outcast. She was hated by the Jews and evidently scorned by her own people. This can be surmised by the hour of the day she came for water and that she was alone. To her surprise Jesus asked for a drink. "Then the woman of Samaria said to Him, 'How is it that You, being a Jew, ask a drink from me, a Samaritan woman? For Jews have no dealings with Samaritans.'"~John 4:9 She used the word *dealings* to convey her wonder. This word means to interact with, but it also means to as much as touch accidently. She was saying to Jesus, "You Jews won't even brush up against us Samaritans, much less drink after us!"

The rest of the story in John 4 tells of her recognizing who Jesus was and telling the people who had scorned her to come see the man who told her all things she had ever done (John 4:39). Who will you brush up against today? Will they all be your regular acquaintances or will you have a need to go through Samaria? Someone's waiting for you at the well!

Lord, help me to stop at some well today and share the gospel.

December 13

The Spirit of Christmas

 I like Charles Dickens's *A Christmas Carol*. The story of the three spirits of Christmas always causes me to stop and reflect on my own reaction to the holiday. Evidence leans toward the fact that Charles Dickens was a Christian. He is quoted as having said, "I have always striven in my writings, to express veneration for the life and lessons of my Savior."

Though this Christmas story is not overtly Christian it is easy to see what happens when a person departs from the real reason for the season. As a matter of fact, there is one Spirit that you must have or it won't matter how jolly your Christmas might be. "But you are not in the flesh but in the Spirit, if indeed the Spirit of God dwells in you. Now if anyone does not have the Spirit of Christ, he is not His."~Romans 8:9

In this season of gift buying, wrapping, and giving make sure that you have been a gift receiver. You may take on the spirit of Christmas and even give the Cratchit family the biggest feast they have ever had. You might pay all of the medical expenses for Tiny Tim, but if you do not have the Spirit of Christ then you will never know the true meaning of Christmas.

Trust Christ today and you will receive the everlasting Spirit of Christ. Without His Spirit you are none of His and that will make for a very sad Christmas, but all who receive His Gift will be forever glad!

Lord, help me to remember the reason for the season.

December 14

Eternal Investments

As one of the credit card companies say in their ad, "What's in your wallet?" More correctly at Christmas, "What's left in your wallet?" It's okay to spend at Christmas, but don't forget to invest in the eternal. You don't have to buy, wrap, or dispose of eternal things because they break or wear out from use.

During the ministry of the prophet Isaiah, God challenged the people to spend their money wisely on the eternal instead of the temporal. "'Ho! Everyone who thirsts, Come to the waters; and you who have no money, come, buy and eat. Yes, come, buy wine and milk without money and without price. Why do you spend money for what is not bread, and your wages for what does not satisfy? Listen carefully to Me, and eat what is good, and let your soul delight itself in abundance.'"~Isaiah 55:1-2

Jesus set the example for us early on in His ministry. He went into the wilderness where He was tempted by Satan. After 40 days of fasting, Jesus was indeed very hungry. It was at this point of basic need for food that Satan tempted Him to turn the stones into bread. I have been to this area of Israel and the stones *do* look like loaves of bread lying on the floor of the desert. Jesus' response was that man does not live by bread alone, but by the very word of God (Luke 4:4).

God calls for us to listen diligently. When we eat that which is good and by implication that which is godly, we will find our souls satisfied. This eternal gift is available to all regardless of social or economic standing. The only requirement is thirst and hunger, the most natural of man's instincts. Most of what we spend our hard earned money on lasts such a short time. There is no satisfaction in what this world has to offer. Buy it and it breaks; eat it and hunger comes again; drink it and you must return to the well. Invest wisely!

Lord, help me to invest my life wisely.

December 15

Anticipating the Gift

 ANTICIPATION! The days leading up to Christmas are always filled with it. Imagine heaven's anticipation as Jesus prepared to be born as man. The anticipation was not primarily from taking on flesh since man was formed by His own hands in the garden. The greater anticipation would be the taking on of man's sin debt. "For He made Him who knew no sin to be sin for us, that we might become the righteousness of God in Him."~2 Corinthians 5:21

Jesus would experience after walking this earth for 33 years the pain and penalty of sin. While Jesus walked here in the days of His earthly ministry, he was fully God and fully man. In being so He voluntarily laid aside some of His attributes. For example, He was restricted to being in one place at a time. His omnipresence was limited while in His manhood.

He also experienced with anticipation the weight of man's sin as He approached the time of His death upon the cross. He even asked that this cup of suffering be taken from Him, but yielded to the Father's will in grace (Matthew 26:39).

If you have never trusted Him as Savior please do so today! His coming into this world was to seek and to save those who were lost. I can tell you this. It will be the greatest gift you have ever anticipated!

Lord, help me present the greatest gift to someone today.

December 16

How to be Happy

In Luke 7 you can read the account of a woman who washed the feet of Jesus with her tears and wiped them with her hair. "And behold, a woman in the city who was a sinner, when she knew that Jesus sat at the table in the Pharisee's house, brought an alabaster flask of fragrant oil, and stood at His feet behind Him weeping; and she began to wash His feet with her tears, and wiped them with the hair of her head; and she kissed His feet and anointed them with the fragrant oil."~Luke 7:37–38 Few of us can fathom this act! Back up the story a little and it might become clearer. Before Jesus came in the flesh, born a babe in Bethlehem, those feet had walked streets of gold in a land of no dust. There is no dust in heaven!

The dust of the ground was part of sin's curse found in man's fall from grace (Genesis 3:14). Imagine those same feet traipsing through the dust of this world for you and for me! Now think for a moment what it meant for Jesus to send this same woman away with her sins forgiven.

Life can be so much fuller if we would spend some time washing the feet of Jesus who came to this world to save me and you! And how you may ask can I wash the feet of Jesus? In John 13 Jesus washed the feet of the disciples and then told them, "If I then, your Lord and Teacher, have washed your feet, you also ought to wash one another's feet. For I have given you an example, that you should do as I have done to you. Most assuredly, I say to you, a servant is not greater than his master; nor is he who is sent greater than he who sent him. If you know these things, blessed are you if you do them."~John 13:14–17

This can be a happy (blessed) day if you are willing to wash a few feet!

Lord, help me to wash someone's feet today.

December 17

Christ's Exaltation

 Can you imagine the angels crowding with anticipation to peer over the banister in heaven as they were awaiting the birth of Jesus? These same angels will gather in one accord at the end of time to declare,"'Alleluia! Salvation and glory and honor and power belong to the Lord our God!'"~Revelation 19:1

Charles Spurgeon spoke on the subject of the exaltation of Christ. Here is a small portion of the sermon he preached on Sunday, November 2, 1856:

"Consider him further still. Do you mark him in your imagination nailed to yonder cross! O eyes! You are full of pity, with tears standing thick! Oh! How I mark the floods gushing down his checks! Do you see his hands bleeding, and his feet too, gushing gore? Behold him! The bulls of Bashan gird him round, and the dogs are hounding him to death! Hear him! 'Eloi, Eloi, lama sabachthani?' The earth startles with fright. ...God is groaning on a cross! ...Each of the thorns becomes a brilliant in his diadem of glory; the nails are forged into his scepter, and his wounds do clothe him with the purple of empire. The treading of the wine-press has stained his garments, but not with stains of scorn and dishonor. The stains are embroideries upon his royal robes forever...and He is the Master of a universe forever. ...Sit down and consider that your Master did not mount from earth's mountains into heaven, but from her valleys. It was not from heights of bliss on earth that he strode to bliss eternal, but from depths of woe he mounted up to glory. Oh! What a stride was that, when, at one mighty step from the grave to the throne of the Highest, the man Christ, the God, did gloriously ascend."

At this Christmas season don't get stuck on a *baby* Jesus. He has ascended and is coming again as LORD! All salvation and glory and honor and power are rightly His!

Lord, help me see You highly exalted and on Your throne.

December 18

Prisoner to the Holidays

One week before Christmas. What will be your complaint today? Amazing in a land of plenty how many complaints will be issued this week before we honor our Lord's birth. We will complain about traffic, lack of courtesy from the clerks, only having a million and one things to choose from for that special person, and even complain about what Santa Claus brought us.

Hear this testimony of two men from prison. "But at midnight Paul and Silas were praying and singing hymns to God, and the prisoners were listening to them."~Acts 16:25 They were imprisoned falsely, had been beaten unmercifully, and they expected nothing under their Christmas tree! Yet they were singing and praying while the other prisoners were listening.

As you negotiate this final week before the big day what will be heard from your life? Complaints or praise? All over the world believers are being persecuted for the sake of the gospel. The experiences of Paul and Silas are being lived out in the here and now. The chances of you and I having a similar experience today here in America are very slim to none. We have every reason to praise His name and yet we may find ourselves complaining in the prison of the holidays.

You probably cannot avoid the holiday, but you can rejoice in the midst of it all. Even in the chains of time constraint and unfinished shopping lists you can break forth at the midnight hour with a hymn of praise and thanksgiving. Never forget there will be other prisoners listening. Who will you be listening to you during this final week of your imprisonment to the holiday? What will be heard from your life as you prepare to celebrate the birth of Jesus?

Lord, help me to sing at the midnight hour.

December 19

No Room

 And the Spirit of God moved upon the face of the deepness and chaos and spoke EVERYTHING into being (Genesis 1). This is the same God who stretched out the lines of the universe. He caused this planet to hang upon nothing at just the right distance from the Sun to sustain His creation. Then He came as Christ in the flesh to save us from our darkness and chaos.

And our response to His graciousness: "She brought forth her firstborn Son, and wrapped Him in swaddling cloths, and laid Him in a manger, because there was no room for them in the inn."~Luke 2:7

NO ROOM! No room in His own creation! This is like Henry Ford needing to hitchhike his way to town. It is like the Wright Brothers being bumped from an overcrowded plane. It is like Dunkin' Donuts not having any varieties to choose from because the glazed donuts have taken up all of the shelf space.

Indeed, we are in a day of no room for God. No room for a Savior. No room for the Spirit's guidance. This is to be expected from a world that has no concept of the real reason for this season. But what about you and me? We are supposed to be the ones who know who Jesus is. We know the real Christmas story and yet it seems that even in our lives there is no room for Him. He has been relegated to the stable of our hearts.

As you approach the holiday season, make room for Jesus. It must be a deliberate choice. Will you make room for Jesus today? I sure hope so…

Lord, help me to make room for You in my life each day.

December 20

To the Uttermost

Only few more days left to this year and then we tear away a page and start over again. No matter how bold the pen which circled the dates of this past year they are gone forever; none have been saved!

On the contrary we have this assurance from Hebrews 7:25, "Therefore He is also able to save to the uttermost those who come to God through Him, since He always lives to make intercession for them." People like days of the year come into being and pass beyond our limited sight, but He lives forever. He is the Ancient of Days!

Yet He is as fresh fallen snow upon the unspoiled field. He covers the rough terrain of our days with His pure grace and makes all things new! It does not matter what twists and turns you may have experienced. It matters not the failures that have plagued your life. He saves to the uttermost. This one word *uttermost* gives us insight into the measure of His intercession for us. That one word means that God saves to the full extent, to completion, to be full-ended. He saves until you are made whole again!

How rough has this past year been for you?

HE SAVES TO THE UTTERMOST!

Today and the coming year can be like new! Praise His name!

Lord, help me to trust in Your daily intercession for me.

December 21

Real Peace

 Peace is a word that comes up a lot at Christmas. Now the world defines peace as an absence of conflict. But think a moment about Jesus in that barnyard environment. Animals were making animal noises, the street vendors were hawking their goods to the crowds, the baby would have been crying. I know the song says no crying He makes, but that's just not the world we live in is it?

Jesus did not come to remove the noise and conflict of the world. He came to give us peace in the midst of all the rancor. The world keeps wishing for peace. The best it has come up with is peace-keeping. The world's peace plan is no more than keeping two parties apart so they that will not kill each other.

Jesus did not come to bring that kind of peace. He said it like this, "Peace I leave with you, My peace I give to you; not as the world gives do I give to you. Let not your heart be troubled, neither let it be afraid."~John 14:27

As we near Christmas Day, you and I have a wonderful opportunity to display this gift of peace that comes from knowing Christ as our Savior. Whether it be in the long lines at the department store or the long line of traffic coursing its way through town, let peace reign in your hearts. "Let not your heart be troubled, neither let it be afraid."

Now go on out there into the fray and show the world what REAL peace looks like. When they see it they just might see JESUS!

Lord, help me to be an example of peace in the world today.

Good Will

"And suddenly there was with the angel a multitude of the heavenly host praising God and saying: 'Glory to God in the highest, and on earth peace, goodwill toward men!'"~Luke 2:13-14 Some say that this verse could have been translated "toward men of good will." I'll not argue the point, but just take it at face value. The word translated *goodwill* is the Greek word *eudokia*. Pronounced yoo-dok-ee-ah. It means those who are well satisfied.

Horatio Spafford authored the old familiar hymn, *It Is Well with My Soul*. The circumstances that allowed him to write the words of that hymn reveal a man who knew what the *goodwill* message of the angels was all about. In November, 1873, Mr. Spafford sent his wife and four daughters across the Atlantic on the *S.S. Ville du Harve*. Since he had been detained he was planning to join them soon. In open ocean the ship was struck by another vessel and sank in 12 minutes. All four of the Spafford daughters—Tanetta, Maggie, Annie and Bessie—were drowned. Mrs. Spafford was among the few who were miraculously saved as over two hundred others were lost to the sea along with their daughters.

Horatio Spafford stood for hours on the deck of the ship carrying him to rejoin his sorrowing wife in Cardiff, Wales. As the ship passed near the place where his precious daughters had drowned, Spafford received sustaining comfort from God that enabled him to write, "When sorrows like sea billows roll ... It is well with my soul." Only a man who knew the *eudokia* of God could write such words which to this day hold comfort for so many. With that in mind, would you be satisfied if there were no tinsel or lights; no presents under the tree or Christmas feasts? Would it be well with your soul if all you had was Jesus?

Lord, help me to say today, "It is well with my soul."

December 23

Not Home Yet

 Are we there yet?

Each morning I take a walk around our neighborhood. It's amazing what you can pick up by just keeping your eyes and ears open. I saw several families packing for road trips to grandma's house—at least I am guessing grandma's house!

Mary and Joseph were required to take a trip back to the home of their birth for the completion of the census. "And it came to pass in those days that a decree went out from Caesar Augustus that all the world should be registered. This census first took place while Quirinius was governing Syria. So all went to be registered, everyone to his own city. Joseph also went up from Galilee, out of the city of Nazareth, into Judea, to the city of David, which is called Bethlehem, because he was of the house and lineage of David, to be registered with Mary, his betrothed wife, who was with child."~Luke 2:1–5

All of these people getting ready to travel to grandma's house got me to thinking about Mary and Joseph's journey back to the city of Bethlehem. Imagine with me the couple nearing Bethlehem. See Mary riding uncomfortably on donkey back. She not only was nearing Bethlehem, she was nearing the time of delivering her child. I wonder if Mary had been asking for a few miles, "Are we there yet?"

As they approached the city the "traffic" certainly must have become congested. Amazing to think that the same Jesus riding safely into the city in Mary's womb would again ride on donkey back into the city of Jerusalem to the hails of HOSANNA IN THE HIGHEST! How about you and I? Are we mistakenly thinking that we have arrived? Presents wrapped, family in place, house filled with holiday smells... yet this is not really home. If we are with family on Christmas morning we can rejoice, but remember--WE'RE NOT HOME YET!

Lord, help me to remember we are not home yet!

December 24

O, Holy Night

"Now there were in the same country shepherds living out in the fields, keeping watch over their flock by night. And behold, an angel of the Lord stood before them, and the glory of the Lord shone around them, and they were greatly afraid. Then the angel said to them, 'Do not be afraid, for behold, I bring you good tidings of great joy which will be to all people. For there is born to you this day in the city of David a Savior, who is Christ the Lord.'" ~Luke 2:8–11

As darkness fell upon the Judean hillside shepherds would have finished gathering their sheep into the fold. One would take his turn to sleep the night in the gap serving as the door to the sheepfold. Hungry and thirsty sheep were now satisfied. Wounded ones were cared for until healed. The shepherds looking into a star-filled sky thought it just another day on the job.

But just inside the walls of Bethlehem The Great Shepherd was being born! He would declare that He would leave the 99 safe in the fold to find the one lost lamb. He would lay Himself down as the door and promise not only the safety of the sheep, but that no one could pass except through Him. He would be food for the hungry and those who drink from Him would thirst no more. The One who would bear the wounded upon His own shoulders was being born just over the hill in Bethlehem as they slept in the silent night under the midnight clear.

All this for you and me. What a gift! O, Holy Night! A night never to be repeated. A night that would change heaven and earth. The boundaries of heaven bulged in anticipation until a multitude of the heavenly host burst forth in a hallelujah chorus. The startled shepherds were the first to hear the glad tidings that a Savior was born, but that same message is available to all who are willing to hear and receive. May the anticipation of those shepherds be yours today as another Christmas arrives.

Lord, help me to have the excitement of the shepherds every day.

December 25

Christmas in October

Christmas 1979. As we celebrate Christmas today I am taken back this morning to 1979. Christmas occurred in October that year. I know. I can hear the gasp and collective, "Huh?" But for me Christmas did come in October that year as I knelt down behind the deli counter in Clark's A.G. Grocery and opened the gift of salvation.

I experienced the truth proclaimed by Peter in his first epistle, "...whom having not seen you love. Though now you do not see Him, yet believing, you rejoice with joy inexpressible and full of glory, receiving the end of your faith—the salvation of your souls."~1 Peter 1:8–9

That day in 1979 must have been a lot like this Christmas morning in Bethlehem long, long ago. I had received the same good news that those shepherds had heard on a dark Judean hillside.

I still remember the weight of sin lifted. The glad tidings of a Savior born in my heart. The sun shone brighter that day. The birds sang sweeter. The trees seem to sway in the breeze to the beat of the hallelujah chorus!

If you have ever opened the gift of salvation for yourself then go tell it on the mountain that Christ is born today! If this Christmas morning finds you in need of a Savior, then you are not reading this by mistake or mere chance. This same Jesus whom Peter spoke of is waiting for you to simply believe and receive Him as your own. There may still be one more present to open today. Go ahead! Open it! It has your name on it! It's from Jesus! MERRY CHRISTMAS!

Lord, help me to share the gift I received with others.

December 26

Day of Returns

Ok! Time for a moment of truth... Did you get what you wanted? All you wanted? NOT what you wanted? Are you heading to the store to return a few things? On this day of returns for better or worse why not take a moment to consider the words of the Lord found in Jeremiah 4:1, "Return unto me!"

That's right before you return stuff, return yourself to the Lord who made you and has called you. Returning to the Lord puts life back into perspective. Things take their place behind the Lord. Our worship is redirected and God is exalted.

The Lord spoke in Jeremiah 4 giving us insight into what takes place when we return; not the world, but us. When we return then we are reestablished. He promises that we shall not be shaken. He promises that the world will take note that our lives demonstrate the fact that God truly is alive and they will give glory unto Him. Amazing! A world that hardly takes note of the Christmas season will give glory when they see us returning to Him.

Here's the great news!

YOU'RE NEXT IN LINE!
YOU DON'T NEED A RECEIPT!
And NO EXCUSES NEEDED!

Return yourself to the Lord today for the best "deal" of your life!

Lord, help me to return unto You today.

December 27

Left-Overs

 By today you are probably a bit tired of turkey and dressing. As a matter of fact the mere mention of left-overs may result in a small riot in the kitchen. There comes a point that yesterday's delicious becomes today's despicable no matter how good it was at the first.

As we near the end of this year, I wonder how many left-overs are being offered to God. The Macedonians were noted by Paul for their sacrificial giving. In the face of poverty and persecution, the members of the church at Macedonia gave liberally to the needs of others in the body of Christ.

But even more noteworthy was the gift of themselves to the Lord. "And not only as we had hoped, but they first gave themselves to the Lord, and then to us by the will of God."~2 Corinthians 8:5 These Christians were not going to give God left-overs! I wonder how despicable some of our gifts may be to the Lord, especially if they are just left-overs warmed up in the microwave and served on spiritual paper plates?

There is still time left in this year to offer to God a gift. YOURSELF! No need for wrapping paper and bows. God already knows what's in the package. Your heart is fully revealed before Him, but He is so ready to receive YOU as a gift even at this late date.

Make a commitment to never again offer God your warmed up left-overs. Be a Macedonian! Offer yourself first and then ask God what you need to offer of your riches even those that come out of your poverty.

Lord, help me to never offer you leftovers.

December 28

Our Real Home

My ministry requires me to travel a lot. I would not want to count the number of beds in which I've slept over the past years. Some of these travels allow me to travel home. Home being that place where family and friends reside. Home being the familiar. Home being the place where everyone knows you by your nickname!

No matter how enjoyable the travel is or the excitement of seeing a new corner of the world, there always comes that moment when you say, "It's time to go home!" You know what I mean. You are home, but you're not. You want your bed.

It must have been the same for Joseph and Mary as the decree went forth requiring them to travel to Bethlehem. They certainly must have rejoiced to get back to Nazareth after the birth of Jesus. But what about Jesus? He would not be home for another 33 years.

He would be like a fox without a hole or a bird without a nest. He would declare that he had no place to lay his head. "And Jesus said to him, 'Foxes have holes and birds of the air have nests, but the Son of Man has nowhere to lay His head.'"~Matthew 8:20

A soft bed beckons us *home*, but as a Christian I am waiting to go HOME! What a glad reunion day that will be when we rest at His feet! Sure hope you will join me there one day on that happy shore!

Lord, help me tell everyone how they can join You in heaven one day.

December 29

Redeeming the Time

 You've probably met the guy who always has the answer to your problem. He's sort of like Mr. Haney on the old television show *Green Acres* (I realize that I just lost half my readers) who always showed up with his truck full of just what Mr. Douglas needed. From fence posts to bouquets of flowers, Mr. Haney would pull down his marquis advertising the latest and the greatest. Of course, the price listed was only good for that day!

The end of a year seems to bring these characters out of the wood work. Because folks are so reflective as we draw nigh to a new year they can hawk their goods to folks who will try to repair what went wrong last year. Sort of like buying a watch to fix yesterday. The watch can only tell you the present time and help you keep the next appointment.

The Bible speaks of time in a very different way: "See then that you walk circumspectly, not as fools but as wise, redeeming the time because the days are evil."~Ephesians 5:15-16

Make up your mind NOW concerning the New Year. Redeem the time. That means to purchase it again. Like a precious item that has been traded at the pawn shop, the price of redemption is to be paid in full for the time that is ours. Claim the new year NOW before you turn around and find yet another holiday time in your memory and yet another new year staring you in the face!

Lord, help me to redeem the time today and every day.

December 30

Patience

Are you thinking about resolutions yet? If so, here's a little item to add to your resolution list for the New Year.

PATIENCE.

Now just be patient and let me explain. No, let the Bible explain, "Now we exhort you, brethren, be patient with all."~1 Thessalonians 5:14 You are probably wishing this verse did not exist, but it does. We are to be patient with ALL. That means everyone!

In Matthew 18 Jesus told the story about a man who owed a large sum and was forgiven all of the debt. This same man later was asked to have patience by one who owed him just a little. Refusing to have patience with this man, his debt was again charged to him by his master and he was placed in debtor's prison.

Patience would have kept him free and forgiven, but he chose instead to enter the prison of impatience and unforgiveness long before he was placed in a debtor's prison. This man should have gained valuable insight from the forgiveness of his master to whom he owed so much, but a hardened heart prevented the salve of patience from penetrating.

Patience is a virtue that should be added to your to-do list for the New Year. You may have been forgiven little or much. The depth of forgiveness matters not. Enjoy a year of freedom and a heart filled with forgiveness. Be patient with all and be amazed how those around you react to you each day of the upcoming New Year.

Lord, help me be patient.

December 31

Times Up

 I awoke this morning thinking of two Biblical characters: Moses and Hezekiah. Moses speaks to us in a prayer recorded in Psalm 90. "For a thousand years in Your sight are like yesterday when it is past, and like a watch in the night. So teach us to number our days that we may gain a heart of wisdom."~Psalms 90:4;12

Moses teaches us to number our days. We are to realize their value, but also their insignificance when measured on God's scale of 1000 years to the day. One needs only peruse the obituary column of the newspaper to realize how temporal this life really is. Included will be those who lived long lives and those who lived only a few days. Yet when all are placed on God's timeline it is only a small blip.

Hezekiah on the other hand begged for an extension to his life and fifteen additional years were granted. This may sound like a great deal, but out of this time frame came Mannasseh, his son, one of the most wicked kings that ever ruled Judah.

I can honestly say that I am seeking no extension of time. Nor am I asking God to take me home today. I am simply going to rest in the assurance that the conclusion to this year is as a thousand years to God and next year is already a part of Heaven's history. Let your prayer be that you will use every day as an extension of your life and another day of opportunity to please the holder of all your days. May the New Year be the best year of service you've ever laid at the feet of Jesus!

Lord, help me to number my days that I might gain wisdom.

ABOUT THE AUTHOR

R.E. CLARK currently serves as an associational missionary in Arkansas. He earned his D.Min. from the Southern Baptist Center in Jacksonville, Florida. He served as a pastor in four churches before beginning his service as the associational missionary to the 70 churches, missions, and ministry points of the Northwest Baptist Association in Bentonville, Arkansas.

His writing comes from life experiences which include over 34 years in ministry. Before his call to ministry he was a business owner. His devotional life deepened and his writing career began in 2008 after the death of his wife Kay from Lou Gehrig's disease. He has written another yearlong devotional entitled *Life Is Not A Snapshot: It's A Mosaic.*

In addition to his devotional writing, he has begun writing a four part series of Bible studies. Each of these helps the reader understand the journey of their life. The first of these Bible studies is *God's Leading: 7 Ways To Know God Is Leading You.* The second, *God's Designing: Evidences for the Christian Life,* and the third *God's Speaking: Responding by Faith to the Voice of God.* The fourth in this series, *God's Giving,* will be released very soon. He has also authored a book on revival. *Expecting Revival* includes a history of revival in America, the biblical basis for revival, and a manual for forming teams that will prepare the church for a heaven-sent revival.

He has been blessed in his second marriage to Trudy. Trudy's first husband, a police officer, was killed in the line of duty. Together they have 8 children, 17 grandchildren, and one great-grandchild. They reside in Centerton, Arkansas.

Contact the author:

Email: reclark@reclarkauthor.com
Facebook: R.e. Clark
Twitter: @GlassesnGrass
Pinterest: reclarkjr
LinkedIn: R.E. Clark

Made in the USA
Charleston, SC
02 October 2015